CONDITIONING, COGNITION, AND METHODOLOGY

Contemporary Issues in Experimental Psychology

Edited by
Joseph B. Sidowski
University of South Florida

UNIVERSITY
PRESS OF
AMERICA

Lanham • New York • London

Copyright © 1989 by

University Press of America,® Inc.

4720 Boston Way
Lanham, MD 20706

3 Henrietta Street
London WC2E 8LU England

British Cataloging in Publication Information Available

Library of Congress Cataloging-in-Publication Data

Conditioning, cognition, and methodology : contemporary issues in experimental
psychology / edited by Joseph B. Sidowski.
p.   cm.
Papers in honor of David A. Grant.
Includes bibliographies and index.
1. Psychology, Experimental.   2. Cognition.   3. Conditioned response.
4. Psychology, Experimental—Methodology.   5. Grant, David A., 1916–1977.
I. Sidowski, Joseph B., 1925–   .   II. Grant, David A., 1916–1977.
BF181.C65   1989   150'.724—dc20   89–9093 CIP

ISBN 0–8191–7496–3 (alk. paper)

CONTENTS

iii

CONTRIBUTORS

NORMAN H. ANDERSON
University of California, San Diego

RAYMOND W. BERRIAN
University of California at Davis

LYLE E. BOURNE, JR.
University of Colorado

ISIDORE GORMEZANO
University of Iowa

JOSEPH B. HELLIGE
University of Southern California

BARRY H. KANTOWITZ
Purdue University

E. JAMES KEHOE
University of New South Wales

RONALD T. KELLOGG
University of Missouri, Rolla

ALAN F. KREISLER
University of California at Davis

NEAL E. A. KROLL
University of California at Davis

PHILIP LICHTENFELS
Bowling Green University

JOAN S. LOCKARD
University of Washington

NANCY ANGRIST MYERS
University of Massachusetts

THOMAS OAKLEY
Bowling Green University

WILLIAM F. PROKASY
University of Illinois at Urbana

HILARY HORN RATNER
Wayne State University

ARTHUR J. RIOPELLE
Louisiana State University

LOWELL SCHIPPER
Bowling Green University

JAMES ZALINSKI
University of California, San Diego

PREFACE

The essays appearing in this book are dedicated to the memory of David A. Grant. All but one chapter (Kellogg and Bourne) were written or co-authored by individuals who received their graduate degrees under his guidance. Lyle Bourne was greatly influenced by Grant. During his tenure virtually every psychology Ph.D. profitted from the experimental design course taught by Grant. The decade of 1950-1960 alone produced a number of noted design oriented experimental psychologists including: R. F. Thompson, J. Voss, W. Batting, J. Myers, L. Gregg, G. Briggs, D. Meyer, M. Shaw, A. Schreier, seven contributors to this volume, and others. The Grant Ph.D. contributors, as they appear in order of the chapters are: W.F. Prokasy, I. Gormezano, N.A. Myers, N.E.A. Kroll, J.B. Hellige, N.H. Anderson, L. Schipper, J.S. Lockard, and A.J. Riopelle. The remaining co-authors are ex-students of several of the above.

It is obvious that not all followed the research interests initially aroused during their associations with Grant. The binding feature in the effort presented here is the common interest to report original works, laboratory research or otherwise, which in some sense will contribute to their specific areas of psychology, while in the process of honoring David A. Grant.

As editor I wish to thank the contributors for the patience shown in accepting delays and in undergoing a revision of their chapters. Bits of the information provided in the introductions to sections two and three were excerpted from material provided by the authors. (Lowell Schipper died during the preparation of this volume.)

Joseph B. Sidowski

INTRODUCTION

This volume consists of eleven chapters divided into three sections. The first section consists of a single chapter written by William F. Prokasy, whose contribution provides a description of the academic work and research of David A. Grant, to whom this book is dedicated.

Section two contains six chapters and is entitled *Conditioning and Cognition.* The contributions contained in this section most clearly reflect the interests of Grant: classical conditioning, learning, concept formation, and cognition. In most instances the authors provide detailed reports of research unreported elsewhere. Theoretical interpretations are provided as required.

The third section, *Methodology,* has four chapters and provides fewer detailed reports of individual research. It is also a section covering a broad spectrum of methods, from the "Measurement of Importance in Multiattribute Models" to a brief description of some of the contributions made by psychologists in the development of a technique described to replace direct questionnaires in personal surveys, some methodology in human ethology, and a treatise covering a topic of international concern, early nutritional deprivation research. All reflect in some way Grant's great concern for methodology.

More detailed statements covering the contents of the chapters in sections two and three are provided in the introductions to those sections.

DAVID A. GRANT, EXPERIMENTAL PSYCHOLOGIST

William F. Prokasy

David A. Grant was born May 17, 1916, and grew up in Des Moines, Iowa. He attended the University of Iowa where he majored in psychology and completed his B.A. in 1938. He completed his M.A. in psychology at the University of Wisconsin in 1939. Two years later, in 1941, he completed his Ph.D. under the direction of Professor Ernest R. Hilgard. Appointed Assistant Professor of Psychology at the University of Wisconsin in 1941, he was promoted to the rank of Associate Professor in 1946 and to the rank of Professor in 1948. In 1970, he was named the Clark L. Hull Professor of Psychology, an appointment in which he took justified pride. Except for visiting appointments elsewhere, Grant spent his entire academic life at the University of Wisconsin. Though he had no liking for administration, he did serve as chairman of the department twice: from 1950 to 1954 and during 1971-72.

Among his many activities were his membership and executive committee role in the Society of Experimental Psychologists, presidency of Division 3 of the American Psychological Association, editorship of the Journal of Experimental Psychology, presidency of the Midwestern Psychological Association, and selection as one of four Lecturer-Scientists under the auspices of the AAAS to exchange with the USSR in 1972-73. Thirty-three experimental psychologists received the Ph.D. under his direction, and three more had nearly completed their work at the time of his death at age 61 on December 28, 1977.

As the late Arthur W. Melton observed, David Grant was an experimental psychologist in the functional tradition. That is, he was empirically and methodologically oriented, he was concerned with human processes and their function in the environment, and his theoretical developments were never far removed from the data.

Grant's empiricism was not the anti-theory empiricism which characterizes radical behaviorism. Rather, it was an empiricism which emphasized the importance of method in answering well-defined questions and, consequently, the value of appropriately gathered data. His experiments were conducted with an eye toward obtaining more information upon which he, or others, could develop an explanatory system. Method was important, and this was reflected in his insistence upon well-designed experiments and well-chosen statistical procedures. However, experimental design and statistics were tools to be used, methods of inquiry, but not science. The more one understands the tools employed, the better the science, but science is neither subservient to nor generated by the tools.

Grant's forty-year research career reflected a major research interest in human cognitive processes in conditioning. His interest in cognitive processes, in particular in Pavlovian second-signalling systems, was not at the expense of response systems. Not only did response output reflect the processes of interest, the consequences of the response were an integral part of the processes (e.g., Grant, 1972). This view is clearly within the functional tradition of Dewey (1896) who interpreted the reflex arc as serving a function which is not evident solely in the description of input and output, and who emphasized the role of feedback in the adjusting organism.

In spite of his years of research in conditioning and learning, Grant did not develop a theory. As noted above, his theoretical predispositions were never far from the data. His style was one of adopting an overall heuristic, or very loose theoretical framework, and then asking very specific questions for experimental purposes. He was most comfortable with an information processing view of the organism. This is evidenced clearly in his early involvement with information theory (e.g., Grant, 1954a, 1954b) and the development of an information processing model of conditioning (Grant, 1968, 1972).

Included among his publications are contributions to Pavlovian conditioning (both autonomic and skeletal responses), perceptual-motor skills, verbal learning, information processing, visual perception, methodology, instrumentation, concept formation, human factors, and instrumental conditioning. He also had been well trained in mathematics and was highly conversant with the literature on sensory psychology. He kept in touch with the latest instrumentation and computer developments, the result being that his laboratory was always a model for others. He had commented more than once that good instrumentation was a cornerstone of scientific inquiry, for developments in instrumentation afforded the opportunity to observe and record phenomena about which there would be otherwise only ignorance or, at best, speculation.

Teacher

It is axiomatic that those who have made contributions to science are our teachers. Similarly, those who have held significant editorial roles have, through their editing, to some extent shaped the character of the science and, consequently, have also taught us much about the scientific enterprise. David Grant as contributing scientist and as editor will be discussed below. His impact as a teacher in other than these two ways, however, does merit some comment.

The course with which Grant was most identified was advanced experimental design. It was, from the post-World War II era to at least into the 1960's, a course through which most Wisconsin graduate students traveled, if not passed. There is no doubt that it was a remarkably successful course, one major indicator being the marked difference between what students knew when they entered and what they had learned by the end of the term. There were several contributing factors to this success: an array of talented students, an atmosphere which enforced the idea that methodology and design were the sine qua non of research, and the principle that research was why the Ph.D. was earned. Such contributing factors can result in successful teaching almost in and of themselves, but Grant's presence lent something to it that made a critical difference. His command of theoretical design and statistics and his ability to put both to use was, to put it mildly, formidable. It provided a marker for students whose own aspirations and plans included research. One of his former students noted that Grant would say that students in the design class might learn less than they learned in other classes but that they had to know more about what they learned than in other classes.

A significant proportion of Grant's students went on to teach design and statistics at other schools, thus extending his influence to a second generation. One further indication of his influence in psychological research can be drawn from Winer's classic work on design and statistics (Winer, 1971): of 30 reference experiments cited by Winer, 11 are to experiments designed by persons who received their design and statistics training largely with Grant.

Teaching includes the supervision of doctoral students. Thirty-three individuals completed degrees with Grant while three were working with him at the time of his death (see Table 1). Different areas or research were pursued by his students: Pavlovian conditioning, perception, child development, infra-human primate behavior, human factors, attitude and impression formation, mathematical models and theory, human memory and verbal learning, and information processing. These differences reflect Grant's own style: he was less concerned with the area of inquiry than he was that the related research be well designed and well executed. Grant's dedication to science as an enterprise helped make it possible for his students to move relatively easily into the variety of research areas that they

3

did. It is in that sense that Grant's contribution through his students is quite broad.

Editor, Journal of Experimental Psychology

Grant edited the Journal of Experimental Psychology from 1963 through 1974, but his association with that journal in a review or editing capacity began in 1951: Consulting Editor, 1951-1956; Associate Editor, 1957-1962; Editor, 1963-1975. It was with the end of his term as editor that the Journal of Experimental Psychology ceased to exist as a single publication for all of experimental psychology and became four separate journals under separate editorships. Sidowski (1978) has written at length about Grant as an editor, and the reader is referred to his paper for additional comment. What follows is drawn in part from the Sidowski paper, in part from comments of Grant's colleagues and editorial associates, and in part from my own experience.

There is little doubt that David Grant was one of the few who had the talents and philosophical orientation to become an outstanding editor for what was at that time the major journal in experimental psychology. What made him a superb editor went well beyond the fact that he had an appreciation for and an understanding of research and theory in general experimental psychology. It had more to do with his view of what a journal is supposed to be and, consequently, his editorial policies.

To begin with, the Journal served the science by being an archival resource continuing the best that experimental psychology had to offer. To optimize the archival value of a journal requires policies which minimize the influence of the idiosyncratic characteristics of any one individual, and Grant's editorship did precisely that.

Given that a submitted paper fell within the general domain of experimental psychology, Grant was indifferent to the particular topic or outcome. The fundamental question was whether or not a paper made a reliable and valid contribution to science. This meant that different scientific strategies were acceptable. For example, papers might be addressed to a tightly drawn experimental hypothesis or theoretical deduction on the one hand, or constitute a carefully conducted empirical inquiry in a topic of contemporary interest on the other. What was a requisite was that the experiments be designed well to test an hypothesis or to extend the empirical base of knowledge: rigor was important. If Grant erred in editing, it was to err in the direction of accepting papers which recounted well executed research but which, in the judgment of some, might not contain sufficiently useful data. This reflects, in part, Grant's recognition of what is an unresolvable issue: Just who is in a position to determine whether or not a set of data, given that it was acquired under appropriately exacting experimental conditions, constitutes a substantial contribution to the discipline? There was, I think, an interesting and important mix of elitism and deference in his editorship. If an investigator had the skills to ask a testable question, design research well to answer it, and produce a sufficient amount of new information to consider the net result to be at the very least a solid empirical gain, then perhaps that investigator's implicit judgment of quality in submitting the paper ought to carry some weight. As any editor knows, it is difficult to say "no" in the face of well-designed, well-executed research, for that decision not only affects individual careers in an adverse way but also runs the risk of denying to the scientific community something which, with the distillation of time, is highly important. Grant's sense of responsibility to science was too great to eliminate all false positives based upon an a priori discounting of the ultimate worth of data obtained from quality empirical inquiry.

Editing a journal is an active process. Reviewing and final judgment are not simply neutral filters, for change is implied in the process and the ultimate contribution is not exclusively the product of an individual author. Grant once observed that associate and consulting editors provide for many authors a high quality post-graduate education. Authors, having been close to the research problem for many months, sometimes need help in making lucid observations about their own data and sometimes, because of the specific focus, miss some issues that can increase the likelihood that a paper has a broader impact. Careful editing can, then, make a first-class contribution even better.

Grant was inclined not to second-guess action editors. If authors were given a careful rationale for a decision, negative or positive, then action editors were to be supported in that decision, subject, of course, to additional information and/or interpretation. His support of action editors was important in another way for the journal and the science: it contributed to the open nature of the system by reducing the possibility that any one theoretical orientation, any one methodological preference, or any one individual's value system dominated manuscript selection. The 11 action editors, 110 consulting editors, and an uncounted number of additional reviewers for the Journal attest to the existence of a journal policy which might result in partial decisions in any given instance but which was impartial in the aggregate.

One final observation about Grant's editorship merits note. He was quite sensitive to the fact that limitations of space and the nature of the overall publishing system made some, perhaps many, papers seem unduly esoteric. This was, as he saw it, bound to be the case as thesis and then counterthesis, support and contradictory findings, find their way into the literature. About continuing investigations on common problems, Grant had this to say: "In many instances, the revelations coming out of these further investigations have led to more complete and more adequate theoretical structures, but until this point is reached the reader who is not thoroughly familiar with the whole story is in for very heavy going and is likely to leap to the conclusion that research in certain problem areas has degenerated into a dull search for esoteric minutiae. And so it is that one reader will see dynamic if saltatory progress, while another reader will see a static if not moribund situation. Just as 'beauty is in the eye of the beholder,' perceptive reading of the Journal requires a considerable apperceptive mass." While Grant demanded much of those who contributed and those who edited, he expected at least as much from us as readers.

Statistician and Methodologist

Of the more than 120 papers published by Grant, only 10 were in statistics and related methodology, a number that may appear to be small considering that he had earned an excellent reputation in the area. Some indication of his breadth of scholarship in statistics and methodology can be obtained from the two chapters (Grant, 1950,1959) which he wrote for the Annual Review of Psychology. Both chapters contained summaries of recent developments in experimental design and analysis, psychometric methods including psychophysics, scaling, correlational analysis, and multidimensional techniques including factor analysis.

One paper (Grant, Kaestner & Schipper, 1955), though reporting the outcome of research on a perceptual-motor learning task, had as its focus a description of the use of the autocorrelation as a method of analyzing gross learning scores. The paper reveals another of Grant's concerns as a laboratory scientist and that is a cost-benefit consideration. He does discuss the costs of conducting these analyses on existing computers (a cost, incidentally, which would be almost immeasurable lower today) and suggests that a feasible way would be the use of power spectrum from which a Fourier transformation could be computed, this being an autocorrelational function.

6

Grant's presidential address to the Midwestern Psychological Association in 1954 concerned time series analysis, this in contrast to the cross-sectional statistical methods typically employed. His view was that time series analysis is particularly important in clinical settings and for the study of "the development of character and personality, normal and pathological, and in the study of the dynamics of behavior." The particular model discussed was the communication model for transmission of information, and Grant drew the analogy of the organism being a transmission system which mapped stimuli into responses. He correctly foresaw such analytic techniques as having a great impact in the following years, though he was careful to observe that they "cannot solve problems in and of themselves any more than the unaided microscope can solve biological problems."

Two of his papers involved identifying in problem solving and learning data, the kind of statistic which would differentiate the theoretical positions taken by Krechevsky and Spence. The former interpreted changes in performance to change in a step-wise fashion following confirmation of an hypothesis. That is, an experimental subject would test hypotheses in trying to solve a learning problem and when the correct hypothesis was obtained performance would move from chance to a very high correct response level. The Spencian interpretation was that there were increments in response strength with reinforcements and decrements following non-reinforcements and that, following a sufficient number of reinforcements, the strength of the correct response was sufficiently great to dominate. Grant (1946, 1947) made use of the binomial theorem to describe how a runs test could be employed to identify sequences of responding. He provided the odds of a particular number of runs (of successes and/or failures), given on a priori p value, and the number of trials over which the examination is to be made.

The main point of Grant's initial paper on statistical methodology was to differentiate between the use of ANOVA as a method of partitioning variance and as a method of assessing the significance of variation, contending that the latter is the appropriate use of ANOVA. A 1949 paper (Grant, 1949) describes the complete analysis of a 2x2 Latin Square design and provides an experimental illustration of its use. All sources of variance and confounding are discussed. His belief, evident in his instruction, was that an important contribution of design was to isolate interactions, for interactions between presumed main effects were, in his judgment, likely to provide the greatest new insights.

Perhaps the best known of Grant's papers in statistical methodology is "Analysis of variance tests in the analysis and comparison of curves" (Grant, 1956). This paper became the focal point of the development and use in psychology of orthogonal polynomial trend tests, a use which now is so routine that it appears in standard statistical software packages for computers. The technique, briefly, involved partitioning the variance into the amounts allocable to the various polynomial orders and in determining the extent to which contrasting experimental treatments differ in curvature across levels of another independent variable. Though the technique partitioned variance into polynomial components, it was clear that Grant intended its use for testing hypotheses and determining if differences in variance were significant. This is nowhere more evident than in his first published use of the technique (Grant & Schiller, 1956). In that study Grant and Schiller examined generalization employing the electrodermal response as a measure and intensity of auditory stimulation as the dimension. The use of orthogonal polynomials permitted the authors to differentiate a linear trend with intensity from the quadratic trend, with peak at the training stimulus, which should characterize a generalization function. Published in 1956, the paper also reflects, indirectly, another fact: Grant taught the use of orthogonal polynomials to graduate students for several years prior to the publication of his 1956 paper. It was but one of a number of instances in which he taught methods which either were not accessible to others or, at least, were little used in the psychological literature. It is indicative, too, of his penchant for being aware of and applying techniques introduced in other fields of inquiry.

Grant's final paper (Grant, 1962) on the use of statistical methods was on the troublesome issue of determining that a theoretical model describes data sufficiently well to permit the conclusions that the model and therefore its theoretical underpinnings merit further consideration. The theorist is in the delicate position of making this assessment under conditions in which the obtained data do not depart significantly from theoretical prediction. The point of departure for the paper was that it is no great feat to design an experiment which either failed to reject or rejected the null hypothesis of no difference between data point and theoretical expectation. Weak experiments with large variances or many sources of uncontrolled variation lent themselves to failure to reject the null hypothesis, hence failure to reject a model; highly precise experiments with many data points contributing to estimates would almost routinely lead to a rejection of the null hypothesis. If accepting a model meant accepting the null hypothesis, how was one to differentiate between a good model and a weak experiment? Grant's argument was that the investigator could make two tests: one would determine whether or not the model accounted for a significant proportion of the variance; the other would determine if there were a significant proportion of the variance yet to be accounted for. It was this latter variance which, with further theory refinement or with alternative theories, was to be reduced in subsequent research. It would similarly be possible to determine if two different models accounted for significantly different amounts of the variance.

Laboratory Scientist

Grant has an extensive bibliography. I have selected several of his contributions for summary and comment. While recognizing that this necessarily excludes some from consideration, the selections should, nonetheless, illustrate Grant's style as a laboratory scientist.

Classical and Operant Conditioning

In the chapter he contributed to Melton's Categories of Human Learning, Grant (1964) discussed four subclasses of classical conditioning: Pavlovian A, Pavlovian B, anticipatory instructed, and sensory preconditioning. In Pavlovian A conditioning, the CS and US are paired, but the UR depends upon an instrumental act by the subject, an act which, in turn, depends upon the subject's motivational state. For example, for food to be a sufficient US for salivary conditioning requires that the organism be food deprived and that it ingest the food US.

Pavlovian B conditioning involves presentation of CS and US independent of the organism's behavior. Grant noted that this particular category was the one in which the CS appeared to substitute for the US, this because the response class learned to the CS is more frequently similar to the UR. The conditioning of cardiac and electrodermal changes of leg or nictitating membrane reflexes are examples of Pavlovian B conditioning.

Anticipatory instructed conditioning is derived from the work of Ivanov-Smolensky (1933). Human subjects are instructed to perform a voluntary act upon presentation of a signal. The signal is preceded by another signal, the CS. As Grant notes, anticipatory instructed conditioning is in effect a reaction time experiment with a constant fore-period signalled by the onset of the CS. It is a uniquely human paradigm in which "the sequence of events in the conditioning situation will therefore depend upon the S's interpretation of the E's instruction and the S's own self-instruction."

The fourth category is sensory preconditioning, the pairing of two "neutral" stimuli. This category was distinguished because there is

9

no apparent motivational component and because the assessment of any associative linkages is made by establishing (usually) Pavlovian B conditioning to one of the stimuli and then later testing to the other. In Grant's view the point of theoretical interest is that conditioning the preconditioning phase produced stimulus substitution in the absence of any particular motivational circumstances in the experiment.

Grant's discussion of the instrumental conditioning paradigm in the Melton volume begins with six examples: reward training, escape training, avoidance conditioning, discriminated operant conditioning, omission training, and passive avoidance. Though all fall within the diagram provided originally by Skinner (1937), the first four variations were operationally distinguished by Hilgard and Marguis (1940) and the latter two were introduced to American researchers through the work of Konorski (1948).

These six variations are differentiated by Grant on the basis of three dimensions: whether or not there is a cue to impending reinforcement; whether or not an active response is required; and whether the reinforcement is a reward or a punishment. These three binary dimensions actually produce eight different sets of experimenter operations, rather than six, and it was through this analysis of experimenter operations that Grant proposed two additional instrumental conditioning variations. The two additions are: "discriminated omission training," and "discriminated punishment training." The former requires that a subject, in the presence of a cue, not perform a response ordinarily performed in order to obtain reward. The latter requires that a subject, in the presence of a cue, not perform an otherwise performed act in order to avoid punishment.

The classical instrumental conditioning taxonomies proposed by Grant are strictly empirical in nature. They are defined exclusively in terms of experimenter operations and in criteria specified by the experimenter for a subject's response. As Grant points out, it might be more desirable to classify experiments in terms of more fundamental psychological operations, but the framework proposed is at least serviceable in being unambiguous.

One value of the taxonomies is that they focus more sharply on experimenter operations, something that is frequently overlooked in attempts to provide theoretical accounts of learning. In addition, even a strictly empirically-based taxonomy can uncover procedures meriting exploration, as his instrumental conditioning taxonomy demonstrates. The most important value of a taxonomy for experimental paradigms, however, is that it forces the experimenter to think more carefully about the operations employed to answer experimental or theoretical questions. As he did statistics and design, Grant viewed experimental paradigms as tools for inquiry. A paradigm for inquiry can be seen, analogically, as a form of microscope: the properties of the microscope must be understood if the biological phenomena being observed are to be seen not only as orderly and theoretically meaningful but as characteristics of the phenomena rather than those of the microscope. Grant's continuing concern with understanding the implications of experimenter operations and their consequences is nowhere more evident than in his research on response systems, one of which (the beta response) is discussed below. He states that it is important to understand irrelevant variables and that "this involves a tremendous amount of methodological experimentation . . . (that) has to be done anew with each different response system . . . It is regrettably the case that for most response systems the basic methodological work simply has not been done."

In the case of classical and instrumental conditioning it is not surprising, according to Grant, that there are many similar phenomena (e.g., acquisition, extinction, external inhibition, spontaneous recovery). This is because the experimenter operations for a specific paradigm may well involve a complicated mix of circumstances which meet the criteria both for classical and instrumental conditioning. Thus, the similarity observed may result strictly from an overlap in the consequences of experimenter operations, these consequences not necessarily having anything to do with the associative processes of interest. Similarly, the overlap might reflect the fact that basic processes are predominantly observed regardless of taxonomic differences. Grant's own view is that the issue remains open and will remain open until it is possible to have "pure" instances of any particular paradigm.

The instrumental conditioning taxonomy provides yet more complications when applied to the human. Grant points out that applying these operations to humans, obstacles must be introduced in order to keep subjects from learning so rapidly that learning cannot be measured. As obstacles are introduced, however, the associative network of interest assumes less and less of a role in the experiment with the consequence that the behavioral laws derived from such experiments may well be quite different and may be comparable only to the extent that they share associative learning which, in turn, may be only a minor portion of the task. "The associative learning may be identical, but the overlay is not."

The Beta Response

Grant's conditioning papers, particularly in the earlier half of his career, reflected an interest in the definition of a conditioned response. How can we be sure that the responses acquired to a conditioned stimulus are indicative of an acquired association? Ultimately an answer to such a question depends upon the theoretical framework from which it is asked. Even the question itself involves a set of heuristic, if not theoretical, assumptions which frequently are not stated in pursuit of answers to what might be misconstrued as purely empirical questions. Given a set of procedures and controls based upon Pavlov's work, however, it was possible to demonstrate what was not associative, and it was within this context that Grant made an important contribution to the human conditioning literature.

By the early 1940's research in human eyelid response conditioning had had substantial influence on theory development and empirical inquiry. It constituted the most reliable preparation for examining Pavlovian conditioning of skeletal responses in humans, and for that reason it was necessary to assure that the response changes measured did, in fact, reflect the pairing of CS and US and neither nonassociative nor other associative influences. There were some puzzling facts, however, which made it difficult to conclude that much of what was observed did reflect an associative system. Grant (1943a) demonstrated that there was an increase in sensitized responding to brightness change in the presence of unconditioned stimuli (air puffs to the cornea) even though the brightness change and the US were not paired. Oddly enough, however, a group of subjects receiving repeated presentations of the stimulus in the absence of the US also exhibited an increase in response levels. It was as though the situation itself produced some form of generalized sensitization. In a subsequent study (Grant, 1943b) Grant compared groups of subjects receiving conditioning, fixation, and pseudo-conditioning treatments. He found no differences among the groups, which is to say that it was not at all clear that the pairing of stimuli produced outcomes other than what would be expected strictly on the basis of sensitization.

A step toward understanding was taken when Grant (1945) demonstrated a secondary response through sensitization procedures. This response, which he labeled the beta response, was thought to be either a secondary reflex to light or as reflecting a pre-existing learned response. beta responses had latencies in the general vicinity of 150 msec, a range which included the mode of the latency distribution in earlier sensitization research (Grant, 1943a, b). Subsequently, Grant and Norris (1946) found that dark adaptation played a role in generating beta responses during sensitization. This particular finding was important for it raised questions about past conditioning research. Subjects had been conditioned in a situation which would result in dark adaptation. Sensitization experience in dark-adapting conditions yielded increases across trials in the frequency of beta responses, an effect which could easily be confused with the associative effects of CS-US pairing. Grant and Norris (1947) then showed that there is a conditioned response with the human eyelid response preparation. This was demonstrated under light adaptation conditions which eliminated beta responses but in which increases in response frequency at latencies longer than the beta response latency occurred. These authors concluded: "It is rash indeed to base theories and principles of associative learning upon the adaptive alterations in a response system whose original characteristics are uncharted."

Grant and his colleagues went on in several additional studies to identify more clearly the role of the beta response. Grant, Norris & Boissard (1947) demonstrated clearly that the US does not result in sensitization or pseudo-conditioning; that, rather, such effects are obtained only when the subject is dark adapted. Of more value for future research with instructional sets, Norris and Grant (1948) found a large impact of inhibitory instructions on conditioning performance. Prior investigators had not found such an effect, apparently because the subjects were run under dark adapting, hence beta-response-inducing, conditions. Not only was it demonstrated that inhibitory instructions influenced conditioned response levels, it was also found (Grant, Norris, & Hornseth, 1948) that inhibitory instructions did not influence beta response levels during sensitization treatments. Since inhibitory instructions did not influence the alpha (or original reflex) response to the CS, Grant and his colleagues concluded that the beta response was more like a reflex response than an acquired response. In the final study of this series, Grant, Hornseth and Hake (1949) found that sensitized beta responses were observed more readily to short wavelength stimuli, from which they concluded that the beta response was very likely a result of increased sensitivity of the rods during dark adaptation. As subjects sat in the experimental room, they became dark adapted and the increased rod sensitivity brought with it an increase in frequency to brightness changes employed as neutral stimuli.

The sequence of studies on the beta response had a substantial impact on research in human conditioning. It isolated a sizable non-associative influence in prior conditioning studies, one which made it difficult to know which studies in the past had been valid inquiries in associative learning. At the same time his results made it possible to investigate influences upon conditioning (notably instructional set, or cognitive, variables) which to that point had been difficult. Grant's continued examination of the beta response not only isolated it as a non-associative response which obscured conditioning effects but also identified its source through a series of elegant investigations. So pervasive was the impact of this research that all subsequent laboratories were routinely designed to avoid the non-associative influences of beta responses.

The V-C Distinction

Spence and Taylor (1951) studied the influence of anxiety on human conditioning and removed from their analysis the data of subjects whom they had designated (with conditioned eyelid responses at the measures) as responding voluntarily. The voluntary responder (a "V" responder) was a subject who yielded rapid-closure responses at a short latency. The rationale for this separation was that the Spence theory was directed at basic laws of associative learning and that subjects who responded voluntarily were reflecting other, pre-learned, associations. The other subjects ("C" responders) exhibited slower rates of acquisition, longer latencies, shallower response slopes, and gave no evidence of self-instructions to respond.

This separation of subjects into V- and C-responders posed difficulties. The criteria for exclusion were relatively arbitrary, even though operationally clean, and certainly did not derive directly from any theory. Under what circumstances were the data of some subjects to be excluded from analysis? How were the criteria to be rationalized? The assumption that V-responders are voluntary responders posed an interesting, and to date never solved, problem. Subjects could hypothetically be considered to be either voluntary or non-voluntary responders. Similarly, they could be operationally distinguished on the basis of either (or both) a response slope or latency criterion. With no independent assessment of the relationship of "voluntariness" to the response measure there was no way to determine the proportions of false positives and false negatives. This is no small problem in view of the fact that the failure to assess false positives and false negatives made it impossible to know whether or not subjects were in any meaningful way being classified as either voluntary or non-voluntary.

The proposed separation of subjects into V and C classes provoked a lot of discussion about the validity and usefulness of the distinction and the criterion by which it was made (e.g., Goodrich, 1966; Gormezano, 1965; Ross, 1965), but it remained for Grant and his colleagues to pursue the issue at an empirical level in a way which

14

made the separation meaningful. The research strategy was to recognize that there were clear and consistent differences in response topography and to develop a criterion for classifying subjects in one category or another, a step taken by Hartman, Grant and Ross (1960). The evidence for a near dichotomy between Vs and Cs is provided by Fleming (1968) in a dissertation done under Grant's supervision. The classification criterion was such that approximately 80 percent of the responses of those subjects classified as V-form responders fell in one category while approximately 80 percent of those of the C-form responders fell in the other category. The elimination of reference to voluntary and non-voluntary was made since separation was strictly on a response form basis. V-form meant that subjects exhibiting this form of response were exhibiting one very similar to that which subjects elicited when they were asked to respond to the onset of a signal.

Having a reliable category of separation between V-form and C-form responders is not in itself a justification for the separation, for it means merely that subjects are reliably different in response characteristics. Whether the difference is trivial or important depends upon other information. The outcome of several experiments illustrates how differentiation on the basis of topography yielded information about human conditioning, in particular about first- and second-signalling systems, which would not otherwise be available. The studies are summarized by Grant (1968) and are reviewed here in part.

When symbolic stimuli are employed as CSs but have no role other than conveying information, the V-form and C-form responders do not differ (Grant, Levy, Thompson, Hickok, & Bunde, 1967; Fleming, Cerekwicki, Grant, 1968; Fleming, Grant, & North, 1968; Fleming, Grant, North, & Levy, 1968). In the first of the cited studies, acquisition, differential performance, and transfer were shown to be more rapid with words than with forms, but Vs and Cs did not differ. In the remaining series of studies correct and incorrect arithmetic problems were used as conditioned stimuli. It was found that when correct arithmetic served as the CS+ and incorrect as the CS-, differential performance was greater than when the reverse relationship existed. Vs and Cs did not differ in this respect.

However, when relatedness of words became the differential stimuli, the differences did appear. For example, when one related set of words (e.g., a set of words with water in common) was used as CS+ and another set of words (e.g., names of different birds) was used as CS-, Vs and Cs did differ (Cerekwicki, Grant, & Porter, 1968). V-form responders rapidly distinguished the two sets and yielded a high

15

degree of differential performance. On the other hand, C-form responders yielded little in the way of terminal performance differences between the CS+ class and the CS- class. When unrelated sets of words were used as CS+ and CS- categories, Vs and Cs did not differ: both yielded limited terminal performance differences. In summary, the Vs were able to use a concept class as a differential stimulus, but the Cs were (or did) not.

More than concept class differentiated the Vs and the Cs. When the verbal stimuli were presented in the form of commands, the two categories of subjects differed substantially. The words BLINK and DON'T BLINK were employed as conditioned stimuli. Terminal level differential performance was the same regardless of which of the two stimuli was the CS+, although with BLINK as the CS+ overall level of performance was higher to both stimuli. On the other hand, when BLINK was the CS+ for Vs, there was a rapid and high level of differential conditioning performance, while when DON'T BLINK was the CS+ differential performance was poor.

The above and other differences between V-form and C-form responders were viewed from an information processing perspective (Grant, 1973, 1968). The subject has a limited processing capacity and this may be occupied primarily either by response shaping for the specific contingencies or by processing of information in the conditioned stimulus. The V-form responders have available a well-formed response, hence their capacity is occupied more by the meaning of the verbal CSs. The C-form responders have to learn the response, hence their processing capacity is occupied largely by the response and its consequences with respect to the US. C-form responders, then, do not process symbolic content to a great extent and therefore do not respond as readily to the command in such words as BLINK and DON'T BLINK and do not detect as readily concepts defined by word sets. Neutral words unrelated to the contingencies in the conditioning situation do not differentiate Cs and Vs since the processing demands are not high. The availability of a pre-formed response, and the lack of any need to process response-consequence information results in a positive response bias in Vs, the result of which is a higher overall level of responding during acquisition and a retarded rate of extinction.

The V-C distinction will be discussed further in the context of Grant's information processing model. The point to treating it separately here is to illustrate how Grant put aside the rhetoric concerning what is appropriate in science and used experimental methods to transform fuzzy constructs into empirically sound experiments yielding highly interesting, and unexpected, results.

Information Processing Model

Grant's combined interest in conditioning and cognitive processes resulted in many papers concerned with Pavlov's second-signalling system, the research on the V-C distinction discussed above being only a part. This interest, together with his orientation toward heuristic models, in particular to information processing models, was reflected in a book chapter (Grant, 1973b), which not only summarized his thinking to that point but also provided a framework for most of the research subsequently conducted in his laboratory.

He was careful to state that his interest in employing symbolic stimuli as CSs was not a way to study verbal learning through the use of a conditioned response as a measure. To the contrary, he was specifically interested in what he viewed to be basic conditioning processes when symbolic stimuli were used as CSs. An insightful student of Pavlov's works and Russian conditioning research in general, Grant noted that there had been a substantial amount of research done in the Soviet Union on the second-signalling system but very little in the United States. This lack was, to him, puzzling for symbols, words in particular, differentiate humans from other species. To understand conditioning processes in humans required, then, that the focus of research not be limited narrowly to neutral, or first signalling system, stimuli.

Trying to account for conditioning phenomena when information is added to the CS is complex since the subject brings with him or her a vast array of prior responses to symbols, verbal and otherwise. The preliminary model adopted by Grant is shown in Figure 1. There are four stages, as described by Smith (1968), with the information flow patterned after a model proposed

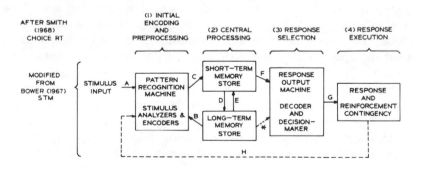

Figure 1. Information processing model for classical conditioning. (Adapted form Grant, 1972, page 38. Reprinted by permission of Appleton Century-Crofts Publishing Co.)

by Bower (1967). There are two features of this model that differentiate it from the Bower model. The first is loop H from response output and reinforcement contingency to stimulus input. This is explicit recognition of the fact that the consequences of a trial (the response topography and its interaction with the US) make a difference in subsequent performance. The second addition is the arrow with an asterisk between long-term memory store and the response output machine. This was to permit long-term store to provide the response machine with some pre-formed responses, e.g., a reflex response elicited by a US or a well developed, prior response such as those exhibited by V-form responders.

Though not doing full justice to Grant's analysis of how the model applies to human conditioning, some sense of his thinking can be obtained through a summary of the way in which he interpreted departures from first-signalling system differential conditioning when second-signalling system CSs were employed.

In one form of departure, the degree of differential performance between CS+ and CS- was reduced because CS- responding was elevated. This he viewed to be a result of subjects, e.g., Vs, having pre-formed responses with little experience at response inhibition. Little central processing capacity is devoted to developing the response and pre-formed responses are available to the response output machine from long-term memory store. In circumstances in which the CS+ and CS- are confusing (such as the word BLUE presented in pink as the CS+ and the word PINK presented in blue as the CS-), central processing is occupied with the confusing nature of the stimuli and the bias toward responding present because of the pre-formed responses manifests itself in elevated response levels to the CS-.

Another form of departure is when terminal differential performance is not different, but overall levels of responding are higher. This reflects, particularly in the case of V-form responders, the response bias resulting from the availability of a pre-formed, adaptive response and the corresponding reduced demand on the central processor.

The third form of departure is an increased differential performance due to elevated responding to CS+ and reduced responding to CS-. This can happen when the encoding resulting from the specific CS-US contingencies is consistent with codes already in long-term store. One example of this is when BLINK is the CS+ and DON'T BLINK is the CS-. Coding of these contingencies is consistent with the previously stored meaning of the words, consequently enhancing differential performance, this particularly the case with V-form responders who attend more to the symbolic nature of the CS. A second example is when a wrong arithmetic problem (e.g., 2+3=6) is used as the CS+ and a right arithmetic problem (e.g., 5+4=9) is used as the CS-. Differential performance is enhanced, according to Grant, because subjects have had a lot of experience with punishment for wrong arithmetic problems and the CS+ is followed by an aversive US.

The fourth form of departure is the reverse of the third form: reduced differential performance. This results when the encoding of the specific CS-US contingencies is inconsistent with codes already present in long-term store and is exhibited in the reverse of the above relationships: when DON'T BLINK is used as the CS+, BLINK as the CS- and when right arithmetic problems are used as the CS+, wrong as the CS-.

The final example discussed by Grant is when overall response levels to CS+ and CS- are depressed. An example of this is when a set of unrelated words is employed as the CS+ and a set of unrelated words is employed as the CS-. Differentiation between CS+ and CS- is then difficult, and there results, in C-form responders a reduced response level. Central processing capacity is devoted more to trying to differentiate CS+ and CS-, thus making it less available for the response development necessary in Cs. The consequence is, with reduced response availability, a lower response level. This negative response bias contrasts, of course, with the bias of Vs who, when confronted with confusing stimuli, exhibit a response bias because little central processing is required for response output.

Grant (1973a) describes in more detail his conception of what takes place during the four information processing stages, and the reader is referred to that paper for a more complete discussion. As noted earlier, the information processing model did provide a general framework to guide his subsequent research. For example, he and his colleagues examined differential conditioning from the perspective of four processing stages (Zajano & Grant, 1974; Zajano, Grant, & Schwartz, 1974; Perry, Grant, & Schwartz, 1977); response topography and the V-C distinction (Zajano, Grant, & Schwartz, 1974; Cody & Grant, 1978); changes in mode of reinforcement (Hellige & Grant, 1974a, b); and hemispheric differences in processing CS meaning (Kadlac & Grant, 1977). His perceptive use of the information processing heuristic in human conditioning did not, it is to be emphasized, constitute a shift away from earlier interests. It provided yet another way to continue his study of what interested him most: the Pavlovian second-signalling system in human conditioning.

Concluding Comment

The preceding sections provided glimpses of David Grant and his works. I hope that the particular events and topics chosen to illustrate his impact are representative of a man who was a superb scientist, demanding teacher, talented editor, and a person of complete integrity and dedication to his profession. In the best sense of the words, he was: David A. Grant, Experimental Psychologist.

REFERENCES

Bower, G. A. (1967). A multicomponent theory of the memory trace. In K. W. Spence & J. T. Spence (Eds.), The psychology of learning and motivation: Advances in research and theory. Vol. 1 (pp. 229-325). New York: Academic Press.

Cerekwicki, L. E., Grant, D. A., & Porter, E. C. (1968). The effect of number and relatedness of verbal discriminanda upon differential eyelid conditioning. Journal of Verbal Learning and Verbal Behavior, 7, 847-853.

Cody, W. J., & Grant, D. A. (1978). Biasing the development of response topography with nonspecific positive and negative evocative verbal stimuli. Journal of Experimental Psychology: Human Learning and Memory, 4, 175-186.

Dewey, J. (1896). The reflex arc concept in psychology. Psychological Review, 3, 357-370.

Fleming, R. A. (1968). Transfer of differentially conditioned eyelid responses as a function of the associative strength between acquisition and transfer CSs and the associative strength between CS+ and CS- in the transfer task. Unpublished doctoral dissertation, University of Wisconsin, Madison.

Fleming, R. A., Cerekwicki, L. E., & Grant, D. A. (1968). "Appropriateness" of the stimulus-reinforcement contingency in instrumental differential conditioning of the eyelid response to the arithmetic concepts of "right" and "wrong." Journal of Experimental Psychology, 77, 295-300.

Fleming, R. A., Grant, D. A., & North, J. A. (1968). Truth and falsity of verbal statements as conditioned stimuli in classical and differential eyelid conditioning. Journal of Experimental Psychology, 78, 178-180.

Fleming, R. A., Grant, D. A., North, J. A., & Levy, C. M. (1968). Arithmetic correctness as the discriminandum in classical and differential eyelid conditioning. Journal of Experimental Psychology, 77, 286-294.

Goodrich, K. P. (1966). Elemental analysis of response slopes and latency as criteria for characterizing voluntary and nonvoluntary responses in eyelid conditioning. Psychological Monographs, 80, No. 14, 1-34.

Gormezano, I. (1965). Yoked comparisons of classical and instrumental conditioning of the eyelid response: And an addendum on "voluntary responders." In W. F. Prokasy (Ed.), Classical conditioning (pp. 47-70). New York: Appleton-Century-Crofts.

Grant, D. A. (1943a). The pseudo-conditioned eyelid response. Journal of Experimental Psychology, 32, 139-149.

Grant, D. A. (1943b). Sensitization and association in eyelid conditioning. Journal of Experimental Psychology, 32, 201-212.

Grant, D. A. (1945). A sensitized eyelid reaction related to the conditioned eyelid response. Journal of Experimental Psychology, 35, 393-402.

Grant, D. A. (1946). New statistical criteria for learning and problem solution in experiments involving repeated trials. Psychological Bulletin, 43, 272-282.

Grant, D. A. (1947). Additional tables of the probability of "runs" of correct responses in learning and problem-solving. Psychological Bulletin, 44, 276-279.

Grant, D. A. (1949). The statistical analysis of a frequent experimental design. American Journal of Psychology, 62, 119-122.

Grant, D. A. (1950). Statistical theory and research design. In C. P. Stone (Ed.), Annual review of psychology, Vol. 1 (pp. 277-296). Palo Alto, CA: Annual Reviews, Inc.

Grant, D. A. (1954a). Information theory and the discrimination of sequences in stimulus events. Current Trends in Psychology, 7, 18-46.

Grant, D. A. (1954b). The discrimination of sequences in stimulus events and the transmission of information. American Psychologist, 9, 62-68.

Grant, D. A. (1956). Analysis-of-variance tests in the analysis and comparison of curves. Psychological Bulletin, 53, 141-154.

Grant, D. A. (1959). Statistical methods. In P. R. Farnsworth (Ed.), Annual review of psychology, Vol. 10 (pp. 131-146). Palo Alto, CA: Annual Reviews, Inc.

Grant, D. A. (1962). Testing the null hypothesis and the strategy and tactics of investigating theoretical models. Psychological Review, 69, 54-61.

Grant, D. A. (1964). Classical and operant conditioning. In A. W. Melton (Ed.), Categories of human learning (pp. 1-31). New York: Academic Press.

Grant, D. A. (1968). Adding communication to the signalling property of the CS in classical conditioning. Journal of General Psychology, 79, 147-175.

Grant, D. A. (1972). A preliminary model for processing information conveyed by verbal conditioned stimuli in classical conditioning. In A. H. Black and W. F. Prokasy (Eds.), Classical conditioning II: Current research and theory (pp. 28-63). New York: Appleton-Century-Crofts.

Grant, D. A. (1973a). Cognitive factors in eyelid conditioning. Psychophysiology. 10, 75-81.

Grant, D. A. (1973b). Reification and reality in the conditioning paradigms: Implications of results when modes of reinforcement are changed. In F. J. McGuigan and D. B. Lumsden (Eds.), Contemporary approaches to conditioning and learning (pp. 49-67). Washington, DC: V. H. Winston & Sons.

Grant, D. A., Hornseth, J. P., & Hake, H. W. (1949). Sensitization of the beta-response as a function of the wavelength of the stimulus. Journal of Experimental Psychology, 39, 195-199.

Grant, D. A., Kaestner, N. F., & Schipper, L. M. (1955). Autocorrelation analysis of gross learning scores. Perceptual and Motor Skills, 5, 53-63.

Grant, D. A., Levy, C. M., Thompson, J., Hickok, C. W., & Bunde, D. C. (1961). Transfer of differential eyelid conditioning through successive discriminations. Journal of Experimental Psychology, 75, 246-254.

Grant, D. A., & Norris, E. B. (1946). Dark adaptation as a factor in the sensitization of the beta response of the eyelid to light. Journal of Experimental Psychology, 36, 390-397.

Grant, D. A., & Norris, E. B. (1947). Eyelid conditioning as influenced by the presence of sensitized beta-responses. Journal of Experimental Psychology, 37, 423-433.

Grant, D. A., Norris, E. B., & Boissard, S. (1947). Dark adaptation and the pseudoconditioned eyelid response. Journal of Experimental Psychology, 37, 434-439.

Grant, D. A., Norris, E. B., & Hornseth, J. P. (1948). Sensitization of the beta response under verbally induced inhibitory set and counter reinforcement. American Journal of Psychology, 61, 66-72.

Grant, D. A., & Schiller, J. J. (1956). Generalization of the conditioned galvanic skin response to visual stimuli. Journal of Experimental Psychology, 55, 9-17.

Hartman, T. F., Grant, D. A., & Ross, L. E. (1960). An investigation of the latency of "instructed voluntary" eyelid responses. Psychological Reports, 7, 305-311.

21

Hellige, J. B., & Grant, D. A. (1974a). Eyelid conditioning performance when the mode of reinforcement is changed from classical to instrumental avoidance and vice versa. Journal of Experimental Psychology, 102, 710-719.

Hellige, J. B., & Grant, D. A. (1974b). Response rate and development of response topography in eyelid conditioning under different conditions of reinforcement. Journal of Experimental Psychology, 103, 574-582.

Hilgard, E. R., & Marguis, D. G. (1940). Conditioning and learning. New York: Appleton-Century.

Ivanov-Smolensky, A. G. (1933). Metodika issledovaniya uslovnykh refleksov u cheloveka. [Methods of investigation of conditioned reflexes in man.] Moscos: Medigz [Medical State Press].

Kadlac, J. A., & Grant, D. A. (1977). Eyelid response topography in differential inter-stimulus interval conditioning. Journal of Experimental Psychology: Human Learning and Memory, 3, 345-355.

Konorski, J. (1948). Conditioned reflex and neuron organization. Cambridge, England: Cambridge University Press.

Norris, E. B., & Grant, D. A. (1948). Eyelid conditioning as affected by verbally induced inhibitory set and counter reinforcement. American Journal of Psychology, 61, 37-49.

Perry, L. C., Grant, D. A., & Schwartz, M. (1977). Effects of noun imagery and awareness of the discriminative cue upon differential eyelid conditioning to grammatical and ungrammatical phrases. Memory and Cognition, 5, 423-429.

Ross, L. E. (1965). Eyelid conditioning as a tool in psychological research: Some problems and prospects. In W. F. Prokasy (Ed.), Classical conditioning (pp. 249-268). New York: Appleton-Century-Crofts.

Sidowski, J. B. (1978). David A. Grant: An appreciation. Journal of Experimental Psychology: General, 107, 115-118.

Skinner, B. F. (1937). Two types of conditioned reflex: A reply to Konorski and Miller. Journal of General Psychology, 16, 272-279.

Smith, E. E. (1968). Choice reaction time: An analysis of the major theoretical positions. Psychological Bulletin, 69, 77-110.

Spence, K. W., & Taylor, J. (1951). Anxiety and strength of the UCS as determiners of the amount of eyelid conditioning. Journal of Experimental Psychology, 42, 183-188.

Winer, B. J. (1971). Statistical principles in experimental design. New York: McGraw Hill.

Zajano, M. J., & Grant, D. A. (1974). Response topography in the acquisition of differential eyelid conditioning. Journal of Experimental Psychology, 103, 1115-1123.

Zajano, M. J., Grant, D. A., & Schwartz, M. (1974). Transfer of differential eyelid conditioning: Effects of semantic and formal features of verbal stimuli. Journal of Experimental Psychology, 103, 1147-1152.

Other Grant Publications

Anderson, N. H., & Grant, D. A. (1957). A test of a statistical learning theory model for two-choice behavior with double stimulus events. Journal of Experimental Psychology, 54, 305-317.

Anderson, N. H., & Grant, D. A. (1958). Correction and reanalysis. Journal of Experimental Psychology, 56, 453-454.

Anderson, N. H., Grant, D. A., & Nystrom, C. O. (1956). The influence of the spatial positioning of stimulus and response components on performance of a repetitive key-pressing task. Journal of Applied Psychology, 40, 137-141.

Anderson, N. H., Kresse, F. A., & Grant, D. A. (1955). Effect of rate of automatically-paced training in a multidimensional psychomotor task. Journal of Experimental Psychology, 49, 231-236.

Beeman, E. Y., & Grant, D. A. (1961). Delayed extinction and spontaneous recovery following spaced and massed acquisition of the eyelid CR. Journal of General Psychology, 65, 239-300.

Beeman, E. Y., Hartman, T. F., & Grant, D. A. (1960). Supplementary report: Influence of intertrial interval during extinction on spontaneous recovery of conditioned eyelid responses. Journal of Experimental Psychology, 59, 279-280.

Borrowman, E. Y., North, J. A., & Grant, D. A. (1967). Stimulus-reinforcement incongruity in differential eyelid conditioning with verbal stimuli. Journal of General Psychology, 76, 43-48.

Bunde, D. C., Grant, D. A., & Frost, M. R. (1970). Differential eyelid conditioning to stimuli that express a response-related command or convey reinforcement-related information. Journal of Verbal Learning and Verbal Behavior, 9, 346-355.

Buxton, C. E., & Grant, D. A. (1939). Retroaction and gains in motor learning: II. Sex differences and further analysis of gains. Journal of Experimental Psychology, 25, 198-208.

Cerekwicki, L. E., & Grant, D. A. (1967). Delay of positive reinforcement in instrumental eyelid conditioning. Journal of Experimental Psychology, 75, 360-364.

Cerekwicki, L. E., Kantowitz, B. H., & Grant, D. A. (1969). Replicability of an optimal delay of reinforcement result in instrumental eyelid conditioning. Journal of Experimental Psychology, 79, 189-190.

Fleming, J. Z., & Grant, D. A. (1961). Influence of intermittent reinforcement upon acquisition, extinction, and spontaneous recovery in eyelid conditioning with fixed acquisition series. Journal of General Psychology, 64, 225-232.

Gormezano, I., & Grant, D. A. (1958). Progressive ambiguity in the attainment of concepts on the Wisconsin card sorting test. Journal of Experimental Psychology, 55, 621-627.

Grant, D. A. (1939). The influence of attitude on the conditioned eyelid response. Journal of Experimental Psychology, 25, 333-346.

Grant, D. A. (1939). A study of patterning in the conditioned eyelid response. Journal of Experimental Psychology, 25, 445-461.

Grant, D. A. (1944). On "The analysis of variance in psychological research." Psychological Bulletin, 41, 158-166.

Grant, D. A. (1946). A convenient alternating current circuit for measuring GSR's. American Journal of Psychology, 59, 149-151.

Grant, D. A. (1948). The Latin square principle in the design and analysis of psychological experiments. Psychological Bulletin, 45, 427-442.

Grant, D. A. (1951). Perceptual versus analytical responses to the number concept of a Weigl-type card sorting test. Journal of Experimental Psychology, 41, 23-29.

Grant, D. A. (1967). classical and instrumental conditioning. In D. B. Lindsley & A. A. Lumsdaine (Eds.), Brain function, Vol. 4, in UCLA Forum in Medical Sciences, No. 6. Berkeley, CA: University of California Press.

Grant, D. A. (1975). W. J. Brogden: The experimentalist. Bulletin of the Psychonomic Society, 6, 238-244.

Grant, D. A. (1976). Wilfred John Brogden: 1912-1973. American Journal of Psychology, 89, 147-159.

Grant, D. A., & Adams, J. K. (1944). 'Alpha' conditioning in the eyelid. Journal of Experimental Psychology, 34, 136-142.

Grant, D. A., & Berg, E. A. (1948). A behavioral analysis of degree of reinforcement and ease of shifting to new responses in a Weigl-type card-sorting problem. Journal of Experimental Psychology, 38, 404-411.

Grant, D. A., & Cost, J. R. (1954). Continuities and discontinuities in conceptual behavior in a card sorting problem. Journal of General Psychology, 50, 237-244.

Grant, D. A., & Curran, J. F. (1952). Relative difficulty of number, form, and color concepts of a Weigl-type problem using unsystematic number cards. Journal of Experimental Psychology, 43, 408-413.

Grant, D. A., & Dittmer, D. G. (1940). An experimental investigation of Pavlov's cortical irradiation hypothesis. Journal of Experimental Psychology, 26, 299-310.

Grant, D. A., & Dittmer, D. G. (1940). A tactile generalization gradient for a pseudo-conditioned response. Journal of Experimental Psychology, 26, 404-412.

Grant, D. A., & Hake, H. W. (1951). Dark adaptation and the Humphreys random reinforcement phenomenon in human eyelid conditioning. Journal of Experimental Psychology, 42, 417-423.

Grant, D. A., Hake, H. W., & Hornseth, J. P. (1951). Acquisition and extinction of a verbal conditioned response with differing percentages of reinforcement. Journal of Experimental Psychology, 42, 1-5.

Grant, D. A., Hake, H. W., Riopelle, A. J., & Kostlan, A. (1951). The effects of repeated pretesting with the conditioned stimulus upon extinction of the conditioned eyelid response to light. American Journal of Psychology, 64, 247-251.

Grant, D. A., Hake, H. W., & Schneider, D. E. (1948). Effects of pre-testing with the conditioned stimulus upon extinction of the conditioned eyelid response. American Journal of Psychology, 61, 243-246.

Grant, D. A., Hornseth, J. P., & Hake, H. W. (1950). The influence of the inter-trial interval on the Humphreys' "random reinforcement" effect during the extinction of a verbal response. Journal of Experimental Psychology, 40, 609-612.

Grant, D. A., Hunter, H. G., & Patel, A. S. (1958). Spontaneous recovery of the conditioned eyelid response. Journal of General Psychology, 59, 135-141.

Grant, D. A., Jones, O. R., & Tallantis, B. (1949). The relative difficulty of the number, form, and color concepts of a Weigl-type problem. Journal of Experimental Psychology, 39, 552-557.

Grant, D. A., Kadlac, J. A., Schwartz, M., Zajano, M. J., Hellige, J. B., Perry, L. C., & Solberg, K. B. (1977). The role of noun imagery in the speed of processing the grammaticality of adjective-noun phrases. Memory and Cognition, 5, 491-498.

Grant, D. A., Kadlac, J. A., Zajano, M. J., Hellige, J. B., Perry, L. C., & Solberg, K. B. (1977). Influence of noun imagery on speed of naming nouns. Bulletin of the Psychonomic Society, 9, 433-434.

Grant, D. A., & Kaestner, N. F. (1955). Constant velocity tracking as a funciton of S's handedness and the rate and direction of the target course. Journal of Experimental Psychology, 49, 203-208.

Grant, D. A., Kroll, N. E. A., Kantowitz, B. H., Zajano, M. J., & Solberg, K. B. (1969). Transfer of eyelid conditioning from instrumental to classical reinforcement and vice versa. Journal of Experimental Psychology, 82, 503-510.

Grant, D. A., McFarling, C., & Gormezano, I. (1960). Temporal conditioning and the effect of interpolated UCS presentations in eyelid conditioning. Journal of General Psychology, 63, 249-257.

Grant, D. A., & Meyer, H. I. (1941). The formation of generalized response sets during repeated electric shock stimulation. Journal of General Psychology, 24, 21-38.

Grant, D. A., & Meyer, D. R., & Hake, H. W. (1950). Proportional reinforcement and extinction of the conditioned GSR. Journal of General Psychology, 42, 97-101.

Grant, D. A., & Mote, F. A. (1949). Effects of brief flashes of light upon the course of dark adaptation. Journal of Experimental Psychology, 39, 610-616.

Grant, D. A., & Patel, A. S. (1957). Effect of an electric shock stimulus upon the conceptual behavior of "anxious" and "non-anxious" subjects. Journal of General Psychology, 57, 247-256.

Grant, D. A., Ripelle, A. J., & Hake, H. W. (1950). Resistance to extinction and the pattern of reinforcement. I. Alternation of reinforcement and the conditioned eyelid response. Journal of Experimental Psychology, 40, 53-60.

Grant, D. A., & Schipper, L. M. (1952). The acquisition and extinction of conditioned eyelid responses as a function of the percentage of fixed-ratio random reinforcement. Journal of Experimental Psychology, 43, 313-320.

Grant, D. A., & Schipper, L. M., & Ross, B. M. (1952). Effect of the intertrial interval during acquisition on extinction of the conditioned eyelid response following partial reinforcement. Journal of Experimental Psychology, 44, 203-210.

Grant, D. A., & Schneider, D. E. (1948). Intensity of the conditioned stimulus and strength of conditioning: I. The conditioned eyelid response to light. Journal of Experimental Psychology, 38, 690-696.

Grant, D. A., & Schneider, D. E. (1949). Intensity of the conditioned stimulus and strength of conditioning: II. The conditioned galfanic skin response to an auditory stimulus. Journal of Experimental Psychology, 39, 35-40.

Grant, D. A., Schneider, D. E., & Goodale, J. C. (1949). Group pre-training for serial rote learning by means of a motion picture technique. Journal of General Psychology, 40, 89-94.

Grant, D. A., & Warren, A. B. (1955). The relation of conditioned discrimination to the MMPI Pd personality variable. Journal of Experimental Psychology, 49, 23-27.

Hake, H. W., & Grant, D. A. (1951). Resistance to extinction and the pattern of reinforcement: II. Effect of successive alternation of blocks of reinforced and unreinforced trials upon the conditioned eyelid response to light. Journal of Experimental Psychology, 41, 216-220.

Hake, H. W., & Grant, D. A., & Hornseth, J. P. (1951). Resistance to extinction and the pattern of reinforcement: III. Effect of trial patterning in verbal "conditioning." Journal of Experimental Psychology, 41, 221-225.

Hansche, W. J., & Grant, D. A. (1960). Onset versus termination of a stimulus as the CS in eyelid conditioning. Journal of Experimental Psychology, 59, 19-26.

Hansche, W. J., & Grant, D. A. (1965). A comparison of instrumental reward and avoidance training with classical reinforcement technique in conditioning the eyelid response. Psychonomic Science, 2, 305-306.

Hartman, T. F., Beeman, E. Y., & Grant, D. A. (1960). The correlation of post-rest recovery in verbal and motor learning. Journal of General Psychology, 63, 199-202.

Hartman, T. F., & Grant, D. A. (1960). Effect of intermittent reinforcement on acquisition, extinction, and spontaneous recovery of the conditioned eyelid response. Journal of Experimental Psychology, 60, 89-96.

Hartman, T. F., & Grant, D. A. (1962). Effects of pattern reinforcement and verbal information on acquisition, extinction, and spontaneous recovery of the eyelid CR. Journal of Experimental Psychology, 63, 217-226.

Hartman, T. F., & Grant, D. A. (1962). Differential eyelid conditioning as a function of the CS-UCS interval. Journal of Experimental Psychology, 64, 131-136.

Hickok, C. W., & Grant, D. A. (1964). Effects of pattern of reinforcement and verbal information on acquisition and extinction of the eyelid CR. Journal of General Psychology, 71, 279-289.

Hickok, C. W., Grant, D. A., & North, J. A. (1965). Differential eyelid conditioning of voluntary form responders. Psychonomic Science, 3, 583-584.

Hickok, C. W., Grant, D. A., & North, J. A. (1967). Factors in the reversal of differential conditioning of the human eyelid response. Journal of General Psychology, 76, 125-137.

Howat, M. G., & Grant, D. A. (1958). Influence of intertrial interval during extinction on spontaneous recovery of conditioned eyelid response. Journal of Experimental Psychology, 56, 11-15.

Kaestner, N. F., & Grant, D. A. (1956). Transfer of training in tracking as a function of the predictability of unidimensional target courses. Journal of General Psychology, 55, 103-116.

Kresse, F. H., Peterson, R. M., & Grant, D. A. (1954). Multiple response transfer as a function of supplementary training with verbal schematic aids. Journal of Experimental Psychology, 48, 381-390.

Kroll, N. E. A., & Grant, D. A. (1968). Cue selection in paired-associate and concept-learning paradigms. Journal of Verbal Learning and Verbal Behavior, 7, 64-71.

Leibowitz, H. W., Myers, N. A., & Grant, D. A. (1955). Frequency of seeing and radial localization of single and multiple visual stimuli. Journal of Experimental Psychology, 50, 369-373.

Leibowitz, H. W., Myers, N. A., & Grant, D. A. (1955). Radial localization of a single stimulus as a function of luminance and duration of exposure. Journal of the Optical Society of America, 45, 76-78.

Levy, C. M., Grant, D. A., & Clark, A. H. (1964). Reversal of conditioned discrimination of the eyelid response. Journal of Experimental Psychology, 67, 80-82.

Lockard, J. S., Lockard, R. B., & Grant, D. A. (1964). Extinction and spontaneous recovery of the eyelid CR as a function of delay of the UCS and the interval between acquisition and extinction. Journal of General Psychology, 71, 161-167.

Morin, R. E., & Grant, D. A. (1955). Learning and performance on a key-pressing task as a function of the degree of spatial stimulus-response correspondence. Journal of Experimental Psychology, 49, 39-47.

Morin, R. E., Grant, D. A., & Nystrom, C. O. (1956). Temporal predictions of motion inferred from intermittently viewed light stimuli. Journal of General Psychology, 55, 59-71.

Mote, F. A., Grant, D. A., & Hoffman, G. K. (1961). The effect of brief flashes of light upon peripheral dark adaptation. Journal of General Psychology, 64, 233-244.

North, J. A., Grant, D. A., & Fleming, R. A. (1967). Choice reaction time to single digits, spelled numbers, and "right" and "wrong" arithmetic problems and short sentences. Quarterly Journal of Experimental Psychology, 19, 73-77.

Novak, D. J., & Grant, D. A. (1965). Semantic generalization of the conditioned eyelid response with two types of training. Psychological Reports, 17, 731-738.

Nystrom, C. O., & Grant, D. A. (1955). Performance on a key pressing task as a function of the angular correspondence between stimulus and response elements. Perceptual and Motor Skills, Monograph Supplement, 1, 113-125.

Nystrom, C. O., Morin, R. E., & Grant, D. A. (1956). Transfer effects between automatically-paced training schedules in a perceptual-motor task. Journal of General Psychology, 55, 9-17.

Nystrom, C. O., Morin, R. E., & Grant, D. A. (1955). The effects of amount, rate, and stage of automatically-paced training on self-paced performance. Journal of Experimental Psychology, 49, 225-230.

Ornstein, P. A., Grant, D. A., & Watters, W. C. (1972). Semantic generalization over a bipolar dimension of meaning. Journal of Experimental Psychology, 95, 202-210.

Patel, A. S., & Grant, D. A. (1964). Decrement and recovery effects in a perceptual-motor learning task as a function of effort, distribution of practice, and sex of subject. Journal of General Psychology, 71, 217-231.

Perry L. C., Ornstein, P. A., & Grant, D. A. (1971). A test of associative generalization of the conditioned eyelid response. Psychonomic Science, 23, 319-320.

Perry, L. C., Ornstein, P. A., Watters, W. C., & Grant, D. A. (1971). Effects of number and type of verbal conditioned stimuli upon differential eyelid conditioning. Journal of Verbal Learning and Verbal Behavior, 10, 459-469.

Prokasy, W. F., Grant, D. A., & Myers, N. A. (1958). Eyelid conditioning as a function of unconditioned stimulus intensity and intertrial interval. Journal of Experimental Psychology, 55, 242-246.

Ross, B. M., Rupel, J. W., & Grant, D. A. (1952). Effects of personal, impersonal, and physical stress upon cognitive behavior in a card sorting problem. <u>Journal of Abnormal and Social Psychology</u>, <u>47</u>, 546-551.

Table 1

**Individuals Completing the Ph.D. Under
David A. Grant's Supervision***

Individuals Completing the Ph.D. Under David A. Grant's Supervision:

Anderson, Norman H.
Bice, Raymond C.
Buckley, Paul
Cerekwicki, Louise
Chodorkoff, Bernard
Fey, Elizabeth T.
Fleming, Robert A.
Gormezano, Isidore
Hake, Harold W.
Hansche, Wesley Jay
Hardtke, Eldred F.
Hartman, Thomas F.
Hellige, Joseph
Hickok, Craig
Hornseth, John P.
Kaestner, Noel F.
Kroll, Neal E. A.

Levy, C. Michael
Lockard, Robert B.
Lockard, Joan
Morin, Robert E.
Myers, Nancy A.
Nystrom, Charles O.
Ornstein, Peter
Patel, Ambalal S.
Peterson, Robert M.
Prokasy, William F.
Riopelle, Arthur J.
Ross, Bruce M.
Schipper, Lowell M.
Sidowski, Joseph B.
Schvaneveldt, Roger
Solberg, Kenneth

*William J. Cody, Jeffrey A. Kadlac, and Michael J. Zajano were in the process of completing their degrees at the time that David Grant died.

CONDITIONING AND COGNITION

In the contribution by Gormezano and Kehoe, it is assumed that laws governing the organization, integration, and selection of stimuli from among the stream of stimuli surrounding biologically significant events is central to the explanation of an organism's behavioral adjustment to its environment. Since conditioning constitutes a fundamental mechanism of individual adaptation, a knowledge of the laws of conditioning in a complex, but well controlled stimulus environment is required. The authors address serial compound conditioning in their reported research since it permits a determination of the degree to which stimulus selection processes interact with contiguity mechanisms.

Kantowitz believes that researchers in Human Information Processing (HIP) regard their techniques in part as a revolution against older more traditional approaches based on learning theory. While some workers in conditioning have tried to apply modern HIP techniques and principles, few have gone the other way. This chapter describes how principles such as response tendencies and generalization gradients drawn from learning theory might improve stage models of double stimulation. The Kantowitz response conflict model is used to illustrate these points.

The general belief of theoreticians over the past years has been that concept learning is a directed analytical process. Although a great deal of research supports that belief, Kellogg and Bourne provide experimental evidence for the use of non-analytical processes in concept formation. They do not deny that concepts are often learned through logic-driven analytic procedures. The data and explanations that they provide, however, strongly support the notion that some concept learning can be best explained in terms of the nonanalytic automatic storage of specific instances.

The fourth contribution to this section deals with research on memory with very young children. Ratner and Myers report on several studies of paired associate learning and delayed response memory, and suggest a tentative model of memory for children between the ages of two and five years.

The comprehension of metaphor has been shown to be a serious problem for "semantic marker" theories of linguistic meaning. Psychological theories of semantic memory are shown to be open to similar criticisms. Kroll, Kreisler, and Berrian point out that the problems center on how appropriate properties of the metaphorical term are selected and how clearly their meaning can be specified since metaphors are necessarily ambiguous. Experiments reported in this chapter attempt to develop an experimental basis for clarifying the processes involved in attribute selection, and the degree to which the resulting representation can be specified.

Performance on many tasks involving visual stimuli depends on whether stimuli are briefly presented to the left or right visual field. Such visual laterality effects are often attributed to information processing differences between the two cerebral hemispheres. In Chapter 7, Hellige examines several variables that influence visual laterality patterns: directional scanning habits, perceptual quality of stimuli, imposition of concurrent tasks, and pure-versus mixed-list presentation of verbal and non-verbal stimuli. Methodological and theoretical implications are discussed.

30

2

CLASSICAL CONDITIONING WITH SERIAL COMPOUND STIMULI

Isidore Gormezano and E. James Kehoe

Introduction

As originally conceived by Pavlov (1927), the classical conditioning paradigm was viewed as a laboratory model for studying behavioral adaptation of organisms to the numerous exigencies of the environment, including the complex array of potential stimuli that typically precede biologically significant events. Subsequently, the use of multiple conditioned stimuli in compound has come to be recognized as an analytically effective means for determining the laws governing the organization, integration, and selection of stimuli in a complex but controlled stimulus environment (e.g., Baker, 1968; Grings, 1972; Hull, 1943; Kehoe & Gormezano, 1980; Razran, 1965; Wickens, 1959).

Historically, investigations of classical conditioning in a complex stimulus environment have involved both compounds of simultaneous and serial conditioned stimuli. However, two major considerations led us to examine the laws governing serial compound conditioning:

1. <u>CR mediation</u>. Students of conditioning have persistently sought to identify classical conditioning mechanisms (e.g., higher-order conditioning, stimulus generalization) that could produce CRs over an extended series of stimuli to mediate "purposeful" or "goal-directed" instrumental behavior (e.g., Hull, 1930, 1934, 1943; Konorski, 1967; Spence, 1956). From this perspective, a serial compound of two CSs followed by a US provides a first approximation to the stimulus analysis of instrumental conditioning found in CR-mediational theories. Thus, serial compounds provide a basis for identifying mechanisms by which classical conditioning can be stretched beyond the bounds of the contiguity gradient for a single CS-US pair to yield responding to members of the serial stimulus sequence long antedating the US (Gormezano & Kehoe, 1984).

2. <u>Stimulus selection</u>. Students of conditioning have long sought to specify mechanisms of "stimulus selection" by which organisms come to respond to a limited subset of the stimuli that are contiguous to a reinforcer (e.g., Gormezano & Kehoe, 1981; Rudy & Wagner, 1975; Sutherland & Mackintosh, 1971). However, investigations of selective conditioning among serial stimuli were rare when we began our

31

investigations (Egger & Miller, 1962; Wickens, 1959, 1965, 1973). Yet, the study of selective conditioning among serial stimuli differing in their respective CS-US intervals permits a more direct determination of the degree to which stimulus selection processes override the operation of CS-US contiguity mechanisms.

The research reviewed in this chapter has extended over ten years and has benefited from contributions by our students and colleagues at both the Universities of Iowa and New South Wales. Hence, the use of "we" in this chapter is meant to include the relevant collaborators as well as the authors of this chapter. Because there were several strands to our research, specific experiments described in this chapter are presented in their "logical" rather than chronological order. To aid discussion of the experiments, each one will be denoted by a Roman numeral.

The Primary Phenomena of Serial Compound Conditioning

Our initial investigation of serial compound conditioning was guided by a question first posed by Wickens (1959) as to whether or not the empirical contiguity gradients obtained for a single CS paired with a US would be sufficient to predict CR acquisition to each of a series of CSs differing in their respective CS-US intervals. In the case of the rabbit nictitating membrane response (NMR) preparation, manipulations of the CS-US interval with a single CS have consistently yielded a sharp gradient, in which CR acquisition occurs most rapidly at CS-US intervals around 250 ms and declines to baseline levels at intervals less than 100 ms and longer than 4,000 ms (Gormezano, Kehoe, & Marshall, 1983; Schneiderman, 1966; Schneiderman & Gormezano, 1964). Using this well-delineated contiguity gradient as the basis for comparison, the NMR preparation has readily revealed the capacity of a reinforced serial compound (CS1-CS2-US) to (a) facilitate CR acquisition to CSs at intervals well beyond the outer bounds of the empirical CS-US contiguity gradient and (b) attenuate CR acquisition to CSs relatively contiguous to the US.

Experiment I

In our first experiment, the serial compound CS consisted of a 400-ms tone CS1 followed after a trace interval by a 400-ms light CS2 and a 50-ms shock US (Kehoe, Gibbs, Garcia, & Gormezano, 1979, Experiment 1). The CS2-US interval was fixed at 350 ms, while the CS1-US interval was manipulated in separate groups over the values of 750, 1,250, 1,750, and 2,750 ms, respectively. The four groups were labeled in terms of the tone CS1 (T), their respective trace intervals between CS1-offset and CS2-onset expressed in seconds (0, 0.5, 1, or 2), and the light CS2 (L). This, the four groups were designated T-O-L, T-.5-L, T-1-L, and T-2-L, respectively. All subjects received 16 days of acquisition training, each day consisting of 60 reinforced serial compound trials interspersed with two nonreinforced test trials to each component and to the compound. On test trials, a constant 2,800-ms observation interval for recording CRs was used.

The major results of the experiment are depicted in Panels a and b of Figure 1. Examination of Panel a indicates that despite the rather large differences in CS1-US interval across groups, initial CR acquisition to CS1 was uniformly rapid. Moreover, all groups attained at least an 80% CRs before groups trained under the longer CS1-US intervals (Groups T-1-L and T-2-L) showed declines in performance. On the other hand, Panel b indicates that the rate of acquisition and terminal level of CRs to CS2 was an inverse function of the CS1-US (or trace) interval.

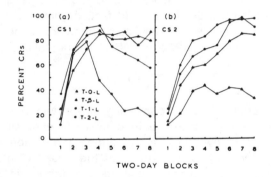

Figure 1. The mean percentage of CRs on CS1 and CS2 test trials in two-day blocks for each of the four groups. Each group was labeled in terms of the tone CS1 (T), their respective trace intervals expressed in seconds (0, 0.5, 1, or 2), and the light CS2 (L).

Serial Facilitation. On the basis of the empirical contiguity gradients for the rabbit NMR, CR acquisition to CS1 in the serial compound should have been a decreasing function of the CS1-US interval. However, as can be seen in Figure 1, rapid CR acquisition to CS1 was observed initially at all CS1-US intervals. Although the high levels of responding to CS1 were not sustained under the longer CS1-US intervals, the observed performance was hardly transient. In particular, at the longest CS1-US interval of 2,750 ms in Group T-2-L, responding to CS1 increased rapidly over the course of six days, or

33

360 reinforced compound trials, before any decline appeared. Accordingly, the high levels of responding to CS1 under the longer CS1-US intervals suggested that serial compounds could bridge long temporal gaps between CSs and USs. Subsequently, Kehoe, Gibbs, Garcia, & Gormezano, (1979, Experiment 4) extended the range of CS1-US intervals to values of 4,750, 8,750, and 18,750 ms, while leaving the CS2-US interval at 350 ms. When responding during CS1 itself was examined, the same pattern of initial increases in responding to CS1 followed by an eventual decline was found even though CS1 was quite remote from both the CS2 and the US.

Serial Attenuation. The deleterious effects of CS1 on CR acquisition to CS2 indicated a stimulus selection effect similar to that observed by Wickens (1959, 1965, 1973) and Egger and Miller (1962). On the basis of empirical contiguity gradients for the rabbit NMR, the fixed 350-ms CS2-US interval should have produced a uniform and high level of responding to CS2 across groups. However, as seen in Panel b of Figure 1, the level of responding to CS2 progressively declined as the CS1-US interval decreased. In fact, the level of responding on CS2 test trials fell below the level of responding to the less contiguous CS1 at the 750-and 1,250-ms CS1-US intervals.

Theory

Although a serial compound consisting of just two CSs might appear to involve only a slight increase in complexity over single CS training, the number of hypotheses concerning interaction between two CSs is staggering. Moreover, many of the possible interactions are compatible with one another and could contribute in an algebraic fashion to the level of responding to each CS. While this state of affairs is theoretically inelegant, the large number of possibilities may truly reflect a multiplicity of processes that enable considerable flexibility in behavioral adaptation to complex environments. In order to identify the contribution of each process to response acquisition in a serial compound, research has focused on three interstimulus relations in a serial compound, namely, CS1-CS2, CS1-US, and CS2-US. Each of the possible processes can be tied to a specific combination of the interstimulus relations. (See Kehoe (1982a) for a review of research using other associative learning procedures.)

CS1-US and CS2-US Relations
Direct Conditioning. Both CS1 and CS2 of a serial compound are subject to direct conditioning according to their individual relations with

the US, especially their CS-US intervals. The level of direct conditioning for each CS can be independently assessed by using single-stimulus control groups, each of which is given CS-US training with either CS1 or CS2. Moreover, the level of responding obtained for each separately-trained CS provides the baseline against which either facilitation or attenuation is detected in a compound conditioning procedure (Kehoe, 1979; Wickens, 1959).

Stimulus Generalization. Stimulus generalization from CS2 to CS1 has been proposed to facilitate responding to CS1 (Levis, 1966; Levis & Stampfl, 1972). The experimental assessment of stimulus generalization requires only CS2-US pairings plus sporadic test presentations of CS1 to observe generalized responses. Although generalization can play a considerable role in serial compound conditioning (Dubin & Levis, 1973), we have deliberately minimized stimulus generalization by the use of CSs from different sensory modalities, namely vision and audition. Empirically, Kehoe, Feyer, & Moses (1981) found that, across three experiments using the rabbit NMR preparation, the maximum levels of cross-modal generalization averaged 17% CRs, which exceeded the baseline level of "spontaneous" responses by approximately 12 percentage points (cf. Kehoe & Holt, 1984; Kehoe, Morrow & Holt, 1984).

General Transfer. General transfer is distinct from stimulus generalization. In particular, its experimental assessment requires both CS1-US and CS2-US pairing. A general transfer mechanism can be conceptualized as a learning-to-learn process analogous to that found in discrimination learning in which acquisition of an "easy" discrimination facilitates acquisition of a "hard" discrimination (e.g., Pavlov, 1927, pp. 121-122). Similarly, CR acquisition to CS2 with its short CS-US interval could facilitate CR acquisition to CS1 with its longer, otherwise ineffective CS-US interval. In fact, Kehoe and Holt (1984, Experiment 1) have demonstrated that training one CS (e.g., tone) at a 400-ms CS-US interval did facilitate subsequent CR acquisition to another CS (e.g., light) at CS-US intervals of 800 ms and 1,800 ms but not 2,800 ms, an interval over which facilitation does occur in a serial compound.

Differential Inhibition. Differential inhibition also relies on the CS1-US and CS2-US pairings and, more particularly, on the disparity between their respective CS-US intervals (Frey, Englander & Roman, 1971; Williams, 1965, p. 341). Pavlov (1927, pp. 103-104) might be regarded as the earliest proponent of a differential inhibition hy-

35

pothesis. In his explanation of "inhibition of delay," Pavlov (1927) argued that a long CS could be regarded as a serial compound with the successive elements arising from the time-dependent processes initiated by the CS. By appealing to the empirical laws of differential conditioning, Pavlov argued that the initial portion of the CS, through its distance from the US, effectively becomes a CS-and accordingly acquires inhibitory properties. Conversely, the later portion of the CS becomes a CS+ and acquires excitatory properties.

The CS1-CS2 Relation

Associative Transfer. The CS1-CS2 relation has usually been thought to facilitate responding to CS1 in a serial compound, specifically through processes of associative transfer as seen in second-order conditioning (Frey, Englander, & Roman, 1971; Rescorla, 1973, p. 145) and sensory preconditioning (Wickens, 1959, 1965, 1973). The experimental demonstration of associative transfer relies on the CS1-CS2 and CS2-US pairings embedded in a serial compound. Demonstrations of second-order conditioning have been obtained in the rabbit NMR preparation using separate but intermixed CS1-CS2 and CS2-US presentations (Gormezano & Kehoe, 1981; Kehoe, Feyer, & Moses, 1981). However, the contrast between unreinforced CS1-CS2 presentations and the CS2-US pairings also permits the acquisition of conditioned inhibitory properties to CS1 as witnessed by an eventual decline in responding to the second-order stimulus (CS1) (Herendeen & Anderson, 1968; Kehoe, Feyer, & Moses, 1981). Thus, procedures for demonstrating associative transfer may underestimate its contribution inside a reinforced CS1-CS2-US sequence.

The CS1-CS2-US Sequence

Although the experimental separation of a serial compound into its constituent interstimulus relations can estimate the contribution by a number of processes, there are additional processes which rely upon the integrity of the entire reinforced serial compound.

Perceptual Integration. Perceptual integration of the compound differs from associative transfer between CS2 and CS1. Instead, CS2 may be thought to "bridge" the longer CS1-US interval, effectively shortening it and thus facilitating direct conditioning of CS1 (Kehoe, Feyer, & Moses, 1981; Kehoe & Morrow, 1984; Rescorla, 1982). To account for serial attenuation of CR acquisition to CS2, other perceptual hypotheses contend that responding to CS2 will suffer a generalization decrement when tested outside the stimulus context provided by CS1 in the compound (e.g., Bond, 1983; Borgealt, Donahoe,

36

& Weinstein, 1972; Hancock, 1982; Kehoe, 1979; Rescorla, 1972; Wickens, 1959, 1965). Under a generalization decrement hypothesis, responding to the initial portion of CS1 would not be subject to a generalization decrement during testing, because the perceptual encoding of CS1 is affected only by the static background stimuli which remain the same whether or not CS2 is subsequently presented.

Discrimination Mechanisms. The simplest discrimination hypotheses contend that response acquisition to CS1 may be facilitated if CS2 fills an otherwise "empty" interval between CS1 and the US, because the reinforced trial will become more distinguishable from the background stimuli (Bolles, Collier, Bouton & Marlin, 1978; Kaplan & Hearst, 1982; Mowrer & Lamoreaux, 1951). In contrast, advocates of temporal discrimination hypotheses contend that a serial compound may hinder response acquisition to CS1 and perhaps facilitate responding to CS2. These hypotheses argue specifically that the sequence of discrete stimuli in a serial compound enhances the precision with which a response can be placed just prior to the onset of the US (Sears, Baker & Frey, 1979; Williams, 1965).

Competition Hypotheses. Competition hypotheses contend that there is a trade-off between concurrent stimuli in their respective associative strengths (Frey & Sears, 1978; Rescorla & Wagner, 1972; Revusky, 1971; Sutton & Barto, 1981) or attentional values (Mackintosh, 1975; Mackintosh & Reese, 1979; Moore & Stickney, 1980; Sutherland & Mackintosh, 1971). Competition hypotheses can account for a variety of outcomes depending on the parameters determining the relative competitive advantages of CS1 and CS2. Specifically, selective attention hypotheses (Sutherland & Mackintosh, 1971) would predict that response acquisition to CS2 will be hindered if CS1 and its traces capture the attention of the subject, thus precluding full attention to CS2 even though it is close to the US (Kehoe, 1979; Kehoe, Schreurs, & Amodei, 1981). However, if attention to CS1 wanes before CS2 appears, then CS2 may be able to attract attention to itself and away from CS1, thus hindering response acquisition to CS1 (Mackintosh & Reese, 1979). Other competition hypotheses generally predict that response acquisition to CS1 will be more greatly impaired than acquisition to CS2 in serial compound conditioning (Mackintosh, 1975; Rescorla & Wagner, 1972; Revusky, 1971, p. 171). These latter competition hypotheses contend that the associative strengths which accrue to each CS depend on their relative associative strengths at the time of US occurrence. Since CS2 is closer to the US, it would gain associative strength faster than CS1 and would thereby gain a competitive advantage over CS1.

Information Hypotheses. Information hypotheses predict that response acquisition to CS2 will suffer as a consequence of serial compound training (Cantor, 1981; Cantor & Wilson, 1981; Egger & Miller, 1962; Seligman, 1966). According to Egger and Miller's original hypothesis, if CS1 and CS2 are equally reliable "predictors" of the US, then associative strength will accrue to the initial CS1 and not the later "redundant" CS2. The more recent information hypotheses contend that CS2 will lose its effectiveness in gaining access to the associative apparatus if its occurrence is well predicted by preceding events, namely CS1 (Cantor, 1981, p. 313; Cantor & Wilson, 1981, p. 262; cf. Pearce & Hall, 1980, p. 535). In the case of Cantor and Wilson's (1981) hypothesis, it implies that response acquisition to CS1 may be facilitated by the ability of CS1 to predict CS2 even though this predictive CS1-CS2 relation would impair the acquisition to CS2. Thus, in a sequence of optimally separated CSs, the earliest stimulus would gain maximal associative strength and the remaining elements would gain less associative strength.

Direct Conditioning and Generalization

Experiment II
   The findings of Experiment I indicated that CR acquisition to CS1 was facilitated at the longer CS1-US intervals while CR acquisition to CS2 was attenuated at the shorter CS1-US intervals. However, unequivocally determining whether the high levels of responding to CS1 arose from the presence of CS2 in the serial compound required a demonstration that responding to CS1 exceeded direct conditioning of CS1 and/or generalization from CS2 to CS1. Similarly, single-CS controls were required to determine whether the depressed level of responding to CS2 at the shorter CS1-US intervals was attributable to the prior presentation of CS1 in the serial compound. Accordingly, our second experiment (Kehoe, Gibbs, Garcia, & Gormezano, 1979, Experiment 2) replicated Groups T-0-L and T-2-L from Experiment I. In turn, Group T-0-L was compared to Group T-0-O, which was trained with only CS1 at a CS-Us interval of 750 ms, and Group O-0-L, which was trained with only CS2 at a CS-US interval of 350 ms. Similarly, Group T-2-L was compared to Group T-2-O, which was trained with CS1 at a CS-US interval of 2,750 ms, and Group O-2-L, which was trained with CS2 at a CS-US interval of 350 ms.

38

The results of Experiment II are presented in the panels of Figure 2. At the 750-ms CS1-US interval, examination of Panels a and c reveals attenuation occurred in CR acquisition to both CS1 and CS2 in Group T-0-L. Panel a indicates that, although Group T-0-L's responding to CS1 rose to a high level, the single-CS1 control, Group T-0-O, reached an even higher level of responding throughout most of training. As can be seen in Panel c, attenuation of CR acquisition to CS2 was more pronounced. That is to say, responding on CS2 test trials by Group T-0-L fell substantially below that of Group O-0-L. At the 2,750-ms CS1-US interval, substantial facilitation of CR acquisition to CS1 in the serial compound appeared. In particular, Panel b reveals that, while Group T-2-O's responding to CS1 averaged only about 15% CRs, Group T-2-L's responding to CS1, as in Experiment I, attained a a level of 88% CRs before showing a decline. Moreover, Group T-2-L's maximal and overall levels of responding to CS1 far exceeded those attributable to generalization from CS2 to CS1 as seen in the single-CS2 control, Group O-2-L. Panel d indicates that Group T-2-L's responding to CS2 was only slightly below that of Group O-2-L, suggesting that little or no attenuation of responding to CS2 occured at the 2,750-ms CS1-US interval.

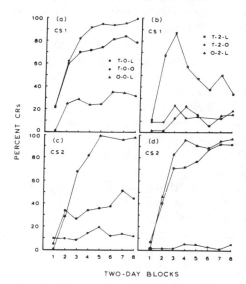

Figure 2. The mean percentage of CRs on CS1 and CS2 test trials over two-day blocks. Groups T-2-L and T-2-L received reinforced tone-light serial compounds with trace intervals of 0 and 2 s, respectively; Groups T-0-O and Groups T-2-O received reinforced tone trials at CS-US intervals of 750 and 2,750 ms, respectively; Groups O-0-L and O-2-L received reinforced light trials each at a 350-ms CS-US interval.

Nonserial Mechanisms

As described the the section on theory, mixed presentations of CS1-US and CS2-US are necessary to engage mechanisms of general transfer and differential inhibition. Moreover, in practice, the use of intermixed CS1-US and CS2-US pairings provides a joint estimate of direct conditioning of CS1, direct conditioning of CS2, and stimulus generalization between the CSs as well as general transfer and differential inhibition. In summary, "uncoupled" training of CS1 and CS2 provides a control for all mechanisms that do not depend on the serial CS1-CS2 relation. In brief, uncoupled training has yielded some facilitation of CR acquisition to CS1 but not enough to account for all the facilitation obtained with reinforced serial compounds.

Experiment III

In our early experiments, CRs initiated during CS1 or the subsequent trace interval were grouped together for purposes of determining the likelihood of a CR to CS1. Recently, Kehoe and Morrow (1984) have examined CR likelihood during the duration of CS1 separately from that of the trace interval. Their serial compound was similar to that used in Group T-2-L of Experiments I and II. That is to say, the serial compound was composed of a 400-ms CS1, a trace interval of at least 2,000 ms, and a brief CS2 prior to the US. Experiment III was conducted in three replications, which entailed joint manipulation of the CS2 duration and CS2-US interval across values of 150, 250, and 400ms. The order of stimulus presentation was counterbalanced so that half the animals in each group received a tone-light series and half received a light-tone series. To assess the contribution of nonserial mechanisms, each serial compound group had a corresponding uncoupled control group, which received separate CS1-US and CS2-US presentations equal in number to those embedded in a serial compound.

Inspection of the CR latencies revealed that the timing of CRs developed differently in the serial compound groups as compared to the uncoupled groups. Within the serial compounds, the distribution of CR latencies showed three distinct modes, namely one during CS1, one during the trace interval, and one during CS2. In contrast, the uncoupled groups showed a mode only during CS1 and not during the trace interval on CS1-US trials. Of course, the uncoupled groups also showed a mode in CR latencies during CS2 on CS2-US trials. Figure 3 shows the likelihood of CRs during CS1, the trace interval, and CS2 across days for the serial compound groups (left column of panels) and the uncoupled groups (right column of panels).

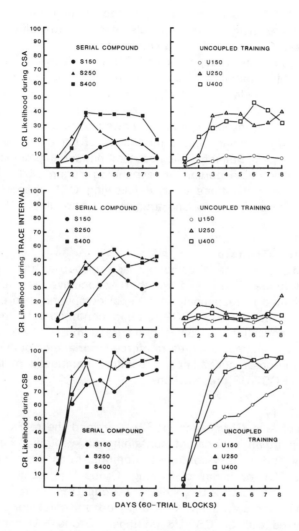

Figure 3. The mean CR likelihood during successive segments of reinforced trials plotted as a function of days. In each row, the left-hand panel shows the data from the serial compound groups, and the right-hand panel shows the data from the uncoupled training groups. The top row shows the CR likelihood during CS1 (designated here as CSA), the middle row shows CR likelihood during the 2,000-ms interval following CS1, and the bottom row shows CR likelihood during CS2 (designated here as CSB).

41

Examination of the top panels reveals that both the serial compound and uncoupled groups trained with the 250- and 400-ms CS2-US intervals showed acquisition of CRs to CS1, which generally reached maximum levels near 40% CRs. The serial compound and uncoupled groups trained with the 150-ms CS2-US interval showed little CR acquisition to CS1. Inspection of CR likelihood during the trace interval as shown in the middle row of panels reveals large differences between the serial compound and uncoupled groups. In particular, all three serial compound groups showed CR acquisition during the trace interval, reaching terminal levels between 30% and 50% CRs. In contrast, the uncoupled groups showed low levels of responding that hovered around 10% CRs. The lower panels indicate that both the serial compound and uncoupled groups showed considerable CR acquisition to CS2. In summary, our comparisons of serial compound training with uncoupled training indicated that nonserial processes could explain a considerable portion of responding during CS1. However, responding during the trace interval following CS1 appears to be a consequence of serial compound training not attributable to nonserial processes.

Associative Transfer

With comparisons of serial compound and uncoupled training in hand, it remained to be determined whether associative transfer mechanisms contributed to responding in a serial compound. To provide direct evidence that the CS1-CS2 relation contributed to the facilitation of CR acquisition to CS1 and its trace interval, we have conducted several comparisons of reinforced serial compound training with a second-order conditioning procedure composed of intermixed CS1-CS2 and CS2-US presentations.

Experiment IV

Gibbs, Cool, and Gormezano (1982) examined the role of the CS1-CS2 relation in an experiment containing six groups. Four of the groups provided a fully-controlled demonstration of second-order conditioning. On each day of training, Group P-P received 30 CS1-CS2 pairings and 30 CS2-US pairings. Group U-P controlled for stimulus generalization and received 30 unpaired presentations of CS1 and CS2 intermixed with 30 CS2-US pairings. Group P-U controlled for any unconditioned stimulus properties of CS1 and received 30 CS1-CS2 pairings intermixed with 30 unpaired presentations of CS2 and the US. Finally, Group U-U served as a control for any nonassociative contributions of the US; Group U-U received 30 CS1, 60 CS2, and 30 US presentations. To assess the contribution of second-order conditioning to the facilitation of CR acquisition to a CS1 in a reinforced serial compound, Group P-P was compared to two serial compound groups. Specifically, Group SC (Serial Compound) received 30 CS1-CS2-US trials per session, and Group PR (Partial Reinforcement) received 30 CS1-CS2-US and 30 CS1-CS2 trials per session in order to determine whether differences between Groups SC and P-P would be attributable to the 50% partial reinforcement schedule in effect for CS2 in Group P-P. The duration of both CS1 and CS2 were 400 ms, the CS1-CS2 interval was 1,400 ms, and the CS2-US interval was 400 ms.

Figure 4 presents the likelihood of CRs during CS1's 400-ms duration. Examination of the figure reveals that Groups U-P, P-U, and U-U, which lacked either CS1-CS2 and/or CS2-US pairings, displayed uniformly low levels of responding during CS1 throughout training. In marked contrast, Groups P-P, PR, and SC each showed consistent increases in responding during CS1 across days of acquisition. Of particular interest, Group P-P attained substantially higher levels of responding than the low levels observed for the unpaired controls, thus demonstrating that CS1-CS2 and CS2-US pairings are sufficient to produce responding during CS1. Moreover, although the response level for Group P-P was much below that of Group SC, the intermediate performance of Group PR indicates that a portion of the difference can be attributed to the decremental effects of the partial reinforcement schedule in operation for CS2 in Group P-P.

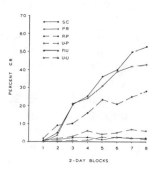

Figure 4. The mean percentage of CRs during CS1 on CS1-CS2 trials over two-day blocks. On each day, Group SC was trained with 30 reinforced serial compound trials (CS1-CS2-US), Group PR received 30 CS1-CS2-US and 30 CS1-CS2 trials per day, Group P-P received 30 CS1-CS2 and 30 CS2-US trials, Group U-P received 30 unpaired CS1-CS2 and 30 CS2-US trials, Groups P-U received 30 CS1-CS2 trials and 30 Unpaired CS2-US trials, and Group U-U received 30 unpaired CS1-CS2 and 30 unpaired CS2-US trials.

43

Experiment V

Kehoe and Morrow (1984, Experiment 2) have also examined the contribution of the CS1-CS2 relation to responding during both CS1 and its trace interval in a reinforced serial compound. Their experiment contained five groups. A serial compound group received on each day 60 reinforced serial compound presentations, in which the duration of CS1 and CS2 were each 400 ms, the CS1-CS2 interval was 2,400 ms, and the CS2-US interval was 400 ms. There was a corresponding second-order conditioning group, which received 60 CS1-CS2 trials and 60 CS2-US trials. In addition, there was an uncoupled training group (60 CS1-US and 60 CS2-US), a CS1 trace conditioning group (60 CS1-US), and a generalization control (60 CS2-US).

Figure 5 presents the CR likelihood during CS1, the trace interval, and CS2 in Panels a, b, and c respectively. In agreement with the findings of Gibbs, Cool, and Gormezano (1982), the level of responding during CS1 (Panel a) tended to be higher in the serial compound group than in the second-order conditioning group. Both the absolute levels of responding during CS1 and the difference between groups were not as large as that seen by Gibbs, Cool, and Gormezano (1982). However, Kehoe and Morrow (1984) used a longer CS1-CS2 interval (2,400 ms) than Gibbs and his colleagues. Because the other parameters of the two experiments were similar, these reductions in responding during CS1 in Kehoe and Morrow's experiment may reflect in part the diminishing effectiveness of associative transfer processes as the CS1-CS2 interval increases. Most notably, investigations of second-order conditioning in the rabbit NMR have revealed that CR acquisition to a second-order CS declines rapidly as the CS-CS interval increases from 400 ms to 2,400 ms (Gormezano & Kehoe, 1984; Kehoe, Feyer, & Moses, 1981). Among the other groups used by Kehoe and Morrow (1984, Experiment 2), the contribution of nonserial mechanisms to responding during CS1 agreed with the estimates that have been described previously. That is to say, the uncoupled training group showed slightly less responding during CS1 than did the serial compound group. In turn, both these groups showed higher levels of responding than either the trace conditioning group or the generalization control group, both of which produced negligible levels of responding.

44

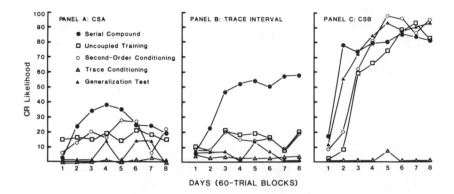

Figure 5. The mean CR likelihood during CS1 (designated here as CSA), the 2,000-ms interval following CS1, and CS2 (designated here as CSB) as a function of days. Separate curves are shown for the serial compound, uncoupled, second-order conditioning, trace conditioning, and generalization control groups.

With respect to the trace interval, the acquisition of CRs appeared to be confined largely to the reinforced serial compound. During the trace interval, the serial compound group showed CR acquisition that reached a terminal level of 54% CRs. The second-order conditioning group and uncoupled training group both reached terminal levels of 20% CRs, whereas the trace conditioning and generalization control groups showed negligible levels of responding around 4% CRs. The singular appearance of CRs in the trace interval of the reinforced serial compound provides provocative evidence that the reinforced serial compound engages processes separate from those attributable to the joint effects of associative transfer and nonserial processes. In the second-order conditioning group, it was curious to see that the CS1-CS2 relation could generate an appreciable number of CRs during CS1 but not during the trace interval. An account of trace-interval CRs in the reinforced serial compound in terms of associative transfer might be mounted by appealing to inhibitory processes that ultimately drive down responding in both serial compound and second-order conditioning procedures. However, an appeal to inhibitory processes would require some additional assumptions. First, the reinforced serial compound presumably retards processes of conditioned inhibition that are engaged by the experimental separation of the

45

CS1-CS2 and CS2-US relations. Second, it would be necessary to assume that, in the second-order conditioning procedure, trace-interval CRs are more susceptible to inhibition than are the CRs during CS1. Perhaps the inhibition of the trace-interval CRs could be explained by appealing to the low salience of CS1's fading trace representation as compared to the high salience of CS1 itself. Third, in the reinforced serial compound, the process of differential inhibition would presumably suppress CRs during CS1, which is remote from the US, while stimuli during the trace interval which are closer to the US would remain excitatory. As may be apparent, a plausible account for the results of serial compound conditioning entirely in terms of associative transfer and differential inhibition becomes increasingly convoluted.

CS2-US Relation: CS2 Strength

Although the experimental partition of a serial compound into its constituent interstimulus relationships has provided estimates of the mechanisms contributing to the facilitation of CR acquisition over long CS1-US intervals, we also sought to determine the manner in which these mechanisms act in concert to determine responding during CS1 and its trace interval in the integrated serial compound. A shared implication of accounts based on generalization and associative transfer is that any operation which alters CR acquisition to CS2 should have parallel effects on CRs to CS1. In contrast, current theories of selective conditioning would clearly expect there to be an inverse relation between responding to CS1 and CS2, as a result of a competition between component CSs for associative strength or attention. For example, an increase in CS2 intensity would be expected to produce overshadowing of CS1 that would counteract the operation of associative transfer mechanisms (Mackintosh & Reese, 1979). Finally, hypotheses concerning facilitation of direct conditioning of CS1 based on the integrity of the CS1-CS2-US sequence are as yet too vague to yield a rigorous prediction regarding manipulations of responding to CS2 (Kehoe, 1982a; Rescorla, 1982).

Experiment VI

Gibbs (1979) conducted an experiment involving the manipulation of CS2 intensity (Weak and Intense) as well CS1-CS2 interval (1,400 and 2,400 ms) and CS1-CS2 contingency (serial compound versus uncoupled training). In the eight groups formed by the factorial combination of the three variables, the CS2-US interval was 400 ms, and the CS2 was a 10-Hz flashing of a strobe light for 400 ms superimposed on a background level of 5.4 lx. Half the groups were trained

46

with a weak (W) light (.3 lx) and half with an intense (I) light (8.1 lx). The CS1 was a 400-ms tone presented at an 1,400-ms CS1-CS2 interval for half the groups and a 2,400-ms CS1-CS2 interval for the other half. Training consisted of eight daily sessions containing 60 reinforced serial compound trials (CS1-CS2-US) in the serial compound condition or 60 reinforced trials for each of the CSs in the uncoupled condition.

The effects of Gibbs's CS2 intensity manipulation on CR acquisition to CS1 are portrayed in Figure 6 with the left- and right-hand panels depicting responding to CS1 at the 1,400- and 2,400-ms CS1-CS2 intervals, respectively. As seen in the previously-described experiments, Figure 6 shows that serial compound (SC) training markedly enhanced CS1 responding relative to the uncoupled (UC) groups. With respect to the effects of CS2 intensity, examination of the right-hand panel indicates that, under the 2,400-ms CS1-CS2 interval, the intense CS2 produced greater responding to CS1 in the serial compound than did the weaker CS2. While this result clearly agrees with the predictions from associative transfer and generalization hypotheses, any positive conclusion must be qualified by the failure of CS2 intensity to have a positive effect of responding to CS1 under the 1,400-ms CS1-CS2 interval as can be seen in the left-hand panel of Figure 6. Moreover, under the 1,400-ms CS1-CS2 interval, the overall mean level of responding to CS1 was slightly higher with the weak CS2 than with the intense CS2, which suggests the operation of an overshadowing mechanism.

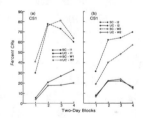

Figure 6. The mean percentage of CRs on CS1 test trials with a 2,800-ms observation interval as a function of two-day blocks. Each group is labeled in terms of (a) their interstimulus relations, namely serial compound (SC) or uncoupled training (UC), (b) CS2 intensity, namely intense (I) or weak (W), and (c) the trace interval between CS1 offset and CS2 onset, namely 1,000 ms (1) or 2,000 ms (2).

Along with Gibbs's (1979) manipulation of CS2 intensity, a series of experiments have been conducted in which the strength of conditioning to CS2 has been manipulated by variations in CS2-US interval, CS2-US training prior to serial compound training, and CS2 extinction

47

after serial compound training. All the manipulations with the exception of prior CS2-US training, produced parallel effects upon responding to CS1 and CS2. In particular, responding to CS1 and CS2 covaried when the CS2-US interval was manipulated over the values of 0, 80, 160, and 320 ms (Kehoe, Feyer, & Moses, 1981). Moreover, extinction of responding to CS2 following serial compound conditioning had an immediate deleterious effect on the level of responding to CS1 during subsequent testing (Gibbs, Cool, & Gormezano, 1982). In contrast, Gibbs (1979) found that prior CS2-US training partially blocked CR acquisition to CS1 during subsequent serial compound conditioning.

Serial Attenuation

Research concerning the mechanisms governing apparent attenuation of CR acquisition to CS2 has revolved around assessing the relative role of generalization decrement as opposed to selective attention, associative competition, and information value. On the one hand, generalization decrement hypotheses contend that the attenuation of responding to CS2 occurs only when CS2 is tested outside the stimulus context provided by CS1 in a serial compound. By the same token, generalization decrement hypotheses content that, within the context of a serial compound, the CS2-US relation is fully effective in producing CR acquisition. On the other hand, all other hypotheses contend that the CS2-US relation will fail to produce CR acquisition because the contiguity-based associative mechanisms have been overridden to some extent by either CS1's capturing the attention of the animal or by CS1's primacy in information value.

Experiment VII

To test generalization decrement hypotheses, Kehoe (1979) examined the effectiveness of the CS2-US relation in the face of serial attenuation of CS2 in two ways: (a) by determining whether the CS2-US interval determined the rate of CR acquisition to the serial compound and (b) by direct measurements of CR likelihood during CS2 within the CS1-CS2-US sequence. Specifically, Kehoe (1979) used a tone-light sequence and manipulated the CS2-US interval across values of 200, 400, 800, and 1,600 ms. To prevent manipulations of the CS2-US interval being confounded with either the CS1-CS2 or CS1-US intervals, the CS1-CS2 interval was manipulated in an orthogonal fashion, those values also being 200, 400, 800, and 1,600 ms. Finally, there was also a CS2 control group for each CS2-US interval.

48

The results of Kehoe's (1979) experiment generally indicated a disparity between the effectiveness of the CS2-US relation as measured on CS2 test trials compared to measurements taken on serial compound trials. On CS2 test trials, the now familiar attenuation of responding appeared. Specifically, CS2 test trials yielded a uniformly low level of responding that was less than that of the corresponding CS2 control at all CS2-US intervals except the 1,600-ms value. In particular, the serial compound groups yielded mean levels of 40%, 51%, 53%, and 49% CRs on CS2 test trials at the 200-, 400-, 800-, and 1,600-ms CS2-US intervals, respectively. In contrast, the CS2 controls yielded mean levels of 71%, 90%, 75%, and 34% CRs at the corresponding CS2-US intervals. In contrast to the attenuation of responding on CS2 test trials, examination of responding during the serial compound indicated that the CS2-US relation was fully effective. For example, the overall levels of responding to the serial compound were 94%, 93%, 84%, and 67% CRs at the 200-, 400-, 800-, and 1,600-ms CS2-US intervals, respectively. Examinations of CR likelihood during CS2 on serial compound trials also revealed a high level of responding, which approximated that of the CS2 controls at all CS2-US intervals. The mean CR likelihoods during CS2 in the serial compound were 60%, 73%, 79%, and 57% CRs at the 200-, 400-, 800-, and 1,600-ms CS2-US intervals, respectively. Although the disparity between the low level of responding on CS2 test trials outside the context of the serial compound and the high level of responding during CS2 inside the serial compound is consistent with generalization decrement hypotheses, some caution must be exercised in identifying the stimulus antecedents for responding during CS2 inside the serial compound. Examination of responding on CS1 test trials revealed that CS1 had residual response-evoking characteristics during the interval occupied by CS2. Thus, the high level of responding during CS2 inside a serial compound may have represented summation of the separate response-evoking capabilities of CS2 and the after-effects of CS1.

Experiment VIII

Kehoe (1983, Experiment 1) further examined the effects of the CS2-US interval by pitting CS2-US contiguity against the salience and informativeness of CS1. CSl was an intense 93-dB, 800-ms tone which was fixed at an 800-ms CS1-US interval. CS2 was either an 800-, 600-, or 400-ms light presented at the corresponding CS2-US interval. These compound groups were designated as TL88, TL86, and TL84, which denote the Tone CS1, the Light CS2, the CS1-US interval (800 ms), and the CS2-US interval (800, 600, and 400ms, respectively). At each level of the CS2-US interval, there was a corresponding CS2 control group. The results revealed that the degree of contiguity between CS2 and the US was a major determinant of responding even in the face of a highly salient CS1. In agreement with Kehoe (1979), the CS2-US interval determined the rate of CR acquisition to the compound even through CS1 completely overlapped CS2. Examination of responding on CS2 test trials revealed that, in Group TL88, in which CS1 and CS2 were simultaneous, the intense tone CS1 completely overshadowed CS2. Across eight days of training, each containing 54 reinforced trials, Group TL88 showed a mean level of 9% CRs to the light, which was 55 percentage points lower than that of the corresponding CS2 control group, which showed 64% CRs to the light. According to information hypotheses, increasing the CS2-US contiguity in Groups TL86 and TL84 should have given CS1 the additional advantage of temporal primacy over CS2, causing additional impairments in CR acquisition to CS2. However, the reverse result appeared; the level of responding on CS2 test trials in Groups TL86 and TL84 showed less impairment than in Group TL88. In particular, Groups TL86 and TL84 showed mean levels of 50% and 57% CRs to the light CS2, which were, respectively, 29 and 24 percentage points lower than those of the corresponding CS2 controls. Thus, increasing CS2-US contiguity partially counteracted the effects of an overshadowing stimulus.

Experiment IX

Although increasing CS2-US contiguity had beneficial effects that exceeded any deleterious effects of CS1's temporal primacy, the level of responding to CS2 still showed substantial attenuation even when the CS2-US interval approached optimal values for conditioning in the rabbit NMR preparation. As a consequence, Kehoe (1983, Experiment 2) conducted a further experiment to determine whether it would be possible to combine the advantages of CS2-US contiguity and CS2 intensity to counteract completely any deleterious effect of CS1's temporal primacy and even perhaps overshadow CS1. There were three serial compound groups labeled LT73, LT85, and LT93, for which CS1 was an 800-ms light and CS2 was a 73-, 85-, or 93-db, 400-ms tone. At each level of tone intensity, there was a corresponding CS2 control group, and there was a CS1 control group for the light. The results revealed that, inside the serial compound, CS2 intensity was an effective variable. In particular, the rate of CR acquisition in the serial compound groups and in the CS2 control groups was as direct function of tone intensity. Although the animals were sensitive to CS2 intensity, the combination of CS2-US contiguity and

CS2 intensity did not eliminate the attenuation of CR acquisition to CS2. The terminal levels or responding on CS2 test trials in Groups LT73, LT85, and LT93 were 1%, 31%, and 32% CRs, respectively. These levels of responding on CS2 test trials were, respectively, 91, 69, and 67 points lower than the terminal levels shown by the corresponding CS2 control group. Furthermore, examination of responding to CS1 yielded no discernable impairment in CR acquisition to the light; the serial compound groups and the CS1-control group all showed terminal levels around 70% CRs. For the light and 93-dB tone, the light-tone serial presentation in the present experiment reversed the results of previous observations that the light was overshadowed by the 93dB tone when they were presented in either a simultaneous compound (Kehoe, 1982b; Kehoe, 1983, Experiment 1) or a tone-light serial compound (Kehoe, 1983, Experiment 1). Thus, temporal precedence proved to be a potent determinant of stimulus selection, overriding the joint effects of CS2 salience and CS2-US contiguity.

Experiment X

Kehoe, Schreurs, and Amodei (1981) examined blocking manipulations in connection with serial compounds. They demonstrated that prior training with CS1 at an 800-ms CS1-US interval blocked CR acquisition to CS2 at a 400-ms CS2-US interval. In fact, the blocking effect of prior training with CS1 combined in an additive fashion with its temporal precedence in the serial compound to eliminate almost all CR acquisition to CS2. On the other hand, pretraining of CS2 produced at best only transient impairments in CR acquisition to CS1 in the serial compound. Thus, prior training with CS1 gave it a dual advantage to the detriment of CS2, while prior training with CS2 failed to offset CS1's temporal advantage, at least when CS1 preceded CS2 by 400 ms.

General Discussion

The body of data from our serial compound studies reveals that even the simplest serial compound composed of merely two components can produce profound interactions. In summary, dramatic facilitation of CR acquisition was obtained even when CS1 was remote from both CS2 and the US (Experiments I - VI). At shorter CS1-US intervals that themselves can produce appreciable CR acquisition, the rabbit NMR preparation occasionally showed a slight impairment of CR acquisition to CS1 (Experiment II). Even when CS2 was given pretraining, blocking of CR acquisition to CS1 was only partial (Gibbs,

1979) and not always obtainable (Experiment X). At the same time, we observed consistent, dramatic attenuations of CR acquisition to CS2 when measured on CS2 test trials (Experiments I, II, VII, VIII), even when CS2 was demonstrably more salient than CS1 (Experiment IX). However, we also obtained repeated indications that, inside the context of the serial compound, CS2 and its temporal relationship with the US exerted a greater impact on CR acquisition than test trial results would suggest. Specifically, the results of Experiment VII indicated that the CR likelihood during CS2 on serial compound trials approximated that of control levels across a broad range of CS2-US intervals. Moreover, both the CS2-US interval and CS2 intensity determined the rate of CR acquisition to the serial compound (Experiments VII, IX).

Mechanisms of Serial Facilitation

Our studies made substantial progress in identifying the mechanisms that facilitate CR acquisition to CS1 at long, otherwise ineffective CS1-US intervals. At present, the total level of responding to CS1 and its trace interval appears to arise from the cumulative contributions of several mechanisms. If anything, responding during CS1 itself may be overdetermined. Considerable responding during CS1 was obtained as a result of both nonserial processes (Experiments III, V, VI) and associative transfer processes (Experiments IV, V). Neither nonserial nor associative transfer mechanisms by themselves can explain all the responding during CS1. However, the combination of nonserial and associative transfer would appear to be more than able to explain responding during CS1, even disregarding the possibility that the separation of a serial compound into its constituent stimulus pairs may engage inhibitory processes that would reduce responding to CS1 in the control procedures. Although responding during CS1 can be analyzed into familiar subprocesses, responding during the trace interval between CS1 and CS2 depends on the integrity of the reinforced serial compound.

It has been realized for some time that the presence of CS2 in a serial compound may act as a catalyst for direct CS1-US conditioning rather than itself entering into a mediated CS1-CS2-US association (Kehoe, Feyer, & Moses, 1981; Kaplan & Hearst, 1982; Rescorla, 1982). In particular, Kaplan and Hearst (1982) have proposed one hypothesis based on Mowrer and Lamoreaux's (1951) explanation for the inferiority of trace conditioning relative to delay conditioning. According to Mowrer and Lamoreaux, the interval between a CS and a US in trace conditioning is operationally identical to the intertrial interval. Thus, the conditioning trial as a whole is poorly differentiated from the background stimuli. Consequently, an event filling the trace interval will more clearly differentiate the CS and its traces from the background stimuli and hence will minimize the intrusion of generalized inhibition from background stimuli. Kaplan and Hearst (1982) along with others (Pearce, Nicholas, & Dickinson, 1981; Rescorla, 1982) have found that filling the entire interval between CS1 and the US produced higher levels of responding to CS1 than did filling only a portion of the gap. However, serial compound conditioning of the rabbit NMR has consistently produced substantial facilitation of responding to CS1 even though CS2 occupied only the final few hundred milliseconds of the trace interval. For example, in one of our more commonly-used serial compounds composed of a 400-ms CS1, a 2,000-ms trace interval, and a 400-ms CS2, the duration of CS2 accounts for only 14% of the 2,400-ms interval between CS1 offset and US onset. Moreover, our studies have revealed that the unique effect of the serial compound is to produce CRs during the unfilled portion of the trace interval, the period least distinct from the background stimuli. At the same time, our data have yielded no evidence that the serial compound procedure increases the likelihood of a response during the intertrial interval (Kehoe & Morrow, 1984, Experiment 1). In conclusion, Kaplan and Hearst's hypothesis does not appear readily applicable to our findings.

Although the acquisition of trace-interval CRs depends on the CS1-CS2-US sequence, the immediate stimulus antecedents for a given CR must be some persistent central representation of CS1, which may be construed as a "short term memory" or CS1's "trace" (Gormezano & Kehoe, 1981; Pavlov, 1927, pp. 39-40). If the stimulus antecedent of a CR is a representation of CS1, the the relevant question is, Why does such a stimulus representation ordinarily fail to become an effective CS at CS-US intervals of 2,800 ms and longer. One class of hypotheses concerning CS-US interval effects in classical conditioning has contended that the rate of CR acquisition is a direct function of the intensity of a stimulus representation at the time of US presentation (Anderson, 1959; Gormezano, 1972: Gormezano & Kehoe, 1981; Hull, 1943; Kamin, 1965; Sutton & Barto, 1981). According to this type of account, the representation of a brief CS fades and becomes too weak to produce conditioning if too much time is allowed to pass before administration of the US. Kehoe and Morrow (1984) have described two possible mechanisms through which CS2 could act as a catalyst for CR acquisition to a weak representation of CS1. First, the weak representation of CS1 may be incorporated into the stronger representation of CS2 in a configural fashion (Konorski & Lawicka, 1959). Even modest generalization from the configural

53

stimulus to the earlier portions of CS1's representation would produce more CRs than trace conditioning by itself could. Second, the rate of conditioning for an individual CS may depend not only on its own intensity but on the total intensity of all stimulus representations present at the time of US administration. Thus, a weak stimulus representation would benefit from the concurrent presence of a strong representation. At first blush, the notion of a weak stimulus representation benefiting from a strong stimulus representation would seem to be contradicted by demonstrations of overshadowing (e.g., Kehoe, 1982b, 1983). However, Kehoe and Morrow (1984) showed that, with minor adjustments, competition theories could account for facilitation without compromising their ability to explain overshadowing outcomes. Specifically, competition models typically assume that the asymptotic level of conditioning is a direct function of US intensity. Instances of serial facilitation can be explained by assuming that the asymptotic level of conditioning depends not only on the US but also on the intensive properties of the CSs. For example, the asymptotic level may be a product of the US intensity multiplied by the total intensity of the concurrent CSs. Thus, the addition of each CS to a compound would raise the asymptotic level. Under a multiplicative rule, a weak CS representation paired with the US would not only suffer from a slow growth rate but also from a very low asymptote no matter how long training continued, as has been seen in CS1 controls at long CS1-US intervals. However, if a weak CS1 representation were trained in compound with a strong representation of CS2, the weak CS's associative strength would still have low growth but its potential asymptote would be substantially raised by the addition of CS2. Although CS1's representation would still suffer from competition with CS2, the growth in CS1's associative strength would nevertheless reach a maximum greater that would otherwise be possible.

Mechanisms of Stimulus Selection

Among the available hypotheses concerning stimulus selection, generalization decrement and selective attention hypotheses would appear to offer the most elegant accounts of serial attenuation of CR acquisition to CS2. Conversely, other competition hypotheses and information hypotheses appear to face a greater challenge in explaining serial attenuation.

Generalization Decrement Hypotheses. Generalization decrement hypotheses assume that all stimuli in a compound have undiminished access to the associative apparatus. Hence, it would be expected that the CS2-US interval and CS2 intensity would determine the rate of response acquisition to a compound as seen in Experiments VII, VIII, and IX. Nevertheless, the relatively low level of responding on CS2 test trials would presumably arise from the disparity between the encoding of CS2 inside the context of the compound and the distinctive encoding of CS2 outside the compound. While a deficit in transfer from compound conditioning to testing with CS2 can explain the low level of responding on CS2 test trials, any impairments in responding to CS1 cannot be attributed to a similar deficit in transfer, because the encoding of the initial portion of CS1 is affected only by static background stimuli, which are the same whether or not CS2 is subsequently presented (e.g., Borgealt, Donahoe, & Weinstein, 1972; Hancock, 1982). However, James and Wagner (1980) have recently offered a generalization decrement hypothesis suitable for explaining impairments in response acquisition to CS1 in a serial compound. Using a stimulus trace account of response acquisition, James and Wagner contend that responding to the initial portion of CS1 depends on generalization of associative strength from the encoding of CS1 at the time of US occurrence (cf. Hull, 1943; Gormezano, 1972; Gormezano & Kehoe, 1981). Consequently, the encoding of CS1 may be altered by the occurrence of CS2 just before US presentation, which would tend to reduce the generalization of associative strength from the point of reinforcement to the earlier portions of CS1.

Even with James and Wagner's extension, generalization decrement hypotheses face difficulties in accounting for blocking of CR acquisition to CS1 and CS2, because the routine control procedures demonstrate that the low level of responding to the added-CS cannot be attributed entirely to generalization decrement from compound training to component testing (Kehoe, Schreurs, & Amodei, 1981; Marchant & Moore, 1973). For a generalization decrement account of blocking, the crucial theoretical question concerns how the pretraining of a CS could lead to a greater alteration in the encoding of the added-CS (cf. Gaioni, 1982).

Selective Attention Theory. As a plausible alternative to a generalization decrement hypothesis, a selective attention hypothesis would contend that the onset of CS1 in a serial compound fully engages the subject's attention but with the passage of time, attention to CS1 wanes (Kehoe, 1979, 1983). Accordingly, response acquisition to CS2 would be most strongly hindered if CS2 were to have an onset shortly after CS1's onset (Kehoe, 1983). However, if the CS2 onset were delayed, more attentional capacity would become available, which CS2 could engage, enabling increased levels of response acquisition to CS2. Moreover, since CS2 would take up unused attentional capacity, the temporal and intensive characteristics of CS2 would make an increasing contribution to overall response acquisition, as was observed in the effects of the CS2-US interval and CS2 intensity on response acquisition to serial compounds (Kehoe, 1979, 1983). Similarly, the level of responding during CS2 inside the serial compound may reflect summation of the separate response tendencies to CS2 and the later portions of CS1 or its traces (Bond, 1982; Kehoe, 1979, 1982a). An account of blocking within a serial compound also follows from a selective attention theory. Moreover, selective attention theory can readily account for what may be an asymmetry in the degree of blocking possible for CS1 and CS2. Specifically, it has been possible to obtain nearly complete blocking of CS2 through prior training of CS1. However, blocking of CS1 through prior training of CS2 has been incomplete (Gibbs, 1979; Kehoe, Schreurs, & Amodei, 1981). Under a selective attention theory, the difficulties encountered in blocking CS1 would be attributed to the fact that the temporal primacy of CS1 would allow it to engage the animal's attention before the onset of CS2 thus offsetting the advantage accrued to CS2 through previous training. Conversely, in blocking of CS2, the primacy of CS1 and the prior training of CS1 would act in concert to preclude attention to CS2.

Associative Trade-off Hypotheses. As alternatives to selective attention hypotheses, the other competition hypotheses (e.g., Mackintosh, 1975; Pearce & Hall, 1980; Rescorla & Wagner, 1972) are more difficult to extend to serial attenuation. Although these theories have detailed trade-off processes which attenuate the associative effects of CS-US contiguity, they deal with "CS-US contiguity" in only a global fashion and do not address explicitly the effects which the degree of CS-US contiguity has on conditioning. However, these models do contain a growth parameter which is a function of CS intensity. To accommodate the precise effects of the CS2-US interval manipulations, it would be possible to assign growth parameters on the basis of the CS-US interval as well as CS intensity. Even using this tactic, the associative trade-off models would not be able to account for serial stimulus attenuation. Specifically, responding to CS1 in the serial compound is frequently higher than responding to CS2. Accordingly, it would be necessary to find some basis for assigning a higher growth parameter to the longer CS1-US interval than to the shorter, more optimal CS2-US interval. However, further developments of "real-time" competitive models (Moore & Stickney, 1980; Sutton & Barto, 1981), which assume continuous processing and modification is associative strengths of CSs, have shown some promise in integrating serial attenuation effects with overshadowing and blocking (Sutton, personal communication, 1984).

Information Hypotheses. Although Egger and Miller's (1962) information hypothesis was inspired by a serial attenuation effect, information hypotheses appear to have great difficulty in encompassing the body of data concerning serial compound conditioning. Most notably, a simple information hypothesis expects that the predictive value of CS1 for the CS2 or the US in a serial compound will impair response acquisition to CS2 (Cantor, 1981; Cantor & Wilson, 1981). Instead, Experiment VIII revealed that there was a higher level of responding to CS2 after serial compound training than after simultaneous compound training in which there was no temporal predictive relation between CS1 and CS2. Furthermore, it would appear difficult for the information hypotheses to account for observations that the CS2-US interval and CS2 intensity determine the overall level of response acquisition to the compound, CS2, and even CS1 (Kehoe, 1979, 1983, but see Cantor & Wilson, 1981).

Conclusions

In considering facilitation and attenuation effects together, the common theoretical theme concerns the nature, function, and temporal dynamics of stimulus representations, particularly the representation of CS1. To account for both facilitation and attenuation, the representation of CS1 may be treated as a fading "sensory trace" or relatively veridical short-term memory of CS1. In connection with perceptual theories, the trace of CS1 presumably interacts in a configural fashion with the representation of CS2, creating a joint stimulus to which associative strength accrues. Subsequently, CR evocation during earlier portions of CS1's trace generally benefit through generalization from the high level of associative strength possessed by the configural stimulus. However, since generalization is never complete, CR evocation during tests of CS2 outside the context provided by CS1 tends to be attenuated relative to a single-CS2 control condition. A similar construction of CS1's representation can be given in terms of a selective attention theory. According to a selective attention theory, the amount of attention to CS1 is, at least, a correlated consequence of the representation's current intensity. Facilitation represents a case in which CS1's representation retains enough of the subject's attention to benefit from the high levels of conditioning promoted by CS2 while not competing strongly for attention with CS2. Conversely, serial attenuation results from strong attention to CS1's representation that leaves little opportunity for CS2 to capture any attention. As may be apparent from these theoretical sketches, a unified account of facilitation and selection involves specifying in a rigorous fashion the fine shifts in parameters that permit the same process to benefit CR acquisition to weak representations and attenuate CR acquisition to strong representations.

REFERENCES

Anderson, N.H. (1959). Response emission in time with applications to eyelid conditioning. In R.R. Brush & W.K. Estes (Eds.), Studies in mathematical learning theory (pp. 125-134). Stanford, CA: Stanford University Press.

Baker, T.W. (1968). Properties of compound conditioned stimuli and their components. Psychological Bulletin, 70, 611-625.

Bolles, R.C., Collier, A.C., Bouton, M.E., & Marlin, N.A. (1978). Some tricks for ameliorating the trace-conditioning deficit. Bulletin of the Psychonomic Society, 11, 403-406.

Bond, N.W. (1983). Reciprocal overshadowing in flavour-aversion learning. Quarterly Journal of Experimental Psychology, 35B, 265-274.

Borgealt, A.J., Donahoe, J.W., & Weinstein, A. (1972). Effects of delayed and trace components of a compound CS on conditioned suppression and heart rate. Psychonomic Science, 26, 13-15.

Cantor, M.B. (1981). Information theory: A solution to two big problems in the analysis of behavior. In P. Harzem & M. Zeiler (Eds.), Advances in the analysis of behaviour, Vol. 2. Predictability, correlation, and contiguity. (pp. 287-320). New York: Wiley.

Cantor, M.B., & Wilson, J.F. (1981). Temporal uncertainty as an associative metric: Operant simulations of Pavlovian conditioning. Journal of Experimental Psychology: General, 110, 232-268.

Dubin, W.J., & Levis, D.J. (1973). Influence of similarity of components of a serial conditioned stimulus on conditioned fear in rats. Journal of Comparative and Physiological Psychology, 85, 304-312.

Egger, D.M., & Miller, N.E. (1962). Secondary reinforcement in rats as a function of information value and reliability of the stimulus. Journal of Experimental Psychology, 64, 97-104.

Frey, P.W., Englander, S., & Roman, A. (1971). Interstimulus interval analysis of sequential CS compounds in rabbit eyelid conditioning. Journal of Comparative and Physiological Psychology, 77, 439-446.

Frey, P.W., & Sears, R.J. (1978). Model of conditioning incorporating the Rescorla-Wagner associative axiom, a dynamic attention process, and a catastrophe rule. Psychological Review, 85, 321-340.

Gaioni, S.J. (1982). Blocking and nonsimultaneous compounds: Comparison of responding during compound conditioning and testing. Pavlovian Journal of Biological Science, 17, 16-29.

Gibbs, C.M. (1979). Serial compound classical conditioning (CS1-CS2-UCS): Effects of CS2 intensity and pretraining on component acquisition. Unpublished doctoral dissertation. The University of Iowa, Iowa City.

Gibbs, C.M., Cool, V., & Gormezano, I. (1982). Second-order conditioning and serial compound conditioning of the rabbit nictitating membrane response. Unpublished manuscript.

Gormezano, I. (1972). Investigations of defense and reward conditioning in the rabbit. In A.H. Black & W.F. Prokasy (Eds.), Classical conditioning II (pp. 151-181). New York: Appleton-Century-Crofts.

Gormezano, I., & Kehoe, E.J. (1981). Classical conditioning and the law of contiguity. In P. Harzem & M.D. Zeiler (Eds.), Advances in analysis of behaviour. Vol 2. Predictability, correlation, and contiguity (pp. 1-45). York: Wiley.

Gormezano, I., & Kehoe, E.J. (1984). Associative transfer in classical conditioning to serial compounds. In M.L. Commons, R.J. Herrnstein, and A.R. Wagner (Eds.), Quantitative analyses of behavior, Vol 3: Acquisition (pp. 297-322). Cambridge: Ballinger.

Gormezano, I., & Kehoe, E.J., & Marshall, B.S. (1983). Twenty years of classical conditioning research with the rabbit. In J. M. Sprague & A.N. Epstein (Eds.), Progress in psychobiology and physiological psychology, Vol. 10 (pp. 197-275). New York: Academic Press.

Grings, W.W. (1972). Compound stimulus transfer in human classical conditioning. In A.H. Black & W.F. Prokasy (Eds.), Classical conditioning II. York: Appleton-Century-Crofts.

Hancock, R.A., Jr. (1982). Tests of the conditioned reinforcement value of sequential stimuli in pigeons. Animal Learning and Behavior, 10, 46-54.

Herendeen, D., & Anderson, D.C. (1968). Dual effects of a second-order conditioned stimulus: Excitation and inhibition. Psychonomic Science, 13, 15-16.

Hull, C.L. (1930). Knowledge and purpose as habit mechanisms. Psychological Review, 37, 511-525.

Hull, C.L. (1934). The rat's speed-of-locomotion gradient in the approach to food. Journal of Comparative Psychology, 17, 393-422.

Hull, C.L. (1943). Principles of behavior. New York: Appleton-Century Crofts.

James, J.H., & Wagner, A.R. (1980). One-trial overshadowing: Evidence of distributive processing. Journal of Experimental Psychology: Animal Behavior Processes, 6, 188-205.

Kamin, L.J. (1965). Temporal and intensity characteristics of the conditioned stimulus. In W.F. Prokasy (Ed.), Classical conditioning (pp. 118-147). Appleton-Century-Crofts.

Kaplan, P.S., & Hearst, E. (1982). Bridging temporal gaps between CS and US in auto-shaping: Insertion of other stimuli before, during and after CS. Journal of Experimental Psychology: Animal Behavior Processes, 8, 187-203.

Kehoe, E.J. (1979). The role of CS-US contiguity in classical conditioning of the rabbit's nictitating membrane response to serial stimuli. Learning and Motivation, 10, 23-38.

Kehoe, E.J. (1982a). Conditioning with serial compound stimuli: Theoretical and empirical issues. Experimental Animal Behaviour, 1, 30-65.

Kehoe, E.J. (1982b). Overshadowing and summation in compound stimulus conditioning of the rabbit's nictitating membrane response. Journal of Experimental Psychology: Animal Behavior Processes, 8, 313-328.

Kehoe, E.J. (1983). CS-US contiguity and CS intensity in conditioning of the rabbit's nictitating membrane response to serial and simultaneous compound stimuli. Journal of Experimental Psychology: Animal Behavior Processes, 9, 307-319.

Kehoe, E.J., Feyer, A., & Moses, J.L. (1981). Second-order conditioning of the rabbit's nictitating membrane response as a function of the CS2-CS1 and CS1-US intervals. Animal Learning and Behavior, 9, 304-315.

Kehoe, E.J., Gibbs, C.M., Garcia, E., & Gormezano, I. (1979). Associative transfer and stimulus selection in classical conditioning of the rabbit's nictitating membrane response to serial compound CSs. Journal of Experimental Psychology: Animal Behavior Processes, 5, 1-18.

Kehoe, E.J., & Gormezano, I. (1980). Configuration and combination laws in conditioning with compound stimuli. Psychological Bulletin, 87, 351-378.

Kehoe, E.J., & Holt, P.E. (1984). Transfer across CS-US intervals and sensory modalities in classical conditioning of the rabbit. Animal Learning and Behavior, 12, 122-128.

Kehoe, E.J., & Morrow, L.D. (1984). Temporal dynamics of the rabbit's nictitating membrane response in serial compound conditioned stimuli. Journal of Experimental Psychology: Animal Behavior Processes, 10, 205-220.

Kehoe, E.J., Morrow, L.D., & Holt, P.E. (1984). General transfer across sensory modalities survives reductions in the original conditioned reflex in the rabbit. Animal Learning and Behavior, 12, 129-136.

Kehoe, E.J., Schreurs, B.G., & Amodei, N. (1981). Blocking acquisition of the rabbit's nictitating membrane response to serial conditioned stimuli. Learning and Motivation, 12, 92-108.

Konorski, J. (1967). Integrative activity of the brain. Chicago: University of Chicago Press.

Konorski, J., & Lawicka, W. (1959). Physiological mechanisms of delayed reactions: 1. The analysis and classification of delayed reactions. Acta Biologiae Experimentalis, 19, 175-197.

Levis, D.J. (1966). Effects of serial CS presentation and other characteristics of the CS on the conditioned avoidance response. Psychological Reports, 18, 755-766.

Levis, D.J., & Stampfl, T.G. (1972). Effects of serial CS presentation on shuttlebox avoidance responding. Learning and Motivation, 3, 73-90.

Mackintosh, N.J. (1975). A theory of attention: Variation in the associability of stimuli with reinforcement. Psychological Review, 82, 276-298.

Mackintosh, N.J., & Reese, B. (1979). One-trial overshadowing. Quarterly Journal of Experimental Psychology, 31, 519-526.

Marchant, H.G., III, & Moore, J.W. (1973). Blocking of the rabbit's conditioned nictitating membrane response in Kamin's two-stage paradigm. Journal of Experimental Psychology, 101, 155-158.

Moore, J.W., & Stickney, K.J. (1980). Formation of attentional-associative networks in real time: Role of the hippocampus and implications for conditioning. Physiological Psychology, 8, 207-217.

Mowrer, O.H., & Lamoreaux, R.R. (1951). Conditioning and conditionality (discrimination). Psychological Review, 58, 196-212.

Pavlov, I.P. (1927). Conditioned reflexes. (Translated by G.V. Anrep.) London: Oxford University Press.

Pearce, J.M., & Hall, G. (1980). A model for Pavlovian learning: Variations in the effectiveness of conditioned but not of unconditioned stimuli. Psychological Review, 87, 532-552.

Pearce, J.M., Nicholas, D.J., & Dickinson, A. (1981). The potentiation effect during serial compound conditioning. Quarterly Journal of Experimental Psychology, 33B, 159-179.

Razran, G. (1965). Empirical codifications and specific theoretical implications of compound-stimulus conditioning: Perception. In W.F. Prokasy (Ed.), Classical conditioning (pp. 226-248). New York: Appleton-Century-Crofts.

Rescorla, R.A. (1972). Informational variables in Pavlovian conditioning. In G.H. Bower (Ed.), The psychology of learning and motivation. Vol. 6 (pp. 1-46). New York: Academic Press.

Rescorla, R.A. (1973). Second-order conditioning: Implications for theories of learning. In F.J. McGuigan & D. Lumsden (Eds.), Contemporary approaches to learning and conditioning (pp. 127-150). New York: Winston.

Rescorla, R.A. (1982). Effect of a stimulus intervening between CS and US in auto-shaping. Journal of Experimental Psychology: Animal Behavior Processes, 8, 131-141.

Rescorla, R.A., & Wagner, A.R. (1972). A theory of Pavlovian conditioning: Variations in the effectiveness of reinforcement and nonreinforcement. In A. Black & W.F. Prokasy (Eds.), Classical conditioning II (pp. 64-99). New York: Appleton-Century-Crofts.

Revusky, S.H. (1971). The role of interference in association over a delay. In W.K. Honig & P.H.R. James (Eds.), Animal memory (pp. 155-213). New York: Academic Press.

Rudy, J.W., & Wagner, A.R. (1975). Stimulus selection in associative learning. In W.K. Estes (Ed.), Handbook of learning and cognitive processes. Vol. 2 (pp. 269-303). Hillsdale, NJ: Lawrence Erlbaum.

Schneiderman, N. (1966). Interstimulus interval function of the nictitating membrane response in the rabbit under delay versus trace conditioning. Journal of Comparative and Physiological Psychology, 62, 397-402.

Schneiderman, N., & Gormezano, I. (1964). Conditioning of the nictitating membrane of the rabbit as a function of CS-US interval. Journal of Comparative and Physiological Psychology, 57, 188-195.

Sears, R.J., Baker, J.S., & Frey, P.W. (1979). The eyeblink as a time-locked response: Implications for serial and second-order conditioning. Journal of Experimental Psychology: Animal Behavior Processes, 5, 43-64.

Seligman, M.E.P. (1966). CS redundancy and secondary punishment. Journal of Experimental Psychology, 72, 546-550.

Spence, K.W. (1956). Behavior theory and conditioning. New Haven: Yale University Press.

Sutherland, N.S., & Mackintosh, N.J. (1971). Mechanisms of animal discrimination learning. New York: Academic Press.

Sutton, R.S. & Barto, A.G. (1981). Toward a modern theory of adaptive networks: Expectation and prediction. Psychological Review, 88, 135-170.

Wickens, D.D. (1959). Conditioning to complex stimuli. American Psychologist, 14, 180-188.

Wickens, D.D. (1965). Compound conditioning in humans and cats. In W.F. Prokasy (Ed.), Classical conditioning (pp. 323-339). New York: Appleton-Century-Crofts.

Wickens, D.D. (1973). Classical conditioning, as it contributes to the analyses of some basic psychological processes. In F.J. McGuigan & D.B. Lumsden (Eds.), Contemporary approaches to conditioning and learning (pp. 213-243). New York: Winston.

Williams, D.R. (1965). Classical conditioning and incentive motivation. In W.F. Prokasy (Ed.), Classical conditioning (pp. 340-357). New York: Appleton-Century-Crofts.

Footnote

Preparation of the manuscript and the research described herein was supported by National Science Foundation Grant BNS 83-09826 to I. Gormezano and Australian Research Grants Committee Grant A28315236 to E. J. Kehoe. The authors thank J. Jensen, L.A. Kehoe, and B.G. Schreurs for their aid in preparing the manuscript.

CAN CONDITIONING CONCEPTS AID THE STUDY OF HUMAN INFORMATION PROCESSING?

Barry H. Kantowitz

For many, if not most, experimental psychologists the study of conditioning and that of human information processing (HIP) represent highly incompatible topics and methodologies with little, if any, overlap. The two areas of study are so divergent that they seldom even bother to criticize one another in any useful dialog. Modern HIPers by and large discard years of research in traditional learning theory as uninteresting, staid, and just plain old-fashioned. Watson and Hull are hardly regarded as models to be emulated by this group of researchers. By the same token many traditional researchers in conditioning and learning theory are puzzled by this new wave of information processing research. They cannot see how it is substantially different from the kinds of experiments they have been doing all along and tend to regard the changes of the last two decades or so as changes in terminology rather than anything really important and new. Indeed, at the 50th annual meeting of the Midwestern Psychological Association, one past president showed in some detail how contemporary terms could be easily translated into S-R concepts of yore. This presentation was enthusiastically received by those experimenters old enough to remember the work of Hull, while younger investigators for whom Hull was primarily one topic in a required History of Psychology course, listened with unbelieving ears making caustic sotto voce remarks to their colleagues.

This chapter is not intended to be a replay of the battle of "hyphen" psychology versus "black box" psychology.[2] Instead, it is a tribute to one man, who, while firmly rooted in classical models of conditioning and learning, could also hear and understand the new sounds of a generation of psychologists not old enough to read about the "Big One" (WWII) in the daily newspaper or to be concerned whether Drive and Habit Strength should be added or multiplied. I was privileged to be a student of David Grant at a time when he was expanding his traditional view of the conditioning process and moving on to incorporating the newer style of HIP into his thinking. As students, we were delighted to see Dave adopting HIP techniques and moving into the mainstream of contemporary psychology. Indeed, Dave often remarked that his information processing models of conditioning (e.g.,

Grant, 1972) were more readily accepted by the HIP contingent than by his peers in conditioning.

So this chapter is primarily directed at my colleagues who regard themselves as modern HIPers. I shall argue that in their unseemly haste to escape the yoke of Watson and rigid Behaviorism they have cast off baby, bathwater, and bathtub. Today even learning theorists know that the human is not a passive organism, adrift helplessly on a tide of incoming stimuli, throwing out reflex responses like so many sea anchors. If David Grant could learn from us, perhaps we can learn from him. In deed, the specific charge given me by the editor was to demonstrate how David Grant's conditioning research has influenced my own research in human information processing.

I shall organize my remarks by first summarizing quite briefly some new ideas about the psychology of conditioning; this section can be skipped by readers aware of current conditioning research. However, most HIPers still have a view of conditioning based upon the simple diagrams they encountered in their first undergraduate psychology course — indeed, those same diagrams are still encountered in today's introductory texts — and I hope to convince them that this is no longer accurate. Then I shall discuss two conditioning principles of particular relevance to HIP: response topography and generalization gradients. The following section takes the bull by the horns and attempts to demonstrate that HIP could immediately benefit by incorporating response topography and generalization gradients into processing analyses of behavior; this section should evoke the greatest amount of friendly skepticism. Finally, I shall at long last conclude with some self-serving admonitions comparing HIP and conditioning models.

Conditioning and the Active Organism

Grant (1973a) compared reification versus reality in conditioning paradigms and this section briefly summarizes his comments. The standard conditioning reifications are shown in Table 1. The representations in Table 1 are consistent with a view of the conditioning process as automatic, passive and even mindless. This is why the HIP researcher finds the conditioning process to be dull and uninteresting; it is the very essence of the HIP approach to deny that the organism is passive. It is a basic tenet of HIP that humans have a plethora of alternative processing strategies that are available: they can process information in serial or in parallel, they can control the allocation of capacity or attention, they can vary patterns of rehearsal, and so forth. Cognitive psychologists go even further and boldly proclaim the virtue of mind. The advent of the computer has

64

made purpose and teleology once again respectable in psychology. If a machine, such as Claude Shannon's mechanical mouse or Grey Walter's tortoise, can clearly exhibit goal-oriented behavior, then so can the human. It is no longer fashionable to complain that the organism has been left "lost in thought inside the maze". It is embarrassing to accuse a machine of behavior that is too mentalistic. So if purposive behavior is philosophically acceptable as a description of automata, we cannot reject goal-directed behavior of humans on the grounds of excessive mentalism. Until quite recently, the HIP researcher would also have objected to the automatic nature of the conditioning process, as well as to its passive and mindless qualities. However, recent research (Logan, 1985) has shown that automaticity is worth studying in its own right so that this is no longer an objection to the study of conditioning.

TABLE 1
Diagrams Commonly Used to Instruct Students About Conditioning

Conditioning procedure	Pattern of reinforcement	Didactic paradigm or diagram
Classical Conditioning	All trials reinforced; i.e., UCS follows CS	CS → OR (to CS) \ → CR UCS → UCR
Classical instrumental avoidance training	UCS follows CS if no CR; UCS omitted if CR occurs	CS → CR (Omission of aversive UCS)
Instrumental reward training	Reward given on trials when CR occurs	CS → CR (reward)

(Adapted from Grant, 1973a. Reprinted by permission of Holt, Rinehart & Winston.)

If Table 1 were an accurate representation of the conditioning process, I would share my HIP colleagues' disdain for models of conditioning. However, Grant (1973b) has shown that Table 2 is a much better description of conditioning. (I will resist the temptation to argue about the details of Table 2; indeed the last time I criticized one of Grant's conditioning taxonomies (Grant, 1964) — on prelims — I regretted it.) The important point to be made salient is how Grant arrived at Table 2. He did so by incorporating the idea of voluntary control within the conditioning model. While volition has always played a large role in the Soviet psychology of conditioning, Ameri-

65

cans have tended to regard conditioning as involuntarily; to reiterate, this is a major reason that HIPers have ignored conditioning entirely. However, by studying the transfer of training from classical to instrumental conditioning and vice versa (Grant, Kroll, and Kantowitz, Zajano, & Solberg, 1969) one finds that the symmetric transfer predicted by the paradigms in Table 1 is not obtained. Without going into detail (see Grant, 1973b) the asymmetries of transfer led to the more accurate paradigms of Table 2. Not only did Grant emphasize the voluntary aspects of conditioning, but he also provided a quantitative model based upon the physics of chemical .pa reactions. This style and analogy is quite similar in spirit to the kinds of analyses performed by HIP researchers as they too borrow models from physical and computer sciences.

TABLE 2
Revised Diagrams of the Conditioning Procedures

Conditioning procedure	Pattern of reinforcement	Didactic paradigm or diagram
Classical Conditioning	All trials reinforced; i.e., UCS follows CS	CS $\rightarrow$ OR (to CS) \ $\rightarrow$ CR UCS $\rightarrow$ UCR complex (incl. CR)
Classical instrumental avoidance training	Avoidance reinforcement and classical extinction trial	Avoidance Response CS $\rightarrow$ (AR) $\rightarrow$ no UCS
	Classically reinforced trial	No Avoidance Response CS $\rightarrow$ no (AR) $\rightarrow$ UCS NOTE: also UCS=produced drive
Instrumental reward training	Reinforced trial	instrumental CS $\rightarrow$ response$\rightarrow$ reward (IR)
	Nonreinforced trial	no instrumental CS $\rightarrow$ response $\rightarrow$ no reward

(Adapted from Grant, 1973a. Reprinted by permission of Holt, Rinehart & Winston.)

I hope this message to my HIP colleagues is clear. First, conditioning is not a passive, mechanical process. It is modulated by voluntary control as is any other cognitive activity. Second, since HIP is defined by its techniques rather than its content (Kantowitz, 1974a), process analysis can be just as readily applied to conditioning as to chess. Throughout the 1970's, David Grant was pioneering precisely this kind of modern analysis.

Two Comely Conditioning Concepts to Countenance

In this section I shall review the concepts of response topography and generalization gradients. In the next section these concepts will be specifically applied to topics usually regarded as being of greater interest to HIP researchers: reaction time and attention.

Response Topography: The Accomplished Analog

Response topography is concerned with the dynamic properties of a response. Responses seldom unfold over time in exactly the same way. Researchers who study response topography must erect classification schemes that distinguish among functionally different types of responses. These taxonomies are then validated by relating them to systematic differences in behavior such as latencies, rates of acquisition or extinction in eyelid conditioning, etc. Another approach is to specify the dynamics of a response (Notterman & Mintz, 1965) and then to condition subjects to emit responses having the desired characteristics.

The great virtue of an awareness of response topography is that it constantly forces the investigator to remember he is sampling from a continuous repertoire of behavior. Most responses and behaviors are graded, that is, they are not step functions like electronic signals in computers and digital logic that are either present or absent. While it is often convenient to represent responses as binary states, this should never be allowed to blind us to the reality that behavior is continuous. Data reduction is surely needed, else we could not even report a percentage of conditioned responses for some particular trial block. But just because, for example, trials 13 and 22 are both counted as CRs (conditioned responses) does not necessarily imply that behavior is equivalent on these two trials. Researchers in conditioning have long been aware of the pitfalls inherent upon reliance of a single measure of behavior such as percent CRs. I shall now review a few of the other dependent variables based upon the analog properties of a conditioned response. The example best-known to the contributors of this volume is, or course, the V- and C-form types of responses in eyelid conditioning.

Response Topography in Eyelid Conditioning. While the percentage of CRs is the dependent variable reported first in studies of eyelid conditioning, it has two major defects. First, because a percentage has upper and lower bounds it is often subject to scale attenuation (ceiling and floor effects); this can be especially irksome in differential conditioning when interactions occur as when responding to the positive conditioned stimulus (CS+) reaches asymptote before responding to the negative stimulus (CS-). Second, all CRs do not have the same topography.

The importance of patterning in the conditioned eyelid response was discussed by Grant (1939) over four decades ago. At that time Grant proposed a taxonomy of six types of CRs based upon (a) the temporal relation between response onset and unconditioned stimulus (UCS) onset, and (b) the number of reversals of eyelid motion during the CR. Grant then discussed implications of his data and taxonomy for the habit-family hierarchy of Hull.

Current evaluations of eyelid topography divide responses into V- and C-forms. The V-form is characterized by a rapid closure of long duration; while V originally designated a voluntary form similar to that obtained when subjects are asked to close their eyes. It is no longer generally believed that the V-form response is a self-instructed voluntary closure (Grant, 1972). Th C-form has a slower rate of closure, often is incomplete and may terminate before UCS onset. While there can be no objection to the operational definition of responses as either V- or C-form (Hartman & Ross, 1961), the common practice of labelling subjects as either V- or C-form persons based upon the majority topography of their responses has been debated. Since almost all subjects respond with both topographies — with relative frequencies of about 80% for the predominant form and 20% for the other — such labeling may indeed be an oversimplification. However, rather than going into messy details of this debate I shall assume that this over-simplification does not seriously distort the reporting of data since I do accept the dichotomy between V- and C-form responses.

Before leaving the definition of V- and C-form responses I would like to touch upon one feature of responding dear to the hearts of HIP researchers. It is often suggested that as part of the definition of the two response types one should incorporate response latency, or reaction time as it is termed in modern HIP research (e.g., Donders, 1869). V-form responses have short latencies and C-form have longer latencies. However, although latency is represented on a continuous dimension — albeit with a lower bound of zero — this is not sufficient to make it a measure of response topography. Latency cannot be measured until one has established some criterion for the onset of a response. While this criterion must take topography into account, the latency itself does not. Indeed, one can record different latencies for the same response depending upon how this criterion is chosen. For example, in eyelid conditioning a criterion of a 2mm deflection of a chart-recorder pen as an index of response onset will not yield the same latencies as a criterion based upon slope (rate of change of eyelid closure).

It is, of course, futile to define two different response topographies unless they can be related successfully to different behavioral outcomes. If V- and C-form responses conditioned, extinguished and transferred in the same way there would be no point in distinguishing between them. Grant and his co-workers have demonstrated numerous instances where V- and C-form responders behave differently, especially with differential conditioning to verbal stimuli (see Grant, 1972 for a review of some of these findings). I shall mention only one illustrative finding that shows why it is advantageous to distinguish between V- and C-form responses. In instrumental conditioning of the eyelid response the V-form usually predominates. But when subjects with pretraining on classical conditioning are transferred to instrumental conditioning (Grant et al., 1969) those who emitted C-form responses during classical training continued to use C-form responses during subsequent instrumental training. In addition, the proportion of C-form instrumental responses varied monotonically with number of pretransfer classical reinforcements. So subjects will emit C-form responses in instrumental training when this topography is in their repertoire whereas most untrained subjects use V-form responses in instrumental conditioning.

In order to interpret this (and any other) finding of differential behaviors on the part of V- and C-form responders, we need a model of the conditioning process. In the context of an information processing model of conditioning Grant (1972) suggested that C-form responses require more central capacity than do V-form CR's. The concept of capacity, although not without its problems (Kantowitz, 1985), is central to current HIP models. Thus, C-form responders would be less able to attend to cognitive and semantic aspects of coded conditioned stimuli. In Grant's words (1972, p.44): "The situation of the C-form responder might be said to resemble the plight of a novice automobile driver who cannot carry on a conversation of any complexity while coping with heavy traffic." The fortunate V-form responder, however, need exert less effort to cope with the UCS and has available capacity to devote to semantic aspects of the stimuli. While degradation of performance in divided attention (Kantowitz, 1974b) is hardly a new concept in HIP research, its application by Grant to eyelid conditioning was indeed novel. But familiarity with attention and capacity should not divert the HIP researcher from an important concept contained in Grant's model: the topography of a response is related to the amount of available processing capacity, and vice versa. There is a trade-off between processing capacity and response topography.

Another more traditional view of basic processes in the conditioning of response topographies was explicated by Grant in an article that appeared shortly after his death (Cody & Grant, 1978). The key concept here was that "development of response topography is determined by the relative contributions of inhibitory and excitatory processes (p. 176)." Inhibitory processes were held to produce C-form responses whereas excitatory processes caused V-form CRs. The results of this study, although not entirely in agreement with expectations, did permit the conclusion that response topography can be manipulated or biased by experimental conditions related to inhibition and excitation. In the following major section on HIP and conditioning I shall return to the concepts of (a) topography and processing capacity, and (b) inhibitory and excitatory processes.

No discussion of topography in eyelid conditioning would be complete without at least mentioning some other dependent variables beside V- and C-form response types. Among these are response amplitude and the PUFAMP/MAXAMP ratio (Hellige & Grant, 1974) where the amplitude of eyelid closure 500 msec after CS onset is divided by the maximum response amplitude between 200 and 700 msec after CS onset. This ratio is a crude index of how effective a CR would be in minimizing the noxious effects of the airpuff UCS. In general, V-form responses are more effective.

The concept of response topography is not limited to eyelid closures and conditioning. Learning theorists have also studied the amount of force exerted by an organism while responding. For this dependent variable, topography refers to the unfolding of a graded response over time just as an eyelid closure develops over time. However, instead of measuring position, as is done for eyelid responses, response force is measured in grams (or on rare occasions more properly in newtons).

Response Force. A typical experimental demonstration of the utility of response force as a dependent variable was conducted by Winnick

70

(1950). She placed a rat in an approach-avoidance conflict where it had to choose between two incompatible responses: pushing a panel to keep an aversive light turned off and pressing a bar to obtain food. Her instrumentation was crude by present standards; the panel was hinged and attached to a kymograph drum so that a continuous record of panel-pushing pressure could be obtained. Even so, her results showed systematic changes in pushing pressure (or response force to use modern terminology) which would not have been apparent had an all-or-none switch closure been instrumented instead.

This methodology was soon improved upon by Notterman (1959) who used a strain gauge and an analog computer to measure force emission during bar pressing. Since then many investigators have studied the dynamics of responding with force as an analog dependent variable. For example, Notterman and Mintz (1965) showed that response force emitted by rats could be controlled by exteroceptive cues and Mintz and Notterman (1965) were able to demonstrate response differentiation in human subjects. Space limitations prevent me from describing some of the force results with conditioning paradigms but it should be clear that response force has been an accepted and useful measure of response topography among learning theorists.

Generalization Gradients and Inhibition

I have already mentioned the possible role of inhibitory and excitatory processes in response topography with reference to V- and C-form responses. These concepts occur with much greater frequency in differential conditioning where one stimulus (S+) is associated with reinforcement and another stimulus (S-) in not. For example, Hilgard, Campbell and Sears (1938) presented an air puff UCS when a left window was illuminated and no UCS when a right window was illuminated. At first subjects responded to both lights, but soon CRs were maintained only for the CS+ and dropped off markedly for the CS-. This typical and familiar finding is often explained by invoking excitatory processes associated with the CS+ and inhibitory processes with the CS-. A serious defect in such models (e.g., Spence, 1937) is speculation about the shapes of assumed excitatory and inhibitory gradients. However, modern operant techniques (Blough, 1975; Rescoria, 1975; Rilling, 1977) allow experimenters to trace these gradients from obtained data, so they are no longer purely hypothetical.

Indeed the very notion of a gradient has become much more refined as new methodologies emerge to measure stimulus gradients. The classic method for obtaining a gradient (Guttman & Kalish, 1956) is probably familiar even to HIP researchers. A response is reinforced in the presence of a single stimulus. Generalization testing is then carried out during extinction. As extinction stimuli become more distant from the training stimulus, response rate drops off. However, this procedure to some extent necessarily confounds the extinction process with measurement of the gradient. Better methods surmount this difficulty and they have been summarized in reviews by Rilling (1977) and by Honig and Urcuioli (1981) and so I shall not discuss them here. However, I do wish to emphasize that gradients now can be empirically obtained by sound and sophisticated behavioral techniques; this puts the concepts of excitation and inhibition on much stronger footings.

There is one new wrinkle in obtaining generalization gradients that should be of particular interest to HIP researchers. Responses can be conditionalized upon interresponse time (IRT), forming classes or bands of the IRT distribution. Within each band a generalization function can be plotted. When this was done by Blough (1969), he found that gradients for short (less than 2 sec) IRTs were flat. Stimulus control occurred only for IRTs in the range of 2-4 sec. This finding, and similar findings by others (see Rilling, 1977), implies that the amount of time since the last response is related to degree of stimulus control. Researchers who are familiar with the repetition effects in choice reaction time research with humans will note an obvious parallel.

Another related classic phenomenon is the peak shift (Hanson, 1959). Four different groups of pigeons were trained with the same S^+ but with different S^- until responding to the S^- stopped. (This, or course, required more training when the S^- was closer to the S^+). The subsequent generalization test revealed maximum responding (the peak) not at the S^+ but instead at a stimulus wavelength never seen previously by the pigeons. This result is as if training on the S^- had pushed the peak away from the S^+. This was initial evidence for inhibitory stimulus control but much more has been accomplished in this area (again see Rilling, 1977; Honig and Urcuioli, 1981). Indeed, Rilling has suggested that "the determinants of the peak shift and the inhibitory gradient are identical".

For reasons that will become clearer in following sections, my interest is in inhibitory processes that have been neglected by HIP researchers. Without delving into the data I will cite one more point from Rillings' review: inhibitory stimulus control can be acquired without extinction. A stimulus associated with a less favorable schedule of reinforcement can work just like a stimulus associated with extinction. Indeed, inhibitory gradients can be established

72

rather quickly.   So inhibitory control is not an absolute property of a stimulus but a relative property.

In closing this section I must apologize to learning theorists for my shockingly brief exposition.   My excuse is that excellent reviews already exist (Rilling, 1977; Honig and Urcuioli, 1981) and I direct interested readers to them.   My goal has been first to remind HIP researchers about generalization gradients and to hint at the progress that has been made in this area: gradients once assumed can now be mapped out and tested.   I also wish to sensitize my HIP colleagues to the possibilities of invoking inhibitory processes as explanatory concepts.[3] This section is intended to reassure them that learning theorists can indeed obtain and measure inhibitory gradients.   Now I turn to HIP research itself and attempt to show how conditioning concepts might be profitably applied.

Human Information Processing: The Abdicated Analog

In this section I take the two conditioning concepts — response topography and generalization gradients — and apply them in the context of a double-stimulation paradigm used to study attention.   In the double-stimulation paradigm (Kantowitz, 1974b) two successive stimuli are presented in close temporal succession, i.e., less than 500 msec apart.   This is one of the simplest ways to overload the human; it accomplishes many of the same goals as presenting two simultaneous tasks to be performed together or time-shared, but without the complications inherent in the analysis of performance on simultaneous tasks (Kantowitz & Knight, 1976; Kantowitz & Roediger, 1978).   The degree of information overload is manipulated by varying the interval between the successive stimuli with briefer intervals imposing greater processing loads.   Since the human is such a flexible and powerful information processor, it is my belief that human capabilities can be best studied in overload situations where demands of the task equal or exceed available resources.   The rationale behind this assumption is taken from engineering where overload situations, such as destructive testing where metals are deformed in powerful hydraulic presses until they fail, are quite common.   Of course, a gentler method of imposing overload is mandated when humans rather than metals or machines, are the object of study.

Response Topography. In HIP research one dependent variable stands out from all others: reaction time (RT) is currently viewed by cognitive psychologists as the window to the soul.   I dare not dispute that RT is indeed a noble and refined variable with a most respectable lin-

73

eage. However, most HIP researchers have forgotten that RT cannot be measured without strong assumptions about response topography. When these assumptions are neglected, hubris begets nemesis. For example, a voice key is frequently used to record RT for spoken responses. But onset time will vary with the initial phoneme of the spoken word whose RT is being measured. Unless care is taken to either use the same initial phoneme for the entire response set or to make other corrections (Klapp, 1974) misleading and incorrect data will be recorded.

Reaction time, although continuous, is not an analog variable. It is typically measured by a switch closure. While some characteristics associated with a switch closure, such as response force, are proper analog signals, the switch closure itself is binary. The binary transition from off to on is hardly studied at all, except by perhaps engineering psychologists interested in the design of keyboards. Yet this transition is quite important because RT cannot be measured without it. The mechanical switch in reality functions as an A-D (analog-digital) converter followed by a Schmitt trigger; that is, a continuous analog signal is replaced by a step function with a constant output. The level of the analog signal chosen to trigger the constant output can be crucial. In mechanical terms, this is very roughly equivalent to the pressure required to close the switch. A "hair trigger" switch will yield fast RT but may also give false alarms; certainly the topography of the response even when considered only as a binary event will consist of a series of pulses. Should RT be measured to the first pulse, the last pulse, or the median pulse? The common practice, dictated for reasons that are much more related to electronics than psychology, is to count only the first pulse and then use devices such as switch filters or flip-flops to ignore subsequent pulses. An alternate strategy would be to use a switch requiring considerable force for closure. This will, of course, yield longer RT. Yet how many researchers bother to even report the static force necessary for a switch closure and how many editors demand this information? It is assumed, usually tacitly, that this is unimportant and just adds or subtracts a constant to RT. While this may be true for simple RT (Klemmer, 1957), it is clear that experimenters need to think a little about their response manipulanda in choice RT situations.

The real problem emerges when we realize that any binary response — regardless of the static force needed to close a switch — in general is not a faithful reproduction of the analog force that produced it. While analog signals can be successfully transformed to digital representations, this requires a knowledge of the frequency of the analog signal to ensure an adequate sampling rate. One binary sample is not enough, yet this is all we have in virtually all studies of RT. For example, the pressure on a response key may rapidly approach the threshold required for closure, then decrease and then finally build up again to exceed the threshold. With this kind of signal the recorded RT may be too long: a lower threshold that would have picked up the early increase in signal intensity would have yielded a shorter RT. Since the RT distribution is skewed, the threshold has implications for higher order moments (variance, etc.) as well as for RT itself. Yet we blithely assume that an RT is an RT is an RT.

The solution to this potential problem is simple. If we record response force on manipulanda and store these data, several families of RT scores can be generated by post hoc analysis using different threshold values. Furthermore, any departure from monotonicity in the force function can be easily discovered. Such departures do exist, as I have found when analyzing force data from choice RT experiments. My point should by now be quite clear: it is naive to measure RT without some consideration of the response topography that produced the RT in the first place. Topography is a more fundamental characteristic of responses than is RT since the same response can have different RT scores depending upon the threshold used to evaluate response onset.

In the remainder of this section I shall illustrate my contention that, at least in some instances, response force data may be more helpful than only RT data by reference to a previously published experiment about double stimulation (Kantowitz, 1973). I do not claim that this is a dramatically novel application since response force has been used by learning theorists (as previously indicated) and also in HIP in studies of short-term motor memory (Pepper & Herman, 1970) and simple RT (Klemmer, 1957).

Response force in double stimulation. In a double-stimulation task, two stimuli are presented in rapid temporal succession. Responses may be required to both stimuli or to only either the first or second stimulus. The general finding in this paradigm is a delay in RT (see Kantowitz, 1974b for a review of double stimulation). Response force is a particularly valuable dependent variable in an S_1 - R_1, S_2 double-stimulation paradigm because no overt response is demanded to S_2. Even when subjects are instructed to ignore the second stimulus, it nevertheless increases reaction time to the first stimulus (RT_1).

The response conflict model (Berlyne, 1957; Kantowitz, 1974b) explains this finding by postulating a set of conflicting response tendencies associated with the set of stimuli. The closer in time the

75

two stimuli are presented — that is, the shorter are interstimulus interval (ISI) — the greater the conflict and hence the greater the RT delay relative to a single-stimulation control condition in which S_2 is not presented ($S_1 - R_1$). since S_2 is presented before R_1 can be completed, response tendencies associated with S_2 hinder the generation and emission of R_1. Because no response is made to S_2 it is obviously impossible to record RT_2, so that conflict is inferred from increases in RT_1. However, if the response conflict model is correct, it may be possible to observe the interaction of competing (hypothetical) response tendencies by recording the force exerted on the manipulandum associated with S_2. Such a finding would bolster the conflict model by providing a converging operation if response force were systematically related to variables such as ISI.

The situation used by Kantowitz (1973) to study force is shown in Figure 1. Any of the four possible stimuli (an X appearing within one of the four boxes) could be S_1. However, S_2 was always selected from the remaining 2-alternative set, e.g., if S_1 had been selected from the left stimulus set on some trial, then S_2 would be a member of the right set. This yielded two bits of stimulus and response uncertainty for $S_1 - R_1$ and one bit of conditional uncertainty for S_2 (given S_1). The response manipulanda were Grass Instruments FT.03C force transducers equipped to yield a force rate of .2 kg/mm of excursion. Since these transducers can move in both directions along an axis, (e.g., up and down), each could be placed in a one-to-one correspondence with a 2-choice stimulus set (e.g., left or right). In order to measure RT_1 a response was defined using a force threshold of 128 grams and forces less than this amount did not terminate the RT counter. The experiment was controlled by a LINC-8 minicomputer; see Kantowitz (1973) for additional details.

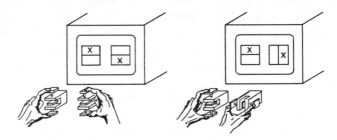

Figure 1. The stimulus display and response manipulanda used by Kantowitz (1973). The parallel condition is on the left and the perpendicular condition on the right. (Adapted from Kantowitz, 1973. Reprinted by permission of the American Psychological Association.)

In the parallel condition both left and right force transducers were oriented so subjects responded by moving them either up or down. In the perpendicular orientation the left transducer remained vertical while the right was horizontal. Any given subject participated in only one of these two conditions. Response force was defined as the observed force on the transducer corresponding to S_2 at RT_1 minus the "resting force" observed 50 microsec prior to S_1 onset.

The response conflict model predicts an interaction among Orientation, ISI and S_1 - R_1 Direction: this is based upon an assumption that incompatible or opposing responses (Up versus Down) are associated with greater conflict than response tendencies associated with the pairs such as Up-Up or Up-Right. (The rationale for this assumption will be discussed in the following section on generalization gradients.) Figure 2 shows this three-way interaction. For the perpendicular orientation response force is basically a flat line around zero grams, as expected. However, in the parallel condition response force on the S_2 transducer (to which no response was demanded) followed the direction of R_1 and, again as expected, this result is magnified at shorter ISI's.

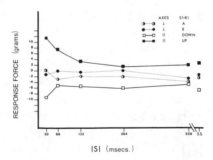

Figure 2. Mean response force as a function of ISI for parallel and perpendicular axis orientations. (The R_1 direction is either up or down for the parallel orientation; for the perpendicular orientation, A and B represent arbitrary combinations of up and down with right and left. S.S. indicates the single-stimulation control condition.)

Similar effects but of lesser magnitude were found when S_2 - r_2 (lower case indicates a response tendency rather than an overt response) direction is the basis for defining axis of (potential) movement. Figure 3 shows small response forces controlled by S_2 in the direction required had an overt response been demanded. It is important to note that a comparison of Figures 2 and 3 reveals S_1 R_1 effects to be more dominant.

77

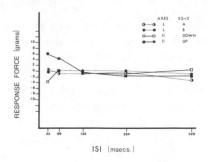

Figure 3. Mean response force for parallel and perpendicular axis orientation as a function of ISI. (The r_2 direction is the direction indicated by S_2 had an overt response been demanded. The r_2 direction is either up or down for the parallel orientation; for the perpendicular orientation, A and B represent arbitrary combinations of up and down with right and left.)

A finer-grained analysis was based upon data from the parallel orientation only (Figure 4). Here S_1 - S_2 pairs may be characterized as **same** or **different**. Again a significant 3-way interaction was predicted and obtained. Strongest effects were found when R_1 and r_2 were the same: both up or both down. Thus, summating response tendencies produced powerful force effects, especially at short ISIs. When R_1 and r_2 were different, reliable force effects were still found but much reduced in magnitude. For example, if R_1 had been up and S_2 - r_2 down, force on the r_2 transducer was still up but only a few grams. This indicates that direct interaction between response tendencies is more powerful than that mediated by S_2. This point will be amplified in the following section on generalization gradients.

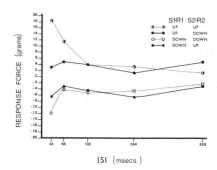

Figure 4. Mean response force as a funciton of ISI for the parallel orientation. (Positive forces represent up movements and negative forces represent down movements.)

78

Finally, single-stimulation (no S_2) data are presented in Table 3. Again response forces are related to S_1 - R_1 direction. Since only one stimulus was presented, these data cannot be explained by any type of stimulus confusion model although such a model has occasionally been presented to explain double-stimulation effects as due to perceptual factors rather than response conflict.

TABLE 3

Mean Response Force (in grams) and S_1 - R_1
Direction for Single-Stimulation Conditions

Axis orientation			
Perpendicular		Parallel	
Left Hand Hand	Right Hand	Left Hand	Right
left -.45 right -2.10 2.33	up -.85 down -.89	up .91 down -8.06	up 5.49 down -

I shall not bother to present RT data since they look like the decreasing monotonic functions usually found in studies of double stimulation and yield no special insights. The force data are much more interesting and paint a far more detailed picture of the processes occurring in the double-stimulation paradigm. Above and beyond and contribution to attention and double stimulation, these data suggest that response topography is a topic that should be pursued by HIP researchers. Although I think it to be more important than RT, I would rest content if HIP researchers paid it the same devotion and care currently exercised in the quest for truth through RT.

Generalization Gradients and Inhibition

Learning theorists have always taken a balanced approach toward excitatory and inhibitory processes. Without inhibitory processes the organism would soon go out of control in a phantasmagoric orgy of myriad responses. However, HIP researchers have been more interested in excitatory processes as information traverses the organism and is variously transformed along its journey. Inhibitory processes have been invoked primarily to account for selectivity in attention as exemplified by perceptual filter mechanisms (e.g., Broadbent, 1958) that inhibit certain classes of stimuli. It is but recently and rarely that inhibitory ideas have been applied to outputs (see Footnote 3), as the category state proposed by Broadbent (1971), as well as inputs.

While the negative feedback loops that are common in HIP models could be used to control inhibitory processes, this aspect of behavior has seldom been stressed enough. Without inhibition, action never ceases. Indeed, one might turn a well-known criticism of S-R psychology and admonish HIP models as leaving the organism lost in action.

An example of an HIP model in which inhibitory processes have been given more than cursory attention is shown in Figure 5. This model was originally proposed to explain RT and error data in double-stimulation tasks, although its generality does not limit it to this topic. The model assumes that all stimulus information makes contact with logogens; these logogens are stored representations that accept stimulus inputs (Morton, 1969). Due to stimulus generalization gradients any particular stimulus will activate several logogens. Hence even though the match between a stimulus and a logogen may be quite close, other logogens will be activated in lesser degree, although on the average, the closest matching logogen will receive the greatest activation. The small boxes within the logogens are intended to represent the accumulator function of the logogens. They can be thought of as so many counters registering the summed activation received by each logogen. Response activation is the process of selecting the output of a single logogen from the set of all possible logogen outputs. For present purposes the exact details of this activation rule are unimportant; regardless of whether a logogen output is activated by a simple rule — select the logogen with the highest count — or a more complex rule — use likelihood ratios to pick an output — the basic excitatory and inhibition processes function as described.

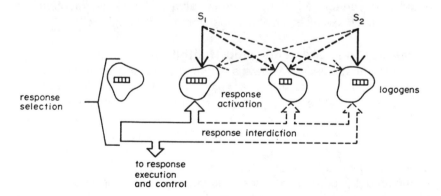

Figure 5. The hybrid model proposed by Kantowitz and Knight (1976). See text for explanation. (Adapted from Kantowitz and Knight, 1976. Reprinted by permission of the American Psychological Association.)

80

As noted, response activation is only half the process of response selection. Eventually all logogens would reach threshold or fire, leaving the organism lost in action. The inhibitory process of response interdiction shown in Figure 5 prevents such an ill-organized state of affairs. An inaccurate (but easy to understand) first approximation of the operation of response interdiction would be that only a single response tendency can be emitted at a time. Thus, the solid arrow in the response interdiction process shown in Figure 5 represents the logogen output that has been successfully connected to later response processing stages. The dotted arrows reveal that all other logogens, although still counting, have temporarily had their outputs disconnected or suppressed so that no response tendency will emerge even if the count merits such. This, however, is an oversimplification because the interdiction mechanism is better conceived of as funded by a limited-capacity source. This implies that a certain amount of parallel processing is possible, if the aggregate demands do not exceed the limited capacity available. (Historically, there has been some confusion between single- and limited-capacity channels. A single-channel can do only one thing at a time, even if that thing is simple. A limited-capacity channel can do several things together as long as its capacity is not exceeded; sometime this implies that the limited-channel can do only one difficult thing.)

The ease with which more than one response can slip by the interdiction process, that is the capacity demands imposed by a subset of responses upon the interdiction process, is measured by response generalization gradients. The more dissimilar are a subset of responses, the easier it is for them to share response initiation (release from interdiction). Putting this another way, the interdiction mechanism requires relatively little capacity to inhibit similar responses. In double-stimulation experiments, for example, the cost of such interdiction will be relatively high RT and/or high error rates. But dissimilar or opposing responses place a greater load on the inhibitory mechanism. So in an S_1 - R_1, S_2 paradigm where R_1 is up and r_2 is down, RT_1 will be higher than if both R_1 and r_2 were up (Way & Gottsdanker, 1968).

There is evidence for at least three types of mediated arousal or release from inhibition in double stimulation. The exact mapping of stimuli onto responses plays a crucial role in such indirect effects and the response conflict model is the only model that makes predictions for S-R mappings. One classification is based upon whether the same physical stimulus (e.g., leftmost lamp) always occurs as, say, S_1 or on some trials can serve as S_1 and as S_2 on others. When a

81

particular stimulus is always S_1 or always S_2 it is said to perform a **unitary** function; stimuli that can alternate role as both S_1 and S_2 perform a **dual** function (Kantowitz, 1974b). Generalization is greater for dual stimuli and this explains the finding of greater RT (e.g., Kantowitz, 1974c).

Another form of mediation occurs when sets of stimuli and responses are placed in conflict. Kantowitz and Sanders (1972) used a partial advance information double-stimulation paradigm where S_1 conveyed information about S_2: S_2 could be red or green, or square or triangle and S_1 indicated whether color or form was the salient dimensions. Thus, S_1 would immediately elicit two competing response tendencies, e.g., red vs. green. This type of mediation differs from the dual-function mediated described above, because it does not depend upon the repeated juxtaposition in time of S_1 and S_2. Thus, Herman and Kantowitz (1970) speculated that unitary-dual arousal required some time to develop (about 50-100 msec) whereas Kantowitz and Sanders (1972) were describing an immediate arousal.

Finally, the response force effects reported earlier (Kantowitz, 1973) are evidence for mediation among responses. In the parallel orientation R_1 direction influenced r_2 force; you will recall that greater forces were observed when both response tendencies were the same than when they were different. These data also illustrated the relative importance of stimulus and response effects. Force on the r_2 transducer was primarily controlled by R_1 direction and not by S_2 direction. So even though S_2 - r_2 effects might have been considered in some sense more direct than R_1 - r_2 effects, results stress the relative importance of response, rather than S - R, effects. This is a happy outcome for any response conflict model which states that competition among responses is responsible for double-stimulation effects.

Learning theorists have long know that there are both excitatory and inhibitory gradients (Rilling, 1977; Honig & Urcuioli, 1981). Hence it is reasonable to expect that the logogen activation gradients represented in Figure 5 be mirrored by inhibitory response interdiction gradients. A recent study completed at Purdue yields strong evidence for selective inhibition (Riegler, Logan, & Kantowitz, 1986). In this study a stimulus mapped to a response would be followed on half the trials by a second stimulus (stop signal) that indicated no response should be made to the first stimulus. The usual finding in this paradigm (Lappin & Eriksen, 1966) is that increases in the inter-stimulus interval decrease the probability of successfully inhibiting the response when the stop signal is presented. Note that the typical stop signal is intended to inhibit any response.

In the Purdue study, we made an important change. For one group of subjects, the stop signal was used in its traditional format and inhibited any response. But for another group of subjects, the stop signal was used to inhibit only one particular response: the right index finger. Thus, for these subjects inhibition was selective because occurrence of the stop signal did not necessarily imply that no response should be made on that trial. For example, if the first stimulus called for a response to the middle finger, presentation of the stop signal would not prevent the response if subjects followed instructions. Our results showed that selective inhibition took longer and required more capacity than blanket inhibition. The probability of response interdiction was greater for the blanket inhibition and stop signal reaction time, estimated from a model of action formulated by Logan and Cowan (1984), was greater for selective inhibition.

To recapitulate, this section makes two important points. First, stimulus and response generalization gradients play important roles in the information processing of double-stimulation tasks. Second, response effects are more important and these appear to be related to inhibition, e.g., response interdiction. My conclusion is that work on inhibitory control and gradients performed by learning theorists could well be applied to double stimulation and perhaps other HIP tasks, especially those related to attention. It is most unfortunate that learning theorists and HIP researchers read and contribute to different journals since many of these researchers are asking almost the same questions. If this chapter increases the awareness of each class of researcher about the other classes' recent doings, it will have served its purpose.

P.S.: Style in HIP and Conditioning Research

I am unable to resist a few parting words on the black box versus the hyphen. I cravenly refuse to take sides and unequivocally state which approach is better since this would only antagonize half my readers without convincing the other half anyway. But I do think it helpful to contrast the two approaches in the same context. So let me briefly return again to the force experiment described previously.

You will recall that in the perpendicular orientation, no effects of R_1 upon r_2 were observed, whereas clear effects were found for the parallel orientation. This was first explained (Kantowitz, 1973) in terms of response-response compatibility, although I now believe that reference to compatibility is more of a description, and that a concept like response interdiction has greater explanatory potential; however, these two rationales for the force effects are entirely consistent with one another. Let me first concentrate upon the compatibility idea to sharpen the stylistic differences between conditioning and HIP models. A conditioning-based explanation would concentrate upon the shape of response generalizational gradients to validate the concept of response compatibility. An HIP-based model might postulate a filter mechanism that attenuated incompatible responses, much like early-selection models of attention attenuated incompatible messages in the unattended ear or unattended channel (e.g., female voice). At first blush, the HIP model appears to be more theoretical but if you agree then all this means is that the extra surplus meaning of a filter is attractive. On the other hand, you might prefer the approach based upon observable generalization gradients because it is more closely tied to data. This argument soon degenerates to inductive versus deductive methods in science, a debate I shall not settle here (but see Kantowitz & Roediger, 1978, Chapter 1). If we take the HIP filter approach to modeling, sooner or later we must ask what makes a filter filter. This embarrassing question takes us back to the general nature of inhibitory processes, itself a theoretical issue. So the distinction between HIP and conditioning approaches depend upon **when** you want your theory, not if you want theory.

Great progress has been made in HIP research by bypassing large theoretical issues — like what is an inhibitory process? — in favor of small stage models that are analogies and not fullblown theories like that of Hull. since analogies are not expected to be 100% correct, they can tolerate flaws that would be fatal to a traditional hypothetico-deductive theory. These HIP models or analogies are still useful, since they organize research findings and suggest new experiments. But they are only first steps towards detailed theoretical explanations. Eventually all our tiny information processing models must be assembled to produce a larger, comprehensive theory of behavior that is not limited to specific experimental paradigms. It is a moot point as to whether this ultimate explanation will be more efficiently produced by piecing together precise and powerful models tied to specific paradigms or by looking at vague theoretical principles like inhibition and trying to sharpen them and to eliminate as many free parameters as possible.

My suggestion is that regardless of which style you prefer, do not ignore those who select a different path to knowledge. If there is one thing I would single out in the example David Grant set for his students, it was his ability to profit from the work of other researchers with a different style. Despite deep roots in the traditional learning theory approaches to conditioning, David Grant was able to reach out and use concepts from HIP researchers. We can all benefit by his example.

REFERENCES

Berlyne, D.E. (1957). Uncertainty and conflict: A point of contact between information-theory and behavior-theory concepts. Psychological Review, 64, 329-339.

Blough, D.S. (1969). Generalization gradient shape and summation in steady-state test. Journal of the Experimental Analysis of Behavior, 12, 91-104.

Blough, D.S. (1975). Steady state data and a quantitative model of operant generalization and discrimination. Journal of Experimental Psychology: Animal Behavior Processes, 104, 3-21.

Broadbent, D.E. (1958). Perception and communication. New York: Pergamon.

Broadbent, D.E. (1971). Decision and stress. London: Academic Press.

Buckolz, E., Deacon, B., & Hall, C. (1984). Response probability and similarity of retrieval response tendencies as determinants of response suppression difficulty. Acta Psychologica, 57, 1-16.

Cody, W.J., & Grant, D.A. (1978). Biasing the development of response topography with nonspecific positive and negative evocative verbal stimuli. Journal of Experimental Psychology: Human Learning and Memory, 4, 175-186.

Donders, F.C. (1869). On the speed of mental processes. (Translated by W.G. Koster). In W.G. Koster (Ed.), Attention and performance II, Acta Psychologica, 30, 412-431.

Grant, D.A. (1939). A study of patterning in the conditioned eyelid response. Journal of Experimental Psychology, 25, 445-461.

Grant, D.A. (1964). Classical and operant conditioning. In A.W. Melton (Ed.), Categories of human learning (pp. 1-31). New York: Academic Press.

Grant, D.A. (1972). A preliminary model for processing information conveyed by verbal conditioned stimuli in classical differential conditioning. In A.H. Black & W.F. Prokasy (Eds.), Classical conditioning II: Current research and theory (pp. 28-63). New York: Appleton-Century-Crofts.

Grant, D.A. (1973a). Reification and reality in conditioning paradigms: Implications of results when modes of reinforcement are changed. In F.J. McGuigan and D.B. Lumsden (Eds.), Contemporary approaches to conditioning and learning (pp. 49-67). Washington: Winston.

Grant, D.A. (1973b). Cognitive factors in eyelid conditioning. Psychophysiology, 10, 75-81.

Grant, D.A., Kroll, N.E.A., Kantowitz, B.H., Zajano, M.J. & Solberg, K.B. (1969). Transfer of eyelid conditioning from instrumental to classical reinforcement and vice versa. Journal of Experimental Psychology, 82, 503-510.

Guttman, J., & Kalish, H.I. (1956). Discriminability and stimulus generalization. Journal of Experimental Psychology, 51, 79-88.

Hanson, H.M. (1959). Effects of discrimination training of stimulus generalization. Journal of Experimental Psychology, 58, 321-334.

Hartman, T.F. & Ross, L.E. (1961). An alternative criterion for the elimination of "voluntary" responses in eyelid conditioning. Journal of Experimental Psychology, 61, 334-338.

Hellige, J.B. & Grant, D.A. (1974). Response rate and development of response topography in eyelid conditioning under different conditions of reinforcement. Journal of Experimental Psychology, 103, 574-582.

Herman, L.M. & Kantowitz, B.H. (1970). The psychological refractory period effect: Only half the double-stimulation story? Psychological Bulletin, 73, 74-88.

Hilgard, E.R., Campbell, E.T. & Sears, R.R. (1938). Conditioned discrimination: The effect of knowledge of stimulus-relationships. American Journal of Psychology, 51, 498-506.

Honig, W.K. & Urcuioli, P.J. (1981). The legacy of Guttman and Kalish (1956): Twenty-five years of research on stimulus generalization. Journal of the Experimental Analysis of Behavior, 36, 405-445.

Kantowitz, B.H. (1973). Response force as an indicant of conflict in double stimulation. Journal of Experimental Psychology, 100, 302-309.

Kantowitz, B.H. (Ed.) (1974a). Human information processing. Hillsdale, N.J.: Erlbaum Associates.

Kantowitz, B.H. (1974b). Double stimulation (pp. 83-131). In B.H. Kantowitz (Ed.), Human information processing. Hillsdale, N.J.: Erlbaum Associates.

Kantowitz, B.H. (1974c). Double stimulation with varying response requirements. Journal of Experimental Psychology, 103, 1092-1107.

Kantowitz, B.H. (1985). Channels and stages of human information processing: A limited analysis of theory and methodology. Journal of Mathematical Psychology, 29, 135-174.

Kantowitz, B.H., & Knight, J.L. (1976). On experimenter-limited processes. Psychological Review, 83, 502-507.

Kantowitz, B.H., & Roediger, H.L. (1978). Experimental psychology. Chicago: Rand McNally.

Kantowitz, B.H., & Sanders, M.S. (1972). Partial advance information and stimulus dimensionality. Journal of Experimental Psychology, 92, 412-418.

Keele, S.W., & Neill, W.T. (1978). Mechanisms of attention. In E.C. Caterette & P. Friedman (Eds.), Handbook of Perception. Vol. 9. New York: Academic Press.

Klapp, S.T. (1974). Syllable-dependent pronunciation latencies in number-naming, a replication. Journal of Experimental Psychology, 102, 1138-1140.

Klemmer, E.T. (1957). Rate of force application in a simple reaction time test. Journal of Applied Psychology, 41, 329-332.

Lappin, J.S., & Ericksen, C.W. (1966). Use of a delayed signal to stop a visual reaction time response. Journal of Experimental Psychology, 72, 805-811.

Logan, G.D. (1985). Skill and automaticity: Relations, implications and future directions. Canadian Journal of Psychology, 39, 367-386.

Logan, G.D., & Cowan, W.B. (1984). On the ability to inhabit thought and action: A theory of an act of control. Psychological Review, 91, 295-327.

McClelland, J.R., & Rumelhart, D.E. (1981). An interactive activation model of context effects in letter perception: Part I. An account of basic findings. Psychological Review, 88, 375-407.

Mintz, D.E., & Notterman, J.M. (1965). Force differentiation in human subjects. Psychonomic Science, 2, 289-290.

Morton, J. (1969). Interaction of information in word recognition. Psychological Review, 76, 165-178.

Notterman, J.M. (1959). Force emission during bar pressing. Journal of Experimental Psychology, 58, 341-347.

Notterman, J.M., & Mintz, D.E. (1965). Exteroceptive clueing of response force. Science, 135, 1070-1071.

Pepper, R.L., & Herman, L.M. (1970). Decay and interference effects in the short-term retention of a discrete motor act. Journal of Experimental Psychology, 83, (2, Pt. 2).

Rescorla, R.A. (1975). Pavlovian excitatory and inhibitory conditioning (pp. 7-35). In W.K. Estes (Ed.), Handbook of learning and cognitive processes, Vol. 2. Hillsdale, N.J.: Erlbaum Associates.

Riegler, G.L., Logan, G.D., & Kantowitz, B.H. (1986). Selective inhibitory control of action. Presented to Midwestern Psychological Association.

Rilling, M. (1977). Stimulus control and inhibitory processes (pp. 432-480). In W.K. Honig & J.E.R. Staddon (Eds.), Handbook of operant behavior. New Jersey: Prentice Hall.

Rumelhart, D.E., & Norman, D.A. (1982). Simulating a skilled typist: A study of skilled cognitive-motor performance. Cognitive Science, 6, 1-36.

Spence, K.W. (1937). The differential response in animals to stimuli varying within a single dimension. Psychological Review, 44, 430-444.

Tipper, S.P., & Cranston, M. (1985). Selective attention and priming: Inhibitory and facilitatory effects of ignored primes. The Quarterly Journal of Experimental Psychology, 37A, 591-611.

Way, T.C., & Gottsdanker, R. (1968). Psychological refractoriness with varying differences between tasks. Journal of Experimental Psychology, 78, 38-45.

Winnick, W.A. (1950). The discriminative function of drive-stimulus independent of the action of the drive as motivation. American Journal of Psychology, 63, 196-205.

Footnotes

1. Revision of this chapter was supported by Cooperative Agreement NCC 2-228 from the National Aeronautics and Space Administration; S.G. Hart was the NASA Technical Officer. I thank my colleague Gordon Logan for espying the more dated segments of the original version. Requests for reprints may be sent to Barry H. Kantowitz, Purdue University, Department of Psychological Sciences, West Lafayette, Indiana 47907.

2. Traditional S-R learning theories have been criticized as "hyphen" theories with nothing explicit to link stimulus and response. Human information processing models have been criticized as "black box" models with unknown mechanisms inside the boxes.

3. Since the original version of this chapter was written in response to the editor's charge, others have reached the same conclusion. Keele and Neil (1978) have stated "The concept of inhibition in the context of selective attention is not well developed and could use more investigation (p.40)." Others have used inhibition as an important concept in HIP models (e.g., McClelland & Rumelhart, 1981; Rumelhart & Norman, 1982; Buckolz, Deacon, & Hall, 1984; Tipper & Cranston, 1985.). I am delighted that editorial delays in bringing this book into print have not inhibited the use of inhibition as an information processing construct.

4

NONANALYTIC-AUTOMATIC ABSTRACTION OF CONCEPTS[1]

Ronald T. Kellogg and Lyle E. Bourne, Jr.

Introduction

Through the late 1970's, it was almost traditional to describe concept learning as a logic-driven analytical process. Examples abound. Levine (1975) argued that the subject's response on any trial of a discrimination or concept learning problem is governed by an hypothesis — selected, modified, or rejected in accord with a "win-stay-loose-shift" strategy, until the correct hypothesis or solution is uncovered. Laughlin (1973) described a variety of complex strategies that human adult subjects exhibit in compound, multi-dimensional problems based on conjunctive, disjunctive, and other logical rules. Bourne (1974) suggested that people learn conceptual rules by ordering and reordering response-controlling procedures which are conditional on the occurrence of individual stimuli or on stimulus classes. Although these examples stem solely from standard feature and rule identification tasks using well defined concepts, Carlson and Dulany (1985) argue that analytical procedures best account even for the learning of ill-defined concepts (Posner & Keele, 1968). Thus, for many theorists, concept learning is based, at least in part, on a deliberate analytical procedure for discovering the defining features and logical rules governing category membership.

Undeniably people can learn concepts by analytical procedures, but we doubt that they always do so. While we can trace the idea back at least as far as Hull (1920), there appears to be a growing re-awakening of the possibility that concept formation is not always logic-driven and can occur by means of non-analytic processes. Several investigators have noted that subjects often emerge form a complex concept learning situation with a working knowledge of the concept but without the ability to verbalize the criterion they use to classify instances correctly (Anderson, Kline, & Beasley, 1979; Kellogg & Dowdy, 1986; Reber, 1976). While not denying the possibility of concept attainment through conscious, deliberate hypothesis testing operations, Anderson, et. al., for example, proposed that learning under some circumstances is controlled by automatic learning mechanisms. One such automatic mechanism in Anderson's model is the build-up of associative strength between a stimulus feature and a category label. This associative strength is based on the processing of probability or frequency of occurrence information regarding features within categories. Hasher and Zacks (1979), among others, have argued that frequency processing is automatic, using their assessment of the literature on frequency judgments in memory experiments as their primary source of information. If feature frequency processing is also automatic in concept learning situations, and if differential feature frequencies serve to identify concepts, then the implication is that a conceptual grouping can enter one's knowledge of the world without conscious effort or intention to learn.

A different nonanalytic means of learning concepts is based on the idea that people represent in memory a few key instances of a given concept and then respond to new potential instances by similarity match or analogy (Brooks, 1979; Hintzman & Ludlum, 1980, Medin & Shaeffer, 1978; Smith & Medin, 1981). Specific instance models maintain that abstraction of category level information such as defining features, prototypes, central tendencies, or feature frequency distributions, is (or might be) unnecessary for classifying instances and noninstances of a concept. Thus, these models are at odds both with analytical hypothesis testing and with nonanalytical frequency processing explanations of concept learning and usage.

There is research to suggest that people sometimes do not abstract category level information, but rather respond appropriately to instances and noninstances of a concept by retrieving specific exemplars. We will return to this literature later in this chapter. Our focus, for the moment is to consider cases where abstraction itself occurs nonanalytically by means of automatic frequency processing. We describe three lines of empirical evidence supporting automatic abstraction where, in each case, memory for specific instances is poor, making it difficult for specific instance models to account for the results. We begin by outlining our theoretical approach, and then take up evidence related to unattended abstraction, incidental abstraction, and failure to remember current hypotheses. We close with a discussion of the known boundary conditions on nonanalytical abstraction, most of which stress the role of specific instances in classification.

Theoretical Approach

Two processes have long been recognized as potentially important in the abstraction of category level information. First, learning relative feature strength or frequency among instances of a category has been suggested as a nonanalytical means for classifying instances of well-defined (Hull, 1920; Bourne & Restle, 1959; Bourne, Ekstrand, Lovallo, Kellogg, Hiew, & Yaroush, 1976) and ill-defined concepts (Anderson et. al., 1979; Fried & Holyoak, 1984). It has also been proposed as a means for determining the typicality of instances of both well-defined (Bourne, 1982) and ill-defined concepts (Chumbley, Sala & Bourne, 1978; Rosch & Mervis, 1975). Rosch's well-known analysis of typicality gradients among members of common taxonomic categories presumes tacitly that people learn feature frequency information, enabling them to compute family resemblance scores. We assume that the basis for knowledge of prototypes or central tendencies is feature frequency information and there is strong evidence supporting this claim (Chumbley et. al., 1978; Goldman & Homa, 1977; Hayes-Roth & Hayes-Roth, 1977, Neumann, 1977). Barsalou (1985) recently verified the importance of family resemblance in explaining typicality for common taxonomic categories, but found that the frequency of whole exemplars, not features, best accounted for typicality in ad hoc, goal derived categories.

Second, as noted, testing hypotheses has been offered as an analytical means of learning how to classify instances of well-defined concepts (Levine, 1975, Bourne, 1974, Laughlin, 1973). Hypothesis testing theory is so well entrenched that we hardly need to review the empirical support for it here. The frequency and hypothesis-testing approaches to abstraction have traditionally been regarded as mutually exclusive alternatives. Our theoretical framework, in contrast, links the two approaches, using the continuum of automatic to controlled processes as a vehicle.

We accept, for the moment that learning event frequencies is an automatic process (Hasher & Zacks, 1979). A single feature, a combination of features, or a complete stimulus may be the event-unit. For instance, people have accurate knowledge of the relative frequencies of single letters (Attneave, 1953), pairs of letters (Underwood, 1971), and English words (Shapiro, 1969), though there seems to be no evidence that they intended to learn these frequencies. Although some evidence raises doubts that frequency processing fulfills all of Hasher and Zack's criteria for a fully automatic process (e.g., Green, 1984), there seems to be no question that better than chance frequency processing occurs even when an individual does not deliberately count events (Kellogg & Dowdy, 1986). We regard all mental operations as falling somewhere on a continuum ranging from automatic and effortless to controlled and effortful. Frequency processing appears to operate reliably if not perfectly without intention or awareness, placing it near, if not on, the automatic end of the continuum.

In contrast to automatic frequency processing, testing hypotheses about defining features is viewed as a fully controlled, effortful process (Hasher & Zacks, 1975; Shiffrin & Schneider, 1977). The term hypothesis testing has been used in a variety of ways, but, in the literature on concept learning, it generally entails attentional processes that leave a record in short-term memory of at least the currently tested hypothesis about what defines the concept. Used in this way, hypothesis testing is a clear example of a controlled strategy that may be allocated varying amounts of attention in particular tasks.

Hypothesis testing is one of numerous controlled processes that a person might attend to while examining instances of a concept. But, as alternatives, a subject might (a) attend to stimuli or specific sensory or semantic features, intentionally attempting to memorize information about each instance, (b) judge the stimulus in terms of attractiveness, familiarity or other dimensions, or simply (c) examine the stimulus without a specific purpose guiding perception. We assume that the manner in which a person allocates attention to controlled processes is heavily influenced by the demands of his or her current task environment.

We speculate that allocating attention to hypothesis testing can carry costs or benefits, depending on the situation. One disadvantage of hypothesis testing is an "opportunity" cost; that is, expended attentional capacity is not free to be allocated to some other important controlled strategy. In a natural environment, the attention demands of hypothesis testing could be troublesome in cases where capacity is needed for alternative parallel activities. Also, when a concept is ill-defined or when the defining features and rules governing a concept are highly complex and difficult to isolate, such as in learning the syntactic rules of natural and artificial languages (Reber, 1976; Reber & Allen, 1978), then hypothesis testing may be fruitless, a waste of effort or worse, debilitating.

On the other hand, there are potential advantages to hypothesis testing. First, testing hypotheses is an efficient way to identify the defining features and rules governing relatively simple, well-defined concepts. Second, after successful hypothesis testing, one can readily state a definition of well-defined concepts in that the aim of testing hypotheses is to discover the defining features and rules. Third, one could use the stored winning hypothesis (concept) as category level information for classifying novel instances instead of, or in addition to, other categorical representations such as a feature frequency distribution.

Except in cases where a task demands that individuals allocate attention to a controlled process of counting, we assume that they do not consciously count and store current feature tallies in short-term memory. Rather, a feature frequency distribution is automatically stored in long-term memory simply as a consequence of encoding enough instances of a particular concept. In the typical laboratory task where individuals have a great deal of background knowledge about the nature of the materials, we assume they enter each problem with a general schema containing empty slots corresponding to all known stimulus dimensions. Over trials, features on irrelevant dimensions occur about equally often among both positive and negative instances of the concept, giving rise to rectangular probability distributions in the corresponding slots of the schema. The only nonrectangular distribution that emerges is the one associated with the relevant dimension or dimensions. Attention may presumably be given to any controlled strategy without affecting the processing of the frequencies of features so-encoded. Even when attention is diverted away from perceiving concept instances, the few features that are encoded under such unattended conditions are presumably added to a frequency distribution. This distribution can then be used to classify instances, judge typicality of instances, estimate feature frequencies, and/or generate a hypothesis about the definition of the concept. Our theoretical approach is not precise enough at this time to allow quantitative prediction or a computer simulation. However, the complexity of explaining human conceptual behavior warrants a broad approach that can qualitatively account for important phenomena as an initial step in theory construction. Drawing a distinction between automatic and controlled processes in concept learning may prove quite useful in this regard. To illustrate its usefulness, we now turn to a discussion of some empirical evidence.

Evidence

Unattended Abstraction. One line of research uses a dual task procedure to control the degree of attention given to instances of a concept in an incidental learning task (Kellogg, 1980). College students were seated in a semi-darkened room and asked to fixate on a small X in the center of a dimly lit gray wall. In dual task conditions, they were instructed to allocate all of their attention to solving difficult mental multiplication problems, which were read to them through earphones. Each problem required the subject to multiply mentally a three-digit number by a single digit number. It took about 2 seconds to read the numbers to the subject, after which he/she had an 8 second calculational period. At the end of that period, signalled by a tone, the subject was required to respond with a 4 digit answer, presumably the product. On some trials, during mental calculation, a schematic face was projected on the subject's visual fixation point, filling the fovea. Subjects had been warned about the possibility of these faces. In some conditions, they were instructed to ignore them. The faces were described as the experimenter's attempt to distract the subjects and that the point of the experiment was to determine the effects of visual distractors on mental multiplication. Subjects were required to keep their eyes open; but they were encouraged to ignore the faces in any way possible under that constraint.

While space does not permit us to present all the details, a variety of controls were exercised in this series of experiments. Two types of multiplication problems were used. The multiplication problems, both easy and difficult, were designed to require full conscious attention and effort. Even in the so-called easy problems, subjects averaged only 65-70% correct product digits. We also examined intention to encode the secondary material by giving subjects instructions either to ignore the face stimuli completely or to attend to the faces if possible with any spare capacity. In both cases, accurate performance on the multiplication task was stressed and the subjects were required to respond overtly to multiplication problems, but not to the faces. After some single task control runs on multiplication problems and 30 multiplication problems accompanied by 30 different faces, the subject was given a surprise recognition test for the faces that included confidence ratings. Also, a single task, faces-only condition was included to examine recognition performance following attended encoding. Finally, subjects were asked to rate, in retrospect, the degree to which they had attended to the faces during acquisition trials, regardless of the instructions they had been given.

Three sources of converging evidence in the data indicate that subjects unintentionally and without conscious effort or attention encoded faces in the dual task condition. First of all, mental multiplication performance, which is sensitive to the influence of attention demanding simultaneous tasks, was at the same level in both control (single task, no faces) and dual task (simultaneous faces) conditions. This suggests that subjects allocated all available conscious resources to mental multiplication even while the faces were presented as distractors. Secondly, intention to encode, manipulated by instructing some subjects to attempt to attend to the faces, failed to affect significantly either multiplication or face recognition performance. Multiplication performance stays high, we think, because of the overt response requirement on each trial. Face recognition did not improve significantly even when subjects were told to attend to them, because the multiplication task consumed most all available capacity. In the absence of sufficient attentional capacity, the intention of the subject should not influence memorial encoding. Thirdly, retrospective ratings of attention to faces were significantly and positively correlated with recognition performance for faces in a single task condition involving face encoding only, r = .55. But, in dual task conditions, where subjects were instructed to treat the faces as distractors, retrospective ratings were uncorrelated with face recognition scores, ranging from r = -0.16 to .21. The interference, intention, and retrospection criteria for distinguishing automatic and effortful processes have proven useful in both our research (Kellogg, Cocklin, & Bourne, 1982; Kellogg, 1985) and in others (Posner & Snyder, 1975; Winter, Uleman, & Cunniff, 1985).

When subjects attended to faces, in a face-only condition, superior recognition performance was achieved. But the unattended conditions also yielded recognition performance statistically better than chance, indicating that conscious attention is useful but not necessary for some minimal long-term storage. We suspect that only a few stimulus features of unattended stimuli are successfully encoded and that the resulting long-term representation is impoverished in these conditions (also see Kellogg, 1985).

TABLE 1
Mean Recognition-Confidence Ratings for
Old, Related, and New Test Faces for Attended and
Various Unattended Encoding Conditions

Condition	Old	Test Type Related	New
ATTENDED ENCODING			
Attended (Experiment 1)	2.32	2.44	-2.53
Attended (Experiment 5)	1.93	2.34	-1.65
UNATTENDED ENCODING			
Easy Ignore (Exp. 2)	.56	.94	-.86
Difficult Ignore (Exp. 2)	.67	.92	-.67
Easy Split (Exp. 2)	1.53	1.57	-.84
Difficult Split (Exp. 2)	.97	1.35	-.69

NOTE: The rating scale ranged from -5 to +5, 0 excluded, with positive values indicating that a face was old, and with greater absolute values indicating greater confidence.

95

It is important to note that, in this study, faces were selected so as to constitute a category based on two defining features related by a disjunctive rule. The reliable recognition achieved by subjects was based on categorical rather than specific face information. On the recognition test the subjects thought they recognized all instances of the category. Instances included both actual, old faces and new, conceptually-related faces exhibiting either one or the other of two defining features. But the subjects correctly rejected new faces that were noninstances of the category; these new faces, of course, exhibited neither of the defining features. Not even attended encoding permitted subjects to distinguish between old and related new faces. The recognition data, taken from Experiments 1, 2 and 5 of this series, are shown in Table 1. Statistical analyses showed that old and related faces were given equivalent ratings both in attended and unattended conditions. Taking the average rating given to instances, both old and related faces, and subtracting the rating given to new faces for each subject yielded a conceptual memory score, reflecting how well the subject learned and used the concept instantiated by acquisition faces. The various unattended encoding conditions failed to differ significantly on this measure; neither did they differ significantly in ratings given to old, related, and new faces when each test type was examined separately. Although there was a tendency toward higher means in the split instructional group receiving easy multiplication problems, the difference was statistically negligible.

We conclude that subjects were able to form a category of faces even under circumstances in which there was little if any allocation of conscious effort to the task. The results indicate that, in dual task conditions, the subjects allocated attention to controlled processes concerned with the multiplication problems, leaving only automatic processes for face encoding. Whatever the process leading to category formation under these circumstances, it can hardly be considered logic-driven. Moreover, the inability of subjects to distinguish specific old instances from new instances does not appear to support the idea that subjects learned by an analytical procedure of storing specific instances.

Incidental Abstraction. We might also expect to find nonanalytic, automatic abstraction of category level information in incidental learning tasks which direct the subject's attention to some controlled process other than hypothesis testing. A recent experiment by Kellogg and Dowdy (1986) examined this possibility. College students were shown 30 letter stimuli belonging to a concept governed by a conjunction of two defining features. Five upper case letters comprised each stimulus. The frequency of stimulus features was varied systematically so that there were features more or less characteristic of the category as well as the two defining features. The orienting task or instructions given to subjects and the rate of stimulus presentation were manipulated. The stimuli were presented either at a 4 or a 8 second rate. Half of the subjects were instructed to test hypotheses about the features that defined the concept and the others were instructed to decide whether the letters of each stimulus formed a word (there were 15 words and 15 nonwords). Unlike subjects in the hypothesis condition, those in the anagram condition were not told that the stimuli were all examples of a concept.

Following the learning phase, subjects estimated the percentage of times that various stimulus features had occurred. The defining features of the concept occurred, of course, in all (100%) the stimuli. Features that were more or less characteristic of the concept occurred on 80%, 60%, 40%, 20%, or 0% of the stimuli. Subject's knowledge of these actual frequencies was the question of interest. Also, to determine whether any category level information was acquired by subjects, a recognition and a definition test were given. Subjects were asked to recognize the instances they had seen from a series of old instances, new instances, and new noninstances of the concept and to give a confidence rating for each stimulus. If subjects learned the concept and used this knowledge in making recognition judgments, then they should judge both old and new instances of the concept as more familiar than new noninstances. The definition test required subjects to name the defining features of the concept. Thus, concept learning was measured both in terms subjects ability to define the concept explicitly and to use the concept tacitly on a recognition test.

According to our theoretical framework, feature frequency information should be automatically learned not only in the intentional concept learning, hypothesis conditions but also under incidental learning, anagram conditions. This information should provide subjects in both conditions with category level information that would lead them to call both old and new instances of the concept familiar and new noninstances unfamiliar on the recognition test. But, only those who allocated attention to controlled hypothesis testing should do well on the definition test. The subjects in the anagram conditions should be able to use their automatically abstracted category knowledge on a recognition test but find it difficult to verbalize the defining features (cf. Anderson, et. al., 1979; Reber, 1976).

To assess accuracy of feature frequency learning, each subject's frequency estimates were correlated (Pearson's r) with actual frequencies with which features occurred in the stimulus acquisition series. Relative to other accuracy measures, this discrimination coefficient is unaffected by criterion differences among conditions in how the rating scale is used (Hasher & Zacks, 1979). That is important here since one can argue that subjects in the hypothesis condition might have been biased to give higher estimates. Unlike anagram subjects, hypothesis subjects were told that some features occurred 100% of the time and that their task was to discover them. The mean discrimination coefficients are presented in Table 2.

TABLE 2
Mean Discrimination Coefficients

Instructions	Presentation Rate	
	Four Seconds	Eight Seconds
Anagram	.65	.74
Hypothesis	.82	.93

NOTE: This measure is the value of Person's r between estimated and actual feature frequencies.

Although both instructions and presentation rate significantly affected the accuracy of feature estimates, all four discrimination coefficients were significantly greater than zero. The percentage of subjects who yielded reliable frequency correlation ($r \geq .58$, $p < .05$) in each condition was as follows: anagram-4 second (70%), hypothesis-4 second (95%), anagram-8 second (80%), and hypothesis-8 second (100%). Thus, feature frequency information was acquired in all conditions, although to a greater degree in some than others.

The mean recognition confidence ratings for the three item types are presented in Table 3. Positive ratings indicate that subjects thought the items were old; the greater the absolute value, the more confident they were. Overall, old instances (1.39) received significantly higher ratings than new instances (.56), which in turn received higher ratings than new noninstances (-2.51). The item type by instructions interaction was also significant; anagram and hypothesis conditions differed little on old instances (1.50 versus 1.28), but the anagram conditions showed less positive new instance (.26 versus .86) and less negative noninstances ratings (-2.15 versus -2.87) than did the hypothesis conditions.

Two statistically orthogonal difference scores clarify the outcome. Memory for specific old instances was measured by calculating the difference in ratings given to old versus new instances for each subject. The mean specific memory difference scores for the anagram-4 second, hypothesis-4 second, anagram-8 second, and hypothesis-8 seconds were 1.17, .35, 1.30, and .49 respectively. Subjects in the anagram conditions remembered significantly more about specific instances at both rates than did those in the hypothesis conditions. In fact, the differences were significantly greater than zero only in the anagram conditions.

TABLE 3
Mean Recognition Confidence Ratings

Instructions	Old Instances	Item Type New Instances	New Noninstances
		Four Seconds	
Anagram	1.38	0.21	-1.89
Hypothesis	1.44	1.09	-2.77
		Eight Seconds	
Anagram	1.61	0.31	-2.40
Hypothesis	1.12	0.63	-2.96

NOTE: The rating scale ranged from -3 to +3, 0 excluded, with positive values indicating that a stimulus was old, and with greater absolute values indicating greater confidence.

The difference in ratings given to both old and new instances versus new noninstances was also calculated for each subject. The mean conceptual memory difference scores (the average given to old and new instances minus the noninstances) for the anagram-4 second, hypothesis-4 second, anagram-8 second, and hypothesis-8 second conditions were 2.60, 4.04, 3.36, and 3.84 respectively. Instances were judged as much more familiar than noninstances in all conditions, indicating that subjects learned the concept. The size of these differences was substantially larger than even the greatest specific memory difference score, and all were significantly greater than zero. The degree of learning was greatest in the hypothesis conditions, particularly under the fast presentation rate.

Definitions were scored on a 4-point scale: 0 = failed to state any defining features, 1 = stated defining feature plus one or more other features, 2 = stated the two defining features plus one or more other features, 3 = stated only the two defining features. Across all subjects, 94% of the definitions included at least two features; so this scale covered nearly all possibilities. The means scores for ability to define the concept are presented in Table 4. The hypothesis condi-

99

tions achieved a significantly higher mean (2.05) on this measure than did the anagram conditions (.73). Presentation rate had no significant effects. Interestingly, subjects in all conditions apparently learned the concept, judging from their ability to differentiate instances and noninstances on the recognition test. However, in general, only hypothesis subjects could define what they had learned. Only 20% of the participants assigned to anagram conditions had scores of 2 or 3 on the definition measure, whereas 87.5% of those assigned to hypothesis conditions had scores indicating knowledge of the defining features.

TABLE 4
Definition Scores

Instructions	Presentation Rate	
	Four Seconds	Eight Seconds
Anagram	.60	.85
Hypothesis	1.95	2.15

NOTE: The measure ranged from 0 (failed to state any defining feature) to 3 (stated two and only two defining features).

These findings demonstrate that a concept can be learned and used on a recognition test, not only under conditions of analytical hypothesis testing, but also under incidental conditions in which attention is directed to problem solving unrelated to the concept being learned. Only when attention is given to hypothesis testing, however, can the individual easily state the defining features of the concept. The amount of specific instance memory was negligible in the hypothesis conditions indicating that category information alone probably mediated their performance. In contrast, subjects in the anagram conditions apparently stored some information about specific instances as well as learning a feature frequency distribution. Their performance, therefore, probably reflected a mixture of category level and specific instance information.

Hypothesis Forgetting. The first two lines of evidence supporting nonanalytic abstraction relied on nontraditional concept learning tasks. The final line of evidence stems from a standard concept identification task in which the subject intentionally tries to learn a concept by classifying instances and receiving feedback. Even in this task, which practically demands analytical abstraction, it is possible to turn up evidence showing learning without hypothesis testing.

100

In the traditional concept identification task, the subject is presented with stimuli, one at a time, and is asked to categorize each as positive or negative. Feedback as to the correctness of each response is supplied on each trial, and the subject's task is to figure out which stimulus feature or combination of features determines category assignments. The dominant interpretation of performance in this problem is based on hypothesis testing (Levine, 1975). The subject enters each trial with an hypothesis of some sort, examines and analyzes the stimulus, finds a match or mismatch between hypothesis and stimulus features, and responds accordingly. If feedback indicates a correct response, the subject keeps the same working hypothesis and may adjust his hypothesis pool (some mental record of still viable hypotheses) accordingly. If feedback indicates an error, the subject drops his/her current hypothesis or revises it for the next trial. Having done that, the subject can purge all information except the updated hypothesis record from working memory, although he/she may maintain information about previously tested and rejected hypothesis as well. If this process model is correct, a memory probe presented during the succeeding trial should reveal high recognition for the hypothesis of the preceding trial and relatively poor recognition for stimulus, response, and feedback from the preceding trial.

We tested these notions in a series of experiments (Kellogg, Robbins, & Bourne, 1978; 1983). Subjects were given a number of simple feature identification problems to solve. Only one feature (upper and lower case letters), of several presented, determined the correct assignment of stimuli. The relevant feature changed randomly from problem to problem. Experimental sessions were conducted on a computer controlled terminal which randomly selected the relevant feature for each problem, the stimulus for each trial, a request for a selection of current hypotheses, the memory probes, and other details.

A memory probe, when presented, was one of four types. To probe memory for the preceding stimulus, one of the letters was randomly selected and presented in both upper and lower case form. The subject's task was to designate with a cursor whether the stimulus of the preceding trial contained an upper or lower case form of that letter. To a response probe, the subject had to indicate, again by moving his cursor, whether the response he/she made on the preceding trial was positive or negative. To a feedback probe, the subject indicated whether his/her response had been correct or incorrect on the preceding trial. Finally, to probe hypotheses, the subject was presented with a letter that had been within his/her hypothesis set on the preceding trial in both upper and lower case form and was asked to designate which of these cases was contained in the actual hypothesis. The instructions emphasized accuracy and speed of problem solving and the importance of memory probes was de-emphasized. Memory probes were administered only on a random half of trials, either at the beginning or 6 seconds into the trial. Because of random sequencing, neither the occurrence or the type of probe could be anticipated. Finally, hypotheses were requested from the subject only on a random one-half of trials.

Subjects responded with differing degrees of accuracy to feedback, response, hypothesis, and stimulus probes. The data from Experiment 1 of Kellogg et. al. (1978) are shown in Table 5. Feedback from the preceding trial was recognized exceedingly well (.98). However, nearly 30% of the time subjects failed to recognize, in a two alternative forced choice test, which feature on a binary dimension had been selected as an hypothesis on the immediately preceding trial. Recognition of the features of the preceding stimulus was equally poor. These figures do not look much different when partitioned into pre- and postsolution data, into early versus late problems, and according to the median number of problem solved.

TABLE 5

Mean Proportion Correct Recognition of
Memory Questions at Each Delay in
Experiment 1

| | Delay | | |
Question Type	Short	Long	M
Feedback	.98	.98	.98
Response	.86	.86	.86
Hypothesis	.76	.68	.72
Stimulus	.66	.72	.69

One explanation of the unexpectedly large number of errors is that our method of identifying the subject's current hypothesis is invalid. This seems unlikely, in view of the fact that the proportion of hypothesis selection trials on which the subject failed to state a hypothesis consistent with his classification was only .03, about the same proportion of "oops" errors as reported by Levine (1975) and others. Another possibility is the subjects return disconfirmed hypotheses to their pool of viable hypotheses for later resampling. If so, recognition errors should occur only on probes following a trial in which wrong feedback is administered. Winning hypotheses would be remembered perfectly according to this account. The mean proportion correct hypothesis recognitions during presolution trials, calculated separately for probes occurring after correct/wrong feedback and after positive/negative response trials, were not contingent on the form of feedback received (see Table 6). But notice, subjects did recognize hypotheses given on positive response trials while performing at chance level if the hypothesis dictated a negative response.

TABLE 6
Proportion Correct Recognition of Hypothesis During Presolution Trials Depending on Previous Response and Feedback in Experiment 1

Feedback	Response	
	Positive	Negative
Correct	.87	.45
	(47)	(41)
Wrong	.84	.48
	(46)	(24)

NOTE: The total number of observations, summed over all subjects and variables, are shown in parentheses.

The second experiment was conducted in part as an attempt to replicate the unusual findings of the first. In addition, we instructed half the subjects to divide their attention and effort between the memory probes and the feature identification task. We did reproduce earlier results but the instructional manipulation had no effect (see Table 7). Once again, we observed a clearcut contingency of correct recognition responses on response type, positive versus negative, but not on type of feedback, correct versus incorrect. Clearly, hypothesis memory, when it occurs, occurs primarily after trials on which the subject made a positive response.

TABLE 7
Mean Proportion Correct Recognition of Memory Questions at Each Delay in Experiment 2

Question Type	Instructions		
	No-memory	Memory	M
Feedback	.95	.97	.96
Response	.84	.84	.84
Hypothesis	.79	.78	.79
Stimulus	.72	.76	.74

In three other experiments, we examined a variety of manipulations to determine the generality of this hypothesis memory failure phenomenon (Kellogg et al., 1978). For example, in one study, we manipulated the number of irrelevant dimensions of the stimuli to be classified. Increasing the number of irrelevant dimensions of the stimuli to be classified. Increasing the number of irrelevant dimensions reduced significantly correct recognition of stimulus features and reduced slightly correct recognition of hypothesis features. No other effects were observed.

It is one thing to replicate a phenomenon under a variety of experimental conditions, but it is quite another to be able to construct circumstances under which the phenomenon will not occur. As Wason and Johnson-Laird (1972) have argued, a true understanding of any phenomenon must encompass both conditions of its occurrence and non-occurrence. The obvious ploy is to change task demands for the utilization of hypotheses. Thus, in one experiment, we manipulated the percentage of trials on which hypotheses were requested from the subject (75% versus 25%) and the percentage of trials on which recognition probes were included (75% versus 25%). Recall that both events occurred on 50% of trials in previous experiments. Much to our surprise, neither of these manipulations did much to change hypothesis memory. These data, taken from Experiment 2 of Kellogg et. al. (1983), are shown in Table 8. It therefore seemed necessary to adopt a brute force approach.

TABLE 8
Mean Proportion of Correct Recognition in Each Probe Type as Functions of the Percentage of Trials on Which Memory Probes Were Delivered and on Which Hypothesis Selections Were Requested

Probe and delivery	Hypothesis selection	
	25	75
Hypothesis		
25	.62	.76
75	.74	.68
Stimulus		
25	.62	.68
75	.70	.69
Response		
25	.69	.80
75	.79	.76
Feedback		
25	.86	.92
75	.95	.94

In the final experiment, subjects were required to state a hypothesis and a memory probe was presented on every trial. For half the subjects, the memory probes were divided equally among stimulus, response, feedback, and hypothesis. For the other half of the subjects, the memory probe inquired about the subjects' hypothesis on every trial. In these conditions, subjects showed excellent hypothesis recognition, averaging 90% accuracy. These data are shown in Table 9. Recognition of correct hypotheses in the hypothesis probe only condition reached an average of 95% accuracy. Clearly, experimental conditions can be arranged so as to induce hypothesis testing and hypothesis memory. Still, under a variety of other conditions, our subjects apparently learned concepts in a way that relies only moderately at best on hypothesis formulation and test.

TABLE 9
Mean Proportion Correct Recognition in
Experiment 3

| | Probe conditions | |
Probe Type	Complete	Hypothesis
Hypothesis	.89	.91
Stimulus	.70	—
Response	.87	—
Feedback	.97	——

The data of these experiments cause us some concern about the adequacy of hypothesis theory as a general account of concept learning. It is worth noting that Kellogg (1980) reported similar results for more complex conjunctive and disjunctive rules, and Schroth (1984) replicated the phenomenon of hypothesis forgetting in an independent laboratory. Even the version of hypothesis theory that makes the weakest assumptions about immediate memory predicts that a confirmed hypothesis is retained from one trial to the next. Other versions go further to assume that subjects remember hypotheses tested on all previous trials or that they remember a confirmed hypothesis plus stimulus, response, and feedback information from the previous one or two trials. Clearly there are circumstances under which people can be induced to solve concept problems by testing hypotheses. But in a context that may, in fact, be more natural — one which does not encourage hypothesis behavior, but rather leaves subjects to their own learning or problem solving devices — hypotheses play, if anything, only a secondary role.

The pattern of results obtained in these less constrained situations is consistent with an alternative interpretation of feature identifica-

105

tion based on nonanalytical frequency learning. The essential idea of this theory is that problem solutions arise out of the repeated occurrence of particular feature-category contingencies. The poor level of hypothesis recognition in our experiments supports such a frequency interpretation, as does the poor level of stimulus recognition. There is no need to remember the exact stimulus features presented on the immediately preceding trial (or probably also, the distinction between stimulus and hypothesis features) as long as the subject stores in long-term memory the relative frequencies of occurrences of features over all previous trials (even subject to some random error function). Note that poor level of stimulus recognition is incompatible with the view that learning is mediated by storage and retrieval of specific instances.

A frequency interpretation concerning information in short-term memory is also consistent with the sensitivity of hypothesis recognition to the manner in which subjects classify stimuli. Negative response trials arise when the stimulus contains a feature opposite to (or different from) the feature hypothesized to be relevant. For instance, if the subject hypothesized B as relevant and the stimulus contained b, the proper classification would be negative. In contrast, on positive response trials, hypothesis (B) and stimulus (B) features match. Subjects recognized their stated hypothesis with high probability if it is represented twice in short-term memory, which is the case after a positive response, but perform poorly if each alternative is represented once, after negative responses. This account assumes, of course, that subjects fail to discriminate perfectly between features of a stimulus and features of an hypothesis (one slot for any feature, regardless of source), which might be too strong an assumption. One finding that indirectly supports such an assumption, however, is that an increase in the number of irrelevant stimulus dimensions yields a decrement in hypothesis as well as stimulus recognition (see Experiment 1 of Kellogg et. al., 1983). If hypothesis and stimulus features were clearly separated in immediate memory, one would not necessarily expect parallel results. The main point to be emphasized is that a frequency analysis of memory in concept problems, if correct, once again renders hypothesis formulation and testing less important than traditional hypothesis theory would lead one to expect.

Boundary Conditions on Abstraction

The three lines of evidence described here suggest that people often learn concepts in a less analytic, less logical way than the major extant theories of abstraction would lead us to believe. As noted earlier, another nonanalytic approach, specific instance models, contends that category level information is not necessary for people to exhibit knowledge of a concept. The data put forth in support of these models (e.g., Medin & Schaeffer, 1978) as well as the results of Carlson and Dulany (1985) establish important boundary conditions on the phenomena of abstraction.

We argue that all encoded stimulus features are automatically stored in long-term memory in the form of a frequency distribution associated with a particular category. Even when attention is not given to hypothesis-testing, this category level information should be stored. Frequency estimation tests should always reveal knowledge of the relative frequencies of occurrence of features within categories. But this claim does not entail that feature frequency distributions will always be sufficiently developed (by virtue of exposure to a reasonable large number of exemplars) to be useful in classifying instances. Also, it does not imply that people always retrieve feature frequency information in classifying instances. For instance, as noted previously, if the learner allocates attention to controlled hypothesis testing, and successfully identifies the defining features and rules governing a well-defined concept, he or she may well retrieve and use only the definition when making classifications. Also if the learner memorizes many of the instances of the concept, in addition to learning feature frequencies automatically, then he or she may retrieve one or more of those instances at test. What then are the boundary conditions on abstraction and use of category level information that we currently know about?

First, the number of different instances of a category experienced seems to be critical. Homa, Sterling, and Trepel (1981) varied the number of different instances (5, 10, or 20) and found that the abstraction of category level information was increasingly important as category size increased. They concluded that a specific instance approach to classification performance is only applicable when a few different exemplars are experienced and testing occurs immediately. Although the conclusions of Homa et. al. have been challenged by Busemeyer, Dewey, and Medin (1984), it is worth noting that most experiments yielding support for specific instance models (e.g., Brooks, 1979; Medin & Shaeffer, 1978) use far fewer than the 30 different instances employed by Kellogg (1980) and Kellogg and Dowdy (in press). Similarly, McAndrews and Moscovitch (1985) recently argued that obtaining evidence of implicit abstraction of the syntactic rules an artificial grammar depends on using a large number of different instances with few repetitions of each. In short, using a

107

small number of instances that are repeated often inhibits abstraction. For us, this reflects the likely use of a controlled strategy to memorize instances and retrieve them at the time of classification when the number of instances is small. People can learn feature frequency information from only a few instances, but the distributions they generate are likely to be too sketchy to be of much use in classification.

A second boundary condition derives from drawing attention to the uniqueness of instances within a category. Medin, Dewey, and Murphy (1983) report that when subjects learn only a last name (a category label) for a group faces, they show evidence of abstracting category level information. However, when they learn both a first and last name for each different face within a category, insuring attention to the distinctive features of each face, then abstraction fails. Once again, we suspect that all individuals in all conditions of Medin et. al. acquired feature frequency information (this was not tested), but that the demands of the task in the first name learning condition encouraged them to retrieve specific instances in classifying test items. A similar outcome was obtained in the anagram conditions of Kellogg and Dowdy (in press). Memory research indicates that the use of anagram problem solving as an orienting task supports excellent retention of specific stimuli (Tyler, Hertel, McCallam, & Ellis, 1979). Our anagram subjects retained significantly more about specific instances than did our hypothesis subjects. The demands of the task dictated how the participants allocated their attention at encoding and at test and this in turn had a major influence on recognition performance. Nevertheless, the anagram subjects still encoded a significant degree of feature frequency information despite their attention to each unique stimulus.

A final boundary condition is represented by insufficient encoding of stimulus features. In an important study, Carlson and Dulany (1985) found that if unattended instances of a concept are presented tachistoscopically for 500 milliseconds then abstraction fails. Their unattended instances were nonreported items in a Sperling-type partial report task. In Kellogg's (1980) study of unattended abstraction each instance appeared for 9.3 seconds while the subject was engaged in an attention demanding mental multiplication task. The ability to distinguish instances from noninstances in Kellogg's unattended conditions was just barely, but statistically better than chance. We suspect that only a few features are successfully encoded under unattended conditions with long exposure durations (several seconds). Degrading the stimulus information available to the subject, by tachistoscopic presentation, by reducing contrast, or by embedding

108

the stimulus signal in noise, probably results in an extremely impoverished encoding of stimulus features. If encoding is too fragile, then frequency information apparently cannot be maintained. Thus, an important boundary condition for abstraction, especially when the individual is not attending to instances, is that sufficient stimulus information be made available for reliable encoding.

Conclusion

Traditional hypothesis testing theories of concept learning have overstated the case for abstraction as a logic-driven, analytic procedure. Evidence that some concept learning can be explained in terms of nonanalytic storage of specific instances, without assuming any abstraction of categorical information, is one way of illustrating this weakness of traditional theories. A second way is to view abstraction itself as mediated by nonanalytic automatic processes. Three lines of evidence were described supporting this approach. We believe that a theory based on **both** automatic frequency processing **and** various controlled strategies is necessary to provide a qualitative account of the important phenomena in the area of concept learning. Lastly, we believe that research on how task demands influence the nature of the controlled strategies employed by an individual is central to understanding the relationships among hypothesis testing, feature frequency learning, and specific instance learning.

REFERENCES

Anderson, J.R., Kline, P.J., & Beasley, C.M. (1979). A general learning theory and its applications to schema abstraction. In G.H. Bower (Ed.) The Psychology of learning and motivation. (Vol. 13). New York: Academic Press.

Attneave, F. (1953). Psychological probability as a function of experienced frequency. Journal of Experimental Psychology, 46, 81-86.

Barsalou, L.W. (1985). Ideals, central tendency and frequency of instantiation as determinants of guided structure in categories. Journal of Experimental Psychology: Learning. Memory and Cognition, 11, 639-654.

Bourne, L.E., Jr. (1982) Typicality effects in logically defined concepts. Memory and Cognition, 10, 3-9.

Bourne, L.E., Jr. (1974). An inference model of conceptual rule learning. In R. Solso (Ed.) Theories in cognitive psychology. Washington, D.C., Erlbaum.

Bourne, L.E., Jr., Ekstrand, B.R., Lovallo, W.R., Kellogg, R.T., Hiew, C.C., & Yaroush, R.A. (1976). A frequency analysis of attribute identification. Journal of Experimental Psychology: General, 105, 294-312.

Bourne, L.E., Jr. & Restle, R. (1959). A mathematical theory of concept identification. Psychological Review, 66, 278-296.

Brooks, L.R. (1979). Nonanalytic concept formation and memory for instances. In E. Rosch & B.B. Lloyd (Eds). Cognition and Categorization (pp. 109-211). Hillsdale, NJ: Erlbaum.

Busemeyer, L.R., Dewey, B.I., & Medin, D.L. (1984). Evaluation of exemplar-based generalization and Deabstraction of categorical information. Journal of Experimental Psychology: Learning Memory and Cognition, 10, 638-648.

Carlson, R.A. & Dulany, D.E. (1985). Conscious attention and abstraction in concept learning. Journal of Experimental Psychology: Learning Memory and Cognition, 11, 45-58.

Chumbley, J.I., Sala, L.S., & Bourne, L.E., Jr. (1978). Memory & Cognition, 6, 217-226.

Fried, L.S. & Holyoak, K.J. (1984). Induction of category distributions: Journal of Experimental Psychology: Learning Memory and Cognition, 10, 234-258.

Goldman, D. & Homa, D. (1977). Integrative and metric properties of abstracted information as a function of category discriminability, instance variability, and experience. Journal of Experimental Psychology: Human Learning and Memory, 3, 375-385.

Greene, R.L. (1984). Incidental learning of even frequency. Memory & Cognition, 12, 90-95.

Hasher, L. & Zacks, R.T. (1979). Automatic and effortful processes in memory. Journal of Experimental Psychology: General 108, 356-388.

Hayes-Roth, B. & Hayes,-Roth, R. (1977). Concept learning and the recognition and classification of examples. Journal of Verbal Learning and Verbal Behavior, 16, 321-328.

Hintzman, D.L. & Ludlam, G. (1980). Differential forgetting of prototypes and old instances; Simulation by an example based classification model. Memory & Cognition, 8, 378-382.

Homa, D., Sterling, S. & Trepel, L. (1981). Limitations of examplar-based generalization and the abstraction of categorical information. Journal of Experimental Psychology: Human Learning and Memory , 7, 418-439.

Hull, C.L. (1920). Quantitative aspects of the evolution of concepts. Psychological Monographs, 281, (Whole No. 123).

Kellogg, R.T. (1980). Feature frequency and hypothesis testing in the acquisition of rule governed concepts. Memory & Cognition, 8, 297-303.

Kellogg, R.T. (1985). Long-term storage of unattended information. Psychological Record, 35, 239-249.

Kellogg, R.T., Cocklin, T. & Bourne, L.E., Jr. (9182). Conscious attentional demands of encoding and retrieval from long-term memory. American Journal of Psychology, 95, 183-198.

Kellogg, R.T. & Dowdy, J. (1986). Automatic learning of the frequency of occurrence of features in concept learning, American Journal of Psychology

Kellogg, R.T., Robbins, D.W., & Bourne, L.E., Jr. (1978). Memory for intratrial events in feature identification. Journal of Experimental Psychology: Human Learning and Memory, 4, 256-265.

Kellogg, R.T., Robbins, D.W., & Bourne, L.E., Jr. (1983). Failure to recognize previous hypotheses in concept learning. American Journal of Psychology, 96, 179-199.

Laughlin, P. (1973). Selection strategies in concept attainment. In R. Solso (Ed). Contemporary issues in cognitive Psychology. Washington, D.C.: Winston & Sons.

Levine, M. (1975). A Cognitive Theory of Learning. Hillsdale, NJ: Erlbaum.

McAndrews, M.P. & Moscovitch, M. (1985). Rule-based and exemplar-based classification in artificial grammar learning. Memory & Cognition, 469-475.

Medin, D.L., Dewey, G.I. & Murphy, T.D. (1983). Relationships between item and category learning: Evidence that abstraction is not automatic. Journal of Experimental Psychology: Learning and Cognition, 9, 607-625.

Medin, D.L. & Shaeffer, M.M. (1978). A context theory of classification learning. Psychological Review, 85, 207-238.

Neumann, P.G. (1977). visual prototype formation with discontinuous representation of dimensions of variability. Memory & Cognition, 5, 187-197.

110

Posner, M.I. & Keele, S.W. (1968). On the genesis of abstract ideas, Journal of Experimental Psychology, 77, 353-363.

Posner, M.I. & Snyder, C.R.R. (1975). Attention and cognitive control in R.L. Solso (Ed). Information Processing and Cognition: The Loyola Symposium. Hillsdale, NJ: Erlbaum.

Reber, A.S. (1976). Implicit learning of synthetic languages: The role of instructional set. Journal of Experimental Psychology: Human Learning and Memory, 2, 88-94.

Reber, A.S. & Allen, R. (1978). Analogical and abstraction strategies in synthetic grammar learning: A functional interpretation. Cognition, 6, 189-221.

Rosch, E.H. & Mervis, C.B. (1975). Family resemblances: Studies in the internal structure of categories. Cognitive Psychology, 7, 573-605.

Schroth, M.L. (1984). Memory for intratrial events in concept formation. Perceptual and Motor Skills, 59, 23-29.

Shapiro, B.J. (1969). The subjective estimation of relative word frequency. Journal of Verbal Learning & Verbal Behavior, 8, 248-251.

Shiffrin, R.M. & Schneider, W. (1977). Controlled and automatic human information processing: II. Perceptual learning, automatic attending and a general theory. Psychological Review, 84, 127-190.

Smith, E.E. & Medin, D.L. (1981). Categories and concepts. Cambridge, MA: Harvard University Press.

Tyler, S.W., Hertel, P.T., McCallum, M.C. & Ellis, H.C. (1979). Cognitive effort and memory. Journal of Experimental Psychology: Human Learning and Memory, 5, 607-617.

Underwood, B.J. (1971). Recognition memory. In H.H. Kendler & J.T. Spence (Eds.), Essays in neobehaviorism: A memorial volume to K.W. Spence. New York: Appleton-Century-Crofts.

Wason, P.C. & Johnson-Laird, P.N. (1972). Psychology of reasoning: Structure and content. Cambridge, MA: Harvard University Press.

Winter, L., Uleman, J.S., Cunniff, C. (1985). How automatic are social judgments? Journal of Personality and Social Psychology, 49, 904-917.

Footnote

1. This research was supported in part by a Contract to the Institute of Cognitive Science from Universal Energy Systems. This chapter is Publication No. 143 from the Institute of Cognitive Science, University of Colorado. Authors contributed equally to the preparation of this chapter and the order of authors was determined by a coin flip.

111

5

MEMORY OF VERY YOUNG CHILDREN IN DELAYED RESPONSE TASKS

Hilary Horn Ratner and Nancy Angrist Myers

The delayed-response paradigm has a long and varied history in psychology as a part of comparative, learning theory, and Piagetian traditions. Since Hunter (1913) first introduced the basic task, it has been useful in characterizing memory capacities of animals and young children, and documenting which cues they remember and use to solve problems. In the earliest studies, the subject observed an object hidden in one of a few, very widely-spaced locations and then either immediately, or with a delay imposed, searched for the hidden lure. Of primary concern was the amount of delay that could be introduced without affecting recall. Length of delays and resulting errors were recorded for each animal or child tested, and if was found that while performance declined as delay increased, delays of some length could be tolerated, and with some species at least, no overt means of mediation, such as maintaining body orientation toward the hidden object, were detected. A system of cues associated with finding the object were thus inferred to be internally maintained and capable of initiating responding after the delay. While Hunter (1917) described this process as an "intra-organic kinesthetic factor", now defined as memory, the recognition that some internal process existed was a valuable one.

The delayed-response paradigm has enjoyed a recent resurgence and has been used to address two primary issues in children's memory development. An initial series of studies was carried out in our laboratory to delineate the types of external cues represented and utilized to mediate delays at various young ages, as well as the reasons for differential cue usage. The primary goal was to determine what information is represented by very young children and to understand how larger conceptual changes affect the child's encoding and retrieval. The second goal, which to a large extent grew out of the first, has been to investigate the rudimentary beginnings of intentional strategy use. Claims made concerning representational limitations experienced by young children led researchers to embed the task in a more meaningful context. This in turn made more evident behaviors that appeared to be deliberate attempts by children to remember the locations of hidden objects. In this chapter then, we will review both lines of research and examine the nature of children's early representational skills, what form early strategies may take, and the relationship between representation and strategy.

Representation

Babska (1965) observed children between eighteen months and five years of age in a task in which a toy was hidden in one box with either a picture, geometric form, or color, as a cover. After a short delay, the child was told to find the toy when the box was re-presented in an array of four boxes, each having a different cover. Almost all 5-year olds responded correctly on all trials; almost all 18-month olds responded randomly, and the largest improvement in correct responding was noted between the ages of 2 and 3. Babska suggested that the youngest children's failure to use the visual cues reflected an inability to remember color, size, or pictorial cues, and concluded that younger children were relying on spatial cues. But location cues were not provided in this task, since the box containing the lure did not appear in a spatial array with other boxes until the time for search, and thus her conclusion did not seem justified. Support for her statement should come from a comparison of younger and older children's performance in a task in which either spatial cues or visual cues or both could be used.

Loughlin and Daehler (1973) used just such a design: a fixed array of four boxes which provided relevant location cues on all trials, and added redundant relevant picture cues on some trials. Their data provided some support for Babska's position that older children rely on visual cues and younger children on spatial cues to find a hidden object, since only the children over three years of age performed significantly better on those trials on which pictures were introduced.

These data suggested that only children over 3 years of age are likely to encode and use discriminative visual cues to remember the location of a hidden object. This may be a result of younger children's difficulty conceptually linking such cues to a hidden object. Our earliest study (Daehler, Bukatko, Benson, & Myers, 1976) was designed to see if young children would be able to utilize some types of visual discriminative cues — those which constitute stable, nonarbitrary, characteristics defining each location. Cues consisting of size and color dimensions of the containers for hidden objects were varied in this experiment, since it was assumed that even the youngest children would have had experience with these perceptual characteristics of containers, and might connect them to the hidden object's location.

At four age levels (mean ages 1.5, 2, 2.5, 3 years) 16 children were each presented a dozen delayed-response test trails, with four boxes arranged in a semicircular array. Three different sets of four boxes were used. The control cue set were all identical in size and color (white). A color cue set of the same size was also used, but each box was a different color (red, blue, green, yellow). Finally, the size cue set were all white but varied in size. The order of trials and location of boxes were randomized with some restrictions to counterbalance cue sets and hidden object positions.

Figure 1 shows mean percentage errorless retrievals as a function of age and cue condition; performance improved with age and when color and size cues were available. Bonferoni t-tests were carried out to evaluate the separate effects further. Significantly more errorless trails were noted for the three older groups that for the youngest, and also significantly more correct.

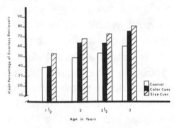

Figure 1. Mean percentage of errorless retrievals as a function of age and cue condition. (Adapted from Daehler, Bukatko, Benson, & Myers, 1976. Reprinted by permission of the Psychonomic Society.)

trials with the size cue set than with the color cue set. The age x cue condition interaction was not significant.

At the end of the test trials two conflict trials, order counterbalanced across subjects, were presented, one involving the size cue set, and the other the color cue set. On these trials the lure was hidden in either the box on the far left or that on the far right, and during the delay the two end boxes were surreptitiously switched so that location cues were no longer appropriate nor redundant with size or color cues. At all four age levels the proportion of location choices was significantly less on conflict trials than on conventional test trials when the end positions contained the hidden objects. Subjects were less likely to search in the end boxes when size or color cues were no longer redundant with location cues. On the other hand, only 25% of even the 3-year olds initiated search on the basis of the color cue, and were not more likely to do this than the younger subjects. Half of the 3-year olds did use size cues to initiate search, however,

115

and were significantly more likely than subjects in each of the younger groups to begin searching in the box of the correct size.

Thus, children under 3 years of age can and do make use of some additional discriminative cues to facilitate memory and search for hidden objects, but it appears that these cues must be intrinsic to the object's location. Furthermore, when these cues are in conflict with location, only children over the age of three appear to use them to initiate search. A subsequent study was conducted to determine more exactly whether 2-year olds rely on spatial cues and 3-year olds on visual or symbolic cues to find hidden objects (Horn & Myers, 1978). In two conditions pictures were either absent, so that only location was relevant, or present, so both pictures and location cues were relevant and redundant. In the remaining conditions, one of the cues was arranged to be relevant in finding the hidden object, and the other, irrelevant. We were interested in whether the younger child, in a condition in which picture cues were solely relevant, but location cues present and irrelevant, would attempt to rely on spatial cues anyway. Further, in a condition where location cues were the only relevant ones, but pictorial cues present and irrelevant, would the young child's performance be unaffected by conflicting pictorial information? Conversely, would 3-year olds perform well with relevant picture cues when location was irrelevant and would the irrelevancy of pictorial cues interfere with the older child's performance when only spatial cues were relevant?

Sixteen children at each age level (within one month of 2 or 3 years) were assigned to each of the four conditions, and received eight delayed-response trials with a 3 x 3 array of boxes, after preliminary training with the appropriate condition-specific procedure. In the no picture-relevant location condition, blank white cards covered the boxes, and the hidden object remained in the same location in which it was hidden before the delay. In the relevant picture-relevant location condition, colored pictures of objects shown in the Peabody Picture Vocabulary Test at the 2-year age level covered the boxes, rather than blank white cards; also the hidden object remained in the location in which it was hidden, so either location or picture cue or both could be used to retrieve the lure. These conditions paralleled those of the Loughlin and Daehler experiment (1973); the major difference was that each child experienced only one type of trial. In the relevant picture-irrelevant location condition, pictures were present, and during the delay the box with the hidden object was moved to a new location. Only the picture could assist the child in finding the hidden object. Finally, in the irrelevant picture-relevant location condition, pictures were present, and the hidden object remained in the location in which it was placed before the delay, but the picture on top of the box was moved to another location. Only by disregarding the picture cue, and remembering the location of the hidden object could the child find it. On each picture test trial one of the nine pictures present in the array was designated the target picture and covered the baited box. These targets had been identified correctly by at least 90% of a separate sample of ten 2-year olds.

Table 1

Mean Percentage of Errorless Retrievals
(First Picture Cue Study)

	No picture Relevant Location	Relevant Picture Relevant Location	Irrelevant Picture Irrelevant Location	Irrelevant Picture Irrelevant Location	Combined over Conditions
Age 2	43.8	56.3	24.2	42.9	41.8
Age 3	50.8	71.2	64.0	25.0	52.8
Combined over ages	47.3	63.8	44.1	34.0	

Once again, as may be seen in Table 1, more errorless retrievals were obtained by the older than the younger children, and the cue conditions resulted in different levels or errorless trials. The conditions produced different effects at the two age levels, however. Bonferoni t-tests indicated that the interaction resulted primarily from the differential effects of the two irrelevant cue conditions at each age level. For the 3-year olds, the irrelevant picture condition resulted in significantly poorer performance than in each of the other three conditions, but for the 2-year olds, the irrelevant location condition produced fewest retrievals, and also differed significantly from performance in each of the three relevant location conditions. In addition, for the older group, performance in the no-picture condition was significantly poorer than in the relevant picture conditions, whereas for the younger group this was not the case.

In this study then, when children experienced only a single cue condition, the results support those of Loughlin and Daehler (1973) and Babska (1965) in demonstrating that only children 3 years of age or older are likely to use pictorial cues to direct initial search, although as we have detailed elsewhere (Horn & Myers, 1978), second-choice data indicate that pictorial information is encoded by younger children, just as locational information is obviously available to the older group. Only after the age of three, then, are children able to spontaneously integrate an arbitrary symbol with a hidden object's location.

Added conceptual knowledge and experience with pictorial information may have encouraged the children in the last experiment to believe that the pictures associated with the hidden objects were reliable predictors of their location. Perhaps supplying labels in conjunction with picture cues would direct attention to the pictures and provide the needed link between the object and picture for even younger children. If so, then performance should improve when relevant pictures are labeled, and deteriorate when irrelevant pictures are labeled for children under 3. Sixteen 2-year olds were tested in each of six conditions, using the same arrays as in the previous experiment, and another set of target pictures, also correctly identified by a separate sample of ten 2-year olds. The relevant picture-relevant location redundant cues condition, and the relevant picture-irrelevant location, and irrelevant picture-relevant location conditions of the last study were replicated, and three new conditions were added in which verbal labels for target pictures were provided.

Table 2

Mean Percentage of Errorless Retrievals (Second Picture Cue Study)

Condition

	Relevant Pictures Relevant Location	Relevant Picture Irrelevant Location	Irrelevant Picture Relevant Location	Combined over Conditions
Unlabeled Pictures	64.8	28.9	39.3	44.3
Labeled Pictures	66.4	57.8	32.3	52.16

In Table 2 the mean percentages of errorless retrievals appear as a function of labeling and condition type. Performance differed significantly among conditions, and although overall performance was slightly better when labels were provided for the targets, the labeling effect was not significant. Labeling did interact with condition type to produce differing effects, however. Bonferoni t-tests showed that performances did not differ in labeled and unlabeled relevant location conditions, but in the relevant picture-irrelevant location condition the percentage of errorless retrievals was significantly higher if the targets were labeled. In fact, when the pictures were labeled, performance was statistically the same as in the redundant relevant cues conditions.

When location is irrelevant, the 2-year old child is able to make use of labeled picture cues. Labeling may provide additional verbal discriminative cues, emphasis on visual cues, or more likely encourages encoding the association between the object and the picture which the child does not ordinarily seem to do himself. Yet when location remains a relevant cue in the task, labeling the pictures neither aids nor interferes with performance.

In several conditions 2-year olds can be observed to use arbitrary picture cues to initiate search for hidden objects, but the considerable environmental manipulation required to encourage this behavior argues for the young child's difficulty in integrating arbitrary cues with location. In our last study (Ratner & Myers, 1980) we manipulated the relation between pictures and hidden objects to see if pictures more closely related to hidden objects would be useful cues to search for 2-year olds where arbitrarily chosen pictures were not.

Sixteen children tested within one month of their second birthday were assigned to each of four cue conditions, and searched in the same arrays used previously, for eight trials. In all conditions location cues were relevant. A baseline no-picture condition in which blank cards covered the boxes was again included because of the changed procedure with respect to hidden objects in this experiment. In all our previous picture cue studies the hidden object had been the same on all test trials; usually a small cracker was used as the lure. In this case the children in all conditions were given a different object lure on each of the eight trials. These hidden objects consisted of a miniature toy telephone, drum, chair, cup, key, shoe, boat, and cow. In the unlabeled matching-picture condition, pictorial representations of the actual objects hidden covered the baited boxes, differing in color and other perceptual features from the lures, but providing alternative exemplars of the same basic-level category. In two related picture conditions, the target pictures over the hidden objects were not exemplars of the objects, but pictures which had been established to be related associates of the target items (e.g., telephone booth, drum sticks, table, etc.). The two related picture conditions differed only with respect to labeling of the picture at the time of hiding the object. In the unlabeled related picture condition the procedure was the same as in the no-picture and matching picture conditions outlined earlier; in the labeled related picture condition the experimenter named the picture as she pointed to it, and hid the object while naming it as well.

Table 3

Mean Percentage of Errorless Retrievals (Non-arbitrary Picture Cue Study)

Condition

No Picture	Matching Picture	Unlabeled Related Picture	Labeled Related Picture
41.4	83.6	43.0	62.5

In Table 3 the mean percentages of errorless retrievals may be seen for each of the four cue conditions. The cue condition effect was significant, although Bonferoni t-tests revealed that while performance in the matching-picture condition was significantly better than in each of the other three conditions, performance in the other conditions did not differ significantly.

Surprisingly, the carefully-selected pictures bearing relationships to the hidden objects which had been easily identified by another sample of 2-year olds, and therefore we assume known to our subjects as well, were not more effective in directing their search than the arbitrarily-assigned unrelated pictures used in our previous experiments. In contrast, performance was truly remarkable when picture cues which matched the hidden object by depicting another form of the same basic-level conceptual referent were made available. Most children retrieved the hidden object correctly on either 6 or 7 of the 8 trials, a level of performance rarely attained by even our oldest 3-year olds in other conditions of previous studies. Quite clearly the matching picture cue was extremely useful in a way that no other pictures were. One possible reason for this was explored in an analysis of children's labeling responses. If the children were labeling the

120

pictures, the labels might serve as powerful additional memory traces and/or links with the hidden object, since the pictures and objects shared the same name. The number of labels provided, however, was on the average less than 1 out of 8 pictures. Rather, the purposeful-looking behavior of the children in this group gave the impression that they readily recognized the picture as a valid cue to the location of the object in this condition. When the tone sounded denoting the end of the delay period, these children returned quickly to the array of boxes, scanned them as though deliberately searching for the target picture, and then confidently removed the box top revealing the lure. This contrasted quite dramatically with performance when pictures bore no relationship to the object. There it seemed that children chose the correct picture by accident—primarily when their glance fell upon the picture and they recognized it. In fact, Perlmutter, Hazen, Mitchell, Grady, Cavanaugh, and Flook (1981) found that 2-year olds' performance was improved when even arbitrary pictures were present if they were forced to search exhaustively. Older children's performance was similar in unrestricted and exhaustive search conditions. Thus, it is not that 2-year olds do not encode information other than location, but rather that they do not integrate the two pieces of information. It appears that only when this integration occurs do children keep the picture cues in mind and use them to initiate search.

How then should we describe the nature of memory representations at ages 2 and 3, and the character of their change? First, we must emphasize no case for representational failure, of the sort suggested by Bruner (Bruner, Olver, & Greenfield, 1966) and Babska (1965), which would limit our youngest children to encoding spatial properties only. The proposition that the very young child can only represent objects in terms of action, next develops spatial representational capabilities independent of action, followed by more imaginal, and finally, verbal codes, is unfounded. (See also Cohen & Gelber, 1975). Nevertheless, our younger children clearly understood the tasks in a different way than the 3-year olds. For those under 3 the delayed response task seemed to translate to "remember the object is in the box located there", and they relied heavily on location cues, and perhaps exclusively on their natural, direct-impression memory. The 3-year olds quite obviously represented the task as "remember the object is with that picture (or color or size)", and they spontaneously and quite consistently used arbitrary cues other than location as memory aids. In fact, the oldest children attempted to utilize pictures even when it was inappropriate do so, indicating an over ro liance on these cues. The child's understanding of the problem

121

changes then in the brief period between 2 and 3 years. What happens?

Our best guess is that in this simple delayed response task we are witnessing the emergence between 2 and 3 of an early form of what the Soviet psychologists call "sign operations" or mediated utilization of external cues. We will relate our findings primarily to those reported by Vygotsky (1978), although Huttenlocher and Higgins (1978) also describe similar early signing processes, and argue for their importance as precursors to adult human symbolic memory representations, and of course Piaget (1954) has detailed early use of signs or signals similarly. Vygotsky (1978) describes "the natural history of the sign" or a developmental series of transitional memory systems from elementary, direct, nonmediated processing of stimuli to high level mediation creating new internalized, relations. At first the child is unable to purposely utilize external signs because the sign does not evoke an internal associative mediator at all. Later, the child will be seen to occasionally but not regularly utilize external signs, such as our picture cues, for example. The cue at this point is, according to Vygotsky, calling forth associative mediated responses, but the sign operation has not progressed to the more advanced level of a culturally-determined standardized conceptual referent. Therefore, only when by chance the same mediator is produced by the external cue each time it appears does the child use the cue. Finally, the sign-significant relations attained the stereotypical control which permits purposeful instrumental use of even arbitrary signs for retrieval.

The Soviet researchers have typically used much more demanding memory tasks, and observe the emergence of sign operations in these difficult situations after age 6, and further development of sign operations until the age of 12 or more. Vygotsky (1978) reports some work of Yussevich and Zankov with 4-6-year olds, however, which demonstrates clear parallels to our findings with 2-year olds in this simple memory paradigm. Zankov for instance, conducted a study in which children were given a list of words to learn, and a series of meaningless figure drawings which they were told could be used to help them in recall. He found preschool children made no attempt to make connections between picture cues and to-be-remembered words, unless they could change the cues or signs into direct copies of the referents for the words. For example, they inverted a trapezoid so it resembled a bucket, and only then, when it was a direct representation of the object, did it serve as an effective clue for the work "bucket". Yussevich also reported that young children looked for direct representations in picture cues, and sought to reproduce the required word "through a process of direct representation rather than mediated symbolization".

In our less demanding delayed-response tasks, even 2-year olds demonstrated some intermediate sign operations. They showed abilities comparable to the considerably older Russian children in that they utilized picture cues to retrieve hidden objects extremely effectively when the cues directly represented the objects or the cues were intrinsic to the objects' locations. Vygotsky (1978) also reviews some findings of Leontiev which show that the ability to form simple associations between sign and to-be-remembered item does not ensure that the child will effectively utilize the associates for recall at intermediate levels of sign operations. Again, out 2-year olds showed exactly this failure to deliberately utilize associatively-related picture cues, although we were reasonably certain they possessed the associations. Their position on a continuum of sign operations use is thus quite clearly defined, as is that of the 3-year old, with clear reliance on even arbitrary cues. In turn, development in memory for hidden objects in the delayed-response paradigm between the ages of 2 and 3 can be characterized by Vygotsky's "natural history of the sign" in the task.

Strategy Use

As indicated above, we found more purposeful-looking behavior during search when a deeper understanding of the task was present. In this section we review a set of studies which examine further the deliberativeness of the child in this task and others. These studies suggest that very young children may even be able to strategically maintain information during the delay before search occurs.

In the first studies of this series (DeLoache, 1980; DeLoache & Brown, 1983) children between the ages of 18 and 30 months participated in a hide-and-seek task. A stuffed toy was hidden in the child's home and after a several-minute delay the child was asked to find the toy. Performance was excellent; 27-month-old children successfully retrieved the toy on 84% of the trails and 21-month-olds, on 69% of the trials. Even when as many as three toys were hidden at once in three different locations 70% of the hidden toys were found. A direct comparison was then made between performance in the standard delayed-response task and the hide-and-seek game. In the delayed-response task a small toy was hidden in one of four boxes with an associated picture cue. The hide-and-seek game was conducted as before. Testing for both was conducted in the child's home. Children retrieved the hidden object 89% of the time in the hide-and-seek game but only 68% of the time in the delayed-response task.

123

A second study was conducted to determine why performance in the hide-and-seek task had been better. One possibility was that the locations in a room allow the child to more easily associate the object with its location, just as the size and color cues had done in the Daehler, Bukatko, Benson, & Myers (1976) study and as the matching pictures cues had done in the Ratner and Myers (1980) study. In this experiment, a third landmark condition was added in which a plain box was placed next to a natural location such as a chair or endtable. In addition, picture cues were removed from the boxes used in the standard delayed-response task (no landmark condition). Again, performance was best in the hide-and-seek game (75% accuracy). Performance in the landmark (60%) and no-landmark (53%) conditions was poorer and appeared not to differ from one another, although this was more true for the younger children. Older children performed similarly in the landmark and hide-and-seek conditions. It was apparent that a familiar location in itself was not adequate to boost performance in the task. Children still were required to associate the hiding place with a landmark which they found difficult to do. Hiding it **in** the familiar location seemed necessary to promote the link between lure and location.

These results clearly mirror our previous findings and strengthen our conclusions. The DeLoache tasks were conducted in a naturalistic setting and within the context of a play activity. In fact, these studies were conducted in part to point out the necessity of examining toddlers' memory performance within a naturalistic context. The preschool child is typically portrayed as cognitively inadequate in comparison to older children (e.g., Gelman, 1978); however, this depiction is based largely upon performance in unfamiliar tasks in unfamiliar settings which may contribute to the image of incompetence. In contrast, children placed in situations which more closely reflect familiar routines can display their abilities rather than their deficiencies.

Although this is an important and valid perspective, we believe that the advantages of naturalistic contexts have been somewhat exaggerated. For example, in the first hide-and-seek study older children retrieved the toy 84% of the time and younger children, 69%. In studies that followed performance was sometimes at 75% accuracy. In the Daehler, Bukatko, Benson, & Myers study (1976) where size and color cues were intrinsic to the lure's location and most comparable to the hide-and-seek game, older children retrieved the object about 79%, and younger children almost 70%, of the time. Clearly, the levels of performance are quite similar. Even when arbitrary pictures cues were used in our laboratory tasks, performance was roughly comparable (71-75% for older children, 57-65% for younger), and when matching picture cues were used, performance was 84% correct, even among 24-month olds. Admittedly, when errorless retrievals in the two tasks were directly compared by DeLoache, performance in the hide-and-seek game was better. Even there, however, the pattern of performance was identical to that obtained in our laboratory tasks. Children in our tasks always seemed to understand what they were to do and enjoyed doing it; we have lost less than 5% of even our youngest age groups due to a lack of understanding or refusal to continue. The general competency of the children was also reflected in quite consistent performance throughout multiple test trials, improvement when further choices were permitted following an error, and almost no evidence of specific cue or position preferences. It is clear then, that laboratory procedures can be effective with this age range (e.g., Myers, 1979) and in fact measure obtained within the laboratory have been found to correlate significantly with performance in the home (e.g., Ratner, 1980).

Nonetheless, the importance of cross-situational testing is evident in a later study carried out by DeLoache, Cassidy, and Brown (1985). Children averaging 20 months of age participated in the hide-and-seek game in either the home or the laboratory. In each setting the child received four trials with a four-minute delay after each. On every trial the toy was hidden in a natural room location (e.g., under a pillow, behind a door). In contrast to other studies, the child was allowed to make contact with the toy and the behaviors the child displayed were recorded. The number of times the child verbalized about the toy, looked, pointed, peeked, hovered, and retrieved the toy was counted. These behaviors were defined as strategic attempts to remember the object locations. Performance in the two settings did not differ, but the number of these target behaviors did. Surprisingly, more target behaviors were performed in the laboratory than at home. In a second experiment this finding was replicated. A third experiment was then conducted to assess whether these behaviors were directed toward remembering the object's location. In two new conditions children were relieved of their responsibility to retrieve the object. In one condition the experimenter found the toy, and in the other the toy remained visible throughout the delay interval. In comparison to the number of target behaviors performed in Experiment 2, children in these conditions were significantly less likely to comment on, gaze at, or interact with the toy during the delay interval. These children then, apparently had not adopted a memory goal and as a result found it unnecessary to maintain the object's location in memory. DeLoache, Cassidy, and Brown (1985) concluded that very young children can adopt remembering as a goal and can carry out behaviors aimed at achieving this goal. In none of the three studies, however, did the number of behaviors performed correlate significantly with recall. Because performance was quite high, a fourth experiment utilizing a more difficult task was carried out, so that the variance would increase and relationships between strategy use and memory would be more easily detected. Three toys were hidden on each trial rather than just one, and indeed accuracy was reduced and variance increased. Again, however, no significant correlation was noted between the two measures. The number of target behaviors was significantly lower on trails when the child failed to retrieve the toy, however, than on trials when successful retrievals occurred. The four studies provide evidence that children under the age of two use rudimentary mnemonic strategies, that strategy use is sensitive to the presence or absence of memory demands, and that strategy use leads to superior memory performance.

The DeLoache et al. studies are not alone in suggesting that preschool children remember deliberately. For example, Wellman (1987) has recently reviewed a number of studies which appear to support the same conclusion. We will briefly summarize this evidence and then go on to examine whether young children indeed adopt memory as a goal and deliberately use strategies to accomplish this goal.

In an early study, Wellman, Ritter, and Flavell (1975) asked 2-and 3-year old children to either remember where a toy was hidden, or to wait with the toy. Three-year olds in the remember condition looked and touched the baited box longer and more frequently than children in the wait condition, and those who used these techniques longer or more often remembered more. This was true, however, only in the remember condition. In contrast, 2-year olds did not differentiate between the baited and unbaited boxes in either condition. Three-year olds then, apparently used external strategies to remember in response to the experimenter's instructions and when these deliberate actions were used performance improved.

Similarly, Baker-Ward, Ornstein, and Holden (1984) found that 4-, 5-, and 6-year-old children played differently with a set of toys that had been asked to remember. Children were told either to play with a full set of toys, to play with a target subset of the toys, or to remember the target subset. Object naming and visual scanning were more frequent, and play and distraction less frequent, by those who had been asked to remember. Even though children at all ages interacted differently with the toys, only the 6-year olds remembered more in the remember condition than in the other two conditions. Wellman argues that preschoolers deliberately direct their behavior toward the goal of remembering, but it is not always effective in accomplishing the goal.

Finally, Somerville, Wellman, and Cultice (1983) asked 2-, 3-, and 4-year olds to remind their parents to do some activity, such as get milk at the store, or take out the wash. The interest the child had in the activity was varied, as well as the delay between instructing the child to remind the parent and the time for reminding. Although children were most successful when the delay was short and when they were highly interested in the activity, even 2-year olds reminded their caregivers often. The authors concluded that at all ages children demonstrated that they were deliberate rememberers because of the effort required to successfully perform the task.

The evidence accrued thus far converges nicely to tell the story that preschool children even as young as 20 months deliberately remember and direct their behavior toward remembering. This contrasts sharply with more traditional views of children's memory development that describe preschoolers as nonplanful and nonstrategic (e.g., Flavell, 1985). Which are we to believe? In partial answer, we will argue that in the spirit of emphasizing the competencies of the preschool child, more intentionality is being attributed than the data warrant. In part the discrepancy may arise because it is difficult to decide which behavioral components, if any, must be present in order to identify an action as strategic. We adopt the position that in order for a behavior to be strategic it must be used to accomplish the conscious goal of remembering and that children must believe that the behaviors they employ will be effective in reaching this goal. Wellman (in press) has proposed these criteria and others have offered similar definitions (e.g., Flavell, 1970; Naus & Ornstein, 1983; DeLoache, 1985). We would add one more. To be fully strategic, the person remembering needs to formulate the memory goal initially and plan how the goal will be accomplished. The goal should not be discovered in the course of carrying out other behaviors. Under our definition it is doubtful that 2-year olds are strategic. It is irrelevant whether effective or relevant behaviors are carried out if the necessary belief system is absent. It is our view that strategic forms may be present but strategic functions probably are not, and that therefore the very young child is prestrategic. However, if the presence of this belief system is not thought to be necessary, then effective or relevant behaviors may be seen as strategic or predecessors of strategic behaviors. We would then classify these early forms as

127

protostrategies.   In the next section we evaluate the available evidence and discuss why very young children appear to be prestrategic.

In two studies (DeLoache & Brown, 1983; DeLoache, Cassidy, & Brown, 1985), children under 2 were found to exhibit behaviors which could help them remember the hidden object's location, and more of these behaviors were enacted in the laboratory than at home. The authors argued that the children performed these behaviors in order to remember and needed to perform more of them in the laboratory because they were more uncertain there.   There is, however, no evidence that children adopted a memory goal independently of the goal to find the object.   The child was told to remember where Big Bird was hiding so he could be found when the bell rang.   It is not clear whether the child responded to the goal of finding, remembering, or both.   Remembering is a means to another end, not a goal in itself, and it is unclear whether two independent goals are generated and whether the child is aware of each.   This is an important distinction to make. In a study that is often cited to support the position that 3- and 4-year olds use strategies in a meaningful context   (e.g., De-Loache, 1985), Istomina (1975) found no evidence that children under the age of five have specific mnemonic goals that are separate from their more general intentions in a particular event.   Three- to seven-year olds' memory for a list of words was tested.   Children either remembered the words as items to buy at the grocery store or as items to repeat back in a standard memory task.   Recall was better in the context of the grocery game, but only for children over the age of four.   Typically only children over the age of five strategically rehearsed the list and were able to indicate that they were beginning to separate remembering and buying as distinct goals.   Istomina (1975) concluded that "when a child has not yet been fully able to view remembering or recall of the content of a message as a conscious objective, when he is still unable to grasp the content of the game role that poses this objective for him, then, of course both remembering and recall of a message will remain equally unintentional and involuntary". (p. 34)

Perhaps, however, children under the age of two can form an independent memory goal when they are asked to remember information external to themselves such as the location of an object, rather than verbal information which has to be internally generated and maintained, as in the Istomina study.   Wellman has suggested that first mnemonic efforts may be directed primarily toward remembering external information, and DeLoache and Brown (1983) report verbalizations and motor behaviors which seemed directed toward keeping object locations in mind.   Did the children purposefully execute

128

these actions in order to remember, however, and did they know that engaging in them would make it more likely that the object would be remembered? Children may have simply wanted the objects or wanted to complete the task of finding, and carried out actions that permitted proximity to the lures. DeLoache points out that Harris (1984) has suggest that these "strategies" may just be components of the terminal response that the child will eventually make. They reject this explanation for several reasons. One is that verbalizations, which is not part of the final response, is the most frequent activity. If children are really behaving strategically, though, why would they choose verbalization as their most frequent strategy? Unless it is the name of the location that is verbalized, it would not appear to be a helpful device. Unfortunately, object and location names were combined , so we cannot ascertain the level of location verbalizations alone. Yet even if verbalizations were primarily concerned with locations, we still don't know that children verbalized in order to remember. Perhaps verbalizations, as well as looks and points, were communicative in nature. We agree with DeLoache that children were probably more wary and uncertain in the laboratory. Perhaps they therefore wanted to be absolutely certain they could receive the toy, and thus communicated more.

The problem of whether to ascribe intentional remembering to very young children also arises in the Somerville, Wellman, & Cultice (1983) study, where 2-year olds reminded mothers to carry out actions. Unfortunately, the design made it just as likely that children were externally cues to remember as that they deliberately maintained the information in memory and generated it at the appropriate time. In order to give children a time marker indicating when they should remind, they were told to remember when certain events occurred, such as when Daddy came home. Clearly their memory for the information could have been externally triggered by this event in a direct stimulus-response fashion. Furthermore, children only remembered when the task was of personal interest to them which again raises the problem of determining whether memory or some other intention was the goal.

DeLoache and her colleagues argue that even if alternative explanations could account for the results of the first two studies, they cannot account for the results of the third, in which memory demands were removed, and children performed fewer target behaviors. Here again, however, the distinction has not been made between adopting the goal of remembering and adopting the goal of finding. The demand that was removed may just as easily been the demand to find as the demand to remember. Also, although the total number of target behaviors was lower in the non-memory conditions, we do not know if some types of behaviors such as looking remained frequent. Looking may have been the only behavior necessary in the visible-toy condition to keep the child in contact with the object. In addition to being unclear, these data contradict those of Wellman, Ritter, & Flavell (1975), who in a very similar task found no evidence that children younger than three directed more behaviors toward a box containing the hidden object when told to remember than when told to wait. Their measure involved a comparison of target behaviors toward baited and empty boxes. This raises the possibility that children in the DeLoache et al. studies (1983, 1985) may have been performing these actions in relation to both types of locations.

In the last study of the series, children directed more target behaviors toward objects they successfully found than those they did not find, and the authors interpret this to mean that the behaviors were directed toward remembering. Yet more interaction with objects regardless of intention has been shown to lead to better recall in numerous incidental learning and levels-of-processing paradigms; clearly, behaviors subordinated to some other goal aid memory nonetheless. Further, the findings are not persuasive for arguing for intentionality. For example, Baker-Ward, Ornstein and Holden (1984) observed that children played differently with objects they were told to remember, but no relationship was found between recall and the target behaviors used. Wellman in turn suggested based on this finding that preschoolers may have faulty strategies, that is, direct behaviors toward a memory goal, but act ineffectively, arguing for intentionality even though no relation between target behaviors and recall emerge. It appears then that intentionality cannot be disproved or supported by evaluating the relation between strategy use and performance.

There are other findings as well which call into question the strategic deliberateness fo the child under age 3. Several studies have shown that only as children approach their third birthday do they begin to use the word remember. Bretherton and Beeghly (1982) surveyed children's use of words to describe internal states as a way of examining their concepts of these categories. Words describing cognitive states were the last to be produced, following five other types (i.e., volition, physiology, perception, affect, moral). At 28 months of age only 30% of the children used the word, and only 10% used it to describe other people. Huttenlocher, Smiley, and Charney (1983) argue that descriptions of others' internal states signals a more advanced or complete understanding of them. Similarly, Limber (1973) found that remember began to be produced around the age of 30 months, and Ratner (1980) observed that even when children this young did use the word, they described only retrospective and not prospective remembering. It is the planning or prospective sense that is important in understanding task instructions in the hiding and finding games we have been considering, and thus it is doubtful that children under the age of two would even understand the concept.

Finally, if children are strategic so young, why do they fail even at age 5 or 6 to maintain strategy use when they are taught to use them (e.g., Flavell, 1985)? Paris, Newman, and McVey (1982) argue that children do not understand the causal relationship between rehearsal and recall, and have shown that maintenance is more likely if children do understand the relationship. Why should much older children have difficulty understanding this relationship if it is established at age 2? Even if the understanding is initially domain-specific (i.e., present only for tasks involving memory for external information), little instruction should be required to produce the desired behavior several years later.

Conclusions

Whether very young children are strategic or not may, however, be more a matter of emphasis than one of substance. DeLoache et al. (1985) conclude that the target behaviors they observed can be seen as a "natural propensity to keep alive what must be remembered". Thus, children may have made contact with the hidden toy as its image, the image of its location, or the symbol of its location began to fade from memory. Children expected to retrieve the toy at some point and may have wanted to interact with it in some way as its representation became less available. This seems a reasonable suggestion. In no way, however, is it necessary to interpret these behaviors as consciously, deliberately, or strategically subordinated to a memory goal. If intentionality is present at all, it is the goal of finding that drives the child's actions. In fact, the reference to the child's actions as "natural" echoes our earlier account of representational change from age two to three. We described the very young child as relying on direct, unmediated memory to find the hidden objects. The earliest signs or symbols used mimicked the object or were part of the object's location. Only at age 3 was there evidence that children were able to transform information to create more arbitrary signs. It is also after age 3 that the evidence for strategy use becomes more persuasive (e.g., Wellman, Ritter, & Flavell, 1975). This suggests that the ability to use arbitrary symbols may be a prerequisite for strategic behavior. Perhaps remembering must be concretely experienced by the child before he can generate it as a goal in itself. Memory may be made concrete by the availability of internal images of cues. Thus, once children can use external cues such as pictures effectively, the stage is set for connecting goal and action. Representational skill now allows strategic development.

REFERENCES

Babska, Z. (1965). The formation of the conception of identity of visual characteristics of objects seen successively. In P.H. Mussen (Ed.), European research in cognitive development. Monographs of the Society for Research in Child Development, 30, (2, Serial No. 100).

Baker-Ward, L., Ornstein, P., & Holden, D. (1984). The expression of memorization in early childhood. Journal of Experimental Child Psychology, 37, 555-575.

Bretherton, I. & Beeghly, M. (1982). Talking about internal states: The acquisition of an explicit theory of mind. Developmental Psychology, 18, 906-921.

Bruner, J., Olver, R., & Greenfield, P. (1966). Studies in cognitive growth. New York: Wiley.

Cohen, L.B. & Gelber, E.R. (1975). Infant visual memory. In L.B. Cohen & P. Salapatek (Eds.), Infant perception: From sensation to cognition. Vol. 1, Basic visual processes (pp. 347-403). New York: Academic Press.

Daehler, M.W., Bukatko, D., Benson, K., & Myers, N.A. (1976). The effect of size and color cues on the delayed response of very young children. Bulletin of the Psychonomic Society, 7, 65-68.

DeLoache, J. (1980). Naturalistic studies of memory for object location in very young children. In M. Perlmutter (Ed.), New directions for child development: Children's memory (pp. 17-32). San Francisco: Jossey-Bass.

DeLoache, J. (1985). Memory-based searching by very young children. In H. Wellman (Ed.), Children's searching: The development of search skill and spatial representation (pp. 151-183). Hillsdale, NJ: Lawrence Erlbaum Associates.

Deloache, J. & Brown, A. (1983). Very young children's memory for the location of objects in a large-scale environment. Child Development, 54, 888-891.

DeLoache, J., Cassidy, D., & Brown, A. (1985). Precursors of mnemonic strategies in very young children's memory. Child Development, 56, 125-137.

Flavell, J. (1970). Developmental studies of mediated memory. In H. Reese & L. Lipsitt (Eds.), Advances in child development and behavior (pp. 182-211). New York: Academic Press.

Flavell, J. (1985). Cognitive development (2nd ed.). Englewood Cliffs, NJ: Prentice-Hall.

Gelman, R. (1978). Cognitive development. In M. R. Rozenzweig & L. W. Porter (Eds.), Annual reviews of psychology (pp. 297-332). Palo Alto, CA: Annual Reviews, Inc.

Harris, P.L. (1984). Commentary: Landmarks and movement. In C. Sophian (Ed.), Origins of cognitive skills (pp. 113-128). Hillsdale, NJ: Lawrence Erlbaum Associates.

Horn, H.A. & Myers, N.A. (1978). Memory for location and picture cues at ages two and three. Child Development, 49, 845-856.

Hunter, W.S. (1913). The delayed reaction in animals and children. Behavior Monographs (Whole No. 1).

Hunter, W.S. (1917). The delayed reaction in a child. Psychological Review, 24, 74-87.

Huttenlocher, J. & Higgings, E.T. (1978). Issues in the study of symbolic development. In A. Collins (Ed.), Minnesota Symposia on Child Psychology, Vol. 11 (pp. 98-140). Hillsdale, NJ: Lawrence Erlbaum Associates.

Huttenlocher, J., Smiley, P. & Charney, R. (1983). The emergence of action categories in the child: Evidence from verb meanings. Psychological Review, 90, 72-93.

Istomina, Z. (1975). The development of voluntary memory preschool-age children. Soviet Psychology, 13, 5-64.

Limber, J. (1973). The genesis of complex sentences. In T.E. Moore (Ed.), Cognitive development and the acquisition of language (pp. 169-185). New York: Academic Press.

Loughlin, K.A. & Daehler, M.W. (1973). The effects of distraction and added perceptual cues on the delayed reaction of very young children. Child Development, 44, 384-388.

Myers, N.A. (1979, March). Exploring the knowledge base of very young children. Paper presented at the Society for Research on Child Development Symposium, Exploring the Knowledge Base, San Francisco.

Naus, M.J. & Ornstein, P. (1983). Development of memory strategies: Analysis, questions and issues. In M. Chi (Ed.), Trends in memory development research, Vol. 9 (pp. 1-30). Basel: Karger.

Paris, S., Newman, R. & McVey, K. (1982). Learning the functional significance of mnemonic actions: A microgenetic study of strategy acquisition. Journal of Experimental Child Psychology, 34, 490-509.

Perlmutter, M., Hazen, N., Mitchell, D., Grady, J., Cavanaugh, J., & Flook, J. (1981). Picture cues and exhaustive search facilitate very young children's memory for location. Developmental Psychology, 17, 104-110.

Piaget, J. (1954). The construction of reality in the child. New York: Basic Books.

Ratner, H. H. (1980) The role of social context in memory development. In M. Perlmutter (Ed.), New directions for child development: Children's memory (pp. 49-68). San Francisco: Jossey-Bass.

Ratner, H. H., & Myers, N. A. (1980). Related picture cues and memory for hidden object locations at age two. Child Development, 51, 561-564.

Somerville, S., Wellman, H., & Cultice, J. (1983). Young children's deliberate reminding. Journal of Genetic Psychology, 143, 87-96.

Wellman, H. (1987). The early development of memory strategies. In F. Weinert and M. Perlmutter (Eds.), Memory development: Universal changes and individual differences. Hillsdale, NJ: Lawrence Erlbaum Associates.

Wellman, H., Ritter, K., & Flavell, J. (1975). Deliberate memory behavior in the delayed reactions of very young children. Developmental Psychology, 11, 780-787.

Vygotsky, L.S. (1978). Mind in society: The development of higher psychological processes. Cambridge, MA: Harvard University Press.

ACKNOWLEDGEMENTS

The work reported here was supported by a grant from the Spencer Foundation and NIMH Grant HD 09346 to Nancy Myers and Marvin Daehler, and by a grant from the W.T. Grant Foundation to the Department of Psychology, Unviersity of Massachusetts. We would like to thank Martha Early and Carol Roitberg for help in running subjects.

6

A METAPHOR IS LIKE A FOGGY DAY: DEVELOPING AN EMPIRICAL BASIS FOR THE UNDERSTANDING OF METAPHORS

Neal E.A. Kroll, Alan F. Kreisler, and Raymond W. Berrian

The use of figurative language has been recognized as one of the most interesting, yet most puzzling, of human activities. Metaphor, in particular, is acknowledged by many as being a device which plays an important role in the growth of language through the elaboration of word meaning. The form, used broadly here to include similes and analogies as well as pure metaphors, invites comparison by ascribing to one term, traditionally called the 'tenor', the properties of another, the 'vehicle'. The basis of comparison, the set of properties being transferred, is usually referred to as the 'ground' of the metaphor. Thus, for example, in the sentence "Richard is a lion", Richard (tenor) is being characterized as lion-like (vehicle), and the ground perhaps consists of his nobility and/or courage.

Curiously, while some philosophers of language have made much of the role of metaphorical thinking in the origin of poetry and myth (e.g., Cassirer, 1953), and in science (e.g., Black, 1962), many others have been bothered by the form's imprecision and have thus attempted to show that such figurative statements are deviant and anomalous (Beardsley, 1967). This latter view has traditionally appealed to those scholars who have aimed at describing the structure of language as a coherent, logical system, a machine designed to match the world, truth for truth. Most recently, this approach has been a characteristic of the 'componential analysis' theory of meaning that has become a part of Chomsky's transformational grammar (Chomsky, 1957; 1965) and which is usually associated with Katz and Fodor (1963). To these linguists, word meanings exist in a mental lexicon and are comprised of hierarchies of 'semantic markers', or features, and rules which describe the proper circumstances for the word's usage. Sentence comprehension consists of discovering the appropriate semantic content by a series of decoding procedures, from surface to deep syntactic structure, and from this, via the lexicon, to the sentence's meaning. Unfortunately, as has been pointed out by several authors (e.g., Bolinger, 1965), the incompatibility of the markers which designate the terms of figurative statements dooms metaphor, in this analysis, to anomaly.

Nevertheless, metaphors are used and understood routinely and in many contexts by both adults and children (Pollio, Barlow, Fine, & Pollio, 1977). Further, it can be argued that in many ways metaphoric comprehension is a paradigm case of language understanding: (a) novel metaphors are very clear examples of language used to inform, (b) they display the remarkable flexibility and openness of the procedures used by comprehenders, and (c) they are rooted in the discovery of resemblances by the comprehender between the tenor and vehicle (Verbrugge & McCarrell, 1977) and, therefore, may share important features with other, more basic psychological processes. For these reasons, it seems clear that a theory of language comprehension will necessarily have to include an understanding of the use of figurative language. In particular, such a theory must address itself to (a) the processes at work within the reading of a sentence, whereby its meaning is derived, (b) characterizing that meaning in terms of what is known that was not known before; i.e., to discovering what the comprehender is prepared to do or say as a result of the interpretive interaction with the language, and (c) the role of context across sentences in preparing the comprehender to select appropriate characteristics for comparison.

Until very recently, there has been little experimental work on the comprehension of non-literal language, and most of the existing research has confined itself to the presentation of context-free sentences, which may have greatly reduced the applicability of the results to real comprehension processes. For example, some of the early psycholinguistic research of Miller and his associates (e.g., Marks & Miller, 1964) used semantically anomalous sentences as stimuli in memory experiments and found that it was much more difficult to memorize these than well-formed, literal, sentences. Pollio (1977), however, reports replicating this research and finding no difference between sentence types. The difference in results occurs because Pollio, unlike the previous researchers, asked the participants of his experiment to interpret the sentences metaphorically when they were presented. Once interpreted, they were not difficult to remember.

Recent research measuring the time required to comprehend sentences that could be interpreted either literally or figuratively, depending upon the context, indicates that with the appropriate context, the figurative meaning of these sentences can be comprehended as rapidly as their literal meanings (Inhoff, Lima, & Carroll, 1984; Ortony, Schallert, Reynolds, & Antos, 1978). In fact, people appear to be unable to ignore figurative meanings of ambiguous sentences when these sentences are placed in contexts which refer to the ground of the figurative meaning (Gildea & Glucksberg, 1983).

In addition, what is judged to constitute a 'good' metaphor is a function of the presence or absence of a context. For example, some researchers (e.g., Ortony, 1979; Tourangeau & Sternberg, 1981) have reported a high correlation existing between the judged metaphoric 'goodness' and the degree of similarity of the metaphor's tenor and vehicle term. However, McCabe (1983) demonstrated that, although such a correlation exists when the metaphors are presented in isolation, no such relationship exists for these same metaphors when they are placed in context.

The work to be reported here is concerned with the role of context in the understanding of figurative language. Although few theorists have addressed themselves to this specific question, progress has been made in the analysis of context of more literal discourse. Chafe (1970; 1972) has proposed that context serves to create a memory which contains both backgrounded and foregrounded components, and that a subsequent sentence contains information that links contextually foregrounded material with additional new information to amend that memory. Chafe describes the linguistic rules which govern this process of smoothly directing the receiver through more and more material. For example, in a familiar fairy tale, the story begins: "Once upon a time there were three bears." This, to Chafe, is all new information and serves to introduce the listener to the bears: They are now foregrounded in memory. The next sentence, "They lived in a cottage in a forest," is linked to the previous statement in memory by means of the pronoun, which can only refer to the foregrounded bears. (The definite article, as in 'the bears' might have been used instead.) This second sentence then adds the new information about where the bears live. As information about the bears accumulates, the listener builds a more elaborate 'picture' in memory which will serve as background for the story when Goldilocks is introduced, and the bears will by then be represented rather fully.

A similar analysis has been proposed and experimentally tested by Clark and his associates (Haviland & Clark, 1974; Clark & Haviland, 1974). To Clark, following connected discourse invites the listener to employ the 'given-new' strategy, by which an accumulating propositional memory representation is built up in a way like that proposed by Chafe. Again, linguistic devices, such as pronominalization and the definite article, are used to indicate links with contextually generated memories. When these links are omitted, the listener must infer the relationship between the current sentence and the referents of its parts, slowing significantly the comprehension of that sentence.

Both of the above analyses help to clarify the ways in which discourse may be followed when it is carefully constructed, literal, and concrete. Unfortunately, when the comprehender must construct bridges from new to old information, the above leave us insufficiently equipped: We still must ask how a particular context enables us, when confronted with new information, to pick out the appropriate characteristics from those entailed by the new term(s). That contexts work in these more subtle ways has been demonstrated by recent experiments; e.g., those of Anderson and Ortony (1975), who found that a recall cue's effectiveness varied as a function of its relationship to particular aspects of background information in the to-be-remembered sentences. In the realm of metaphor, similar results were reported by Verbrugge and McCarrell (1977), who successfully used statements of the ground relationship as recall cues for metaphors.

The two studies just cited demonstrate that subject-generated constructions are not limited to logical bridging between propositions. Rather the component terms of sentences are taken in situation-specific ways. In the Verbrugge and McCarrell (1977) experiments, for example, the cue "are tubes which conduct water where it's needed" was a quite effective prompt for the recall of the sentence "Tree trunks are like straws", but not for "Tree trunks are like pillars", even though the water-transporting property is 'always' applicable to tree trunks. Thus, the vehicle 'straws' has constrained the understanding of 'tree trunks' such that the latter is remembered with a certain straw-like bias rather than as either a neutral concept node or an activated feature list. As a result of their experiments, Verbrugge and McCarrell concluded that in metaphor comprehension, "the vehicle domain guides a novel schematization of the topic domain" and that the resulting memory representation is abstract and relational.

Although the above studies contribute to our understanding of the nature of what is interpreted as people interact with language, more work is needed on how that comprehension is achieved, particularly with sentences in a linguistic context. Specifically, how do contexts contribute to the information of abstract, biased construction? In a previous study (Kroll, Berrian, and Kreisler, 1978), the participants were presented with pairs of sentences. The first sentence, the context, was to be read aloud. The second was in the simile form: "(Subject) is like (Predicate)", with the Subject equivalent to the traditional tenor and the Predicate being the vehicle. Only half of the second sentences were actually similes, however. The other half,

138

while in simile form, were deliberately obscure and unlikely pairings of terms. Upon presentation of this second sentence, participants were asked to decide, as quickly as possible, whether the 'similes' were 'Good' or 'Bad', and their decision times were recorded. To measure the effect of context on ease of comprehension, three types of context sentences were constructed for each Good Simile. One type, the Relevant, presented the implicit grounds and included either the Subject or the Predicate terms from the upcoming simile. Additionally, there were Misleading contexts which stated a property shared by the upcoming simile's Subject and Predicate, but not pertinent to the simile's figurative meaning, and Irrelevant contexts which stated a property of the Subject or the Predicate not easily shared by the other. For example, the simile "The refugees were like windblown leaves" could be preceded by any of the following context sentences: "The refugees scatter aimlessly" (Subject-Relevant), "Windblown leaves scatter aimlessly" (Predicate-Relevant), "The refugees were numerous" (Subject-Misleading), "Windblown leaves were numerous" (Predicate-Misleading), "The refugees arrived by boat" (Subject-Irrelevant), or "Windblown leaves fell from the Maple" (Predicate-Irrelevant). The participants were instructed to ignore the context sentence, which was often irrelevant or misleading. Pilot work had demonstrated that, with any less extreme instructions regarding the context, participants routinely misconstrued the task, judging as 'good' only those similes whose context literalized them. The question remained, in what ways and to what degree would the context continue to play a role even under these extreme instructions?

Following the classification phase of the experiment, participants were given a booklet containing a list of sentences that contained either the Subject or the Predicate of a simile they had previously seen. These were actually chosen from the list of context sentences, although only half were sentences previously read by any single participant. This phase of the experiment was a cued recall task where participants were asked to try to recall the appropriate simile for each of the sentences in the booklet. The results of the experiment demonstrated that, as in the research of Verbrugge and McCarrell (1977), recall cues stating the ground of the simile (here, the Relevant context sentences) were the best recall cues. Interestingly, this occurred even when the participant had not seen the Relevant context in the first part of the experiment.

The memory data was further analyzed in terms of whether the cue contence included the Subject or the Predicate of the to-be-remembered simile. Here, when the cue had been seen previously, Subject contexts were superior to the Predicate contexts, while just the reverse was true if the cue differed from the previously seen context. These results were interpreted in terms of the respective functional roles of Subject and Predicate in sentence comprehension: It appeared that upon reading the context sentence during the first phase of the experiment, the Subject guided the interpretation of the Predicate, which then acted back upon the Subject to enrich it with a particular meaning. For example, in the context sentence "The refugees were numerous", the predicate 'numerous' is first taken in a particular way, a way applicable to humans (and not, say, grains of sand, which would entail a much greater number). Once the Predicate is so understood, it can be meaningfully ascribed to the Subject, emphasizing certain characteristics of the Subject. The result of this is a unitary representation of masses of refugees. When the simile now appears, the participant is 'armed' with the representation constructed during the reading of the context. This construction will help or hinder the participant, depending upon the relationship between the context and the simile. Both the decision time data and the misclassification data support the above analysis: When the context was about the simile's Predicate, the context type had relatively little effect on simile comprehension (as measured by the participant's decision time or percentage of misclassifications). This follows from the above since the simile interpretation begins with the Subject and, therefore, the previously constructed representation of the Predicate is essentially ignored. That is, the reader makes sense of the simile's Predicate only in terms of the simile's Subject. On the other hand, when context and simile have identical subjects, the meaning carried over from the context is assumed to be relevant; i.e., the two sentences are assumed to be about the same thing. Thus, with a Relevant-Subject context, simile comprehension is fast and accurate. However, with Irrelevant-Subject contexts, and even more with Misleading-Subject ones, the participant is hampered since, as it turns out, the two sentences are *not* about the same thing.

Returning to the memory data, the above predicts that Relevant cues will always be the best, since they capture the appropriate ground of the simile. Further, when the cue had been seen before in either a Relevant or an Irrelevant context, the Subject cues should be superior to the Predicate cues since the Subject bears most of the meaning as a result of the Predicate-domain transfer during comprehension and since neither the Relevant nor Irrelevant context sentence, now used as a recall cue, contradicts the to-be-recalled simile. (This advantage of the Subject as a recall cue is lost with the Misleading context as a cue.) When the cue is a new sentence, then

140

Predicate superiority should occur with Relevant contexts since the Predicate's domain of meaning is the source of the Subject's enrichment and, therefore, the simile should be most easily retrieved on the basis of the properties suggested by the Predicate. The results of the first experiment fit very nicely with the above expectations.

In the research reported below, we were interested in examining additional consequences of the constructed representation derived from reading similes in context. In particular, we reasoned that if a participant's comprehension of similes was essentially in the form of the Subject elaborated by the Predicate domain, then this representation should affect subsequent interactions with sentences about that Subject or Predicate. To investigate this, we constructed a recognition task in which participants would be presented with sentences that may or may not have been context sentences in the classification phase of the experiment. The questions we hoped to answer in this way were: (a) Would participants tend to falsely 'recognize' sentences that stated the ground of the previously seen similes? (b) Would recognition judgments be a function of what appeared in the test-sentence: the simile's Subject or its Predicate? and, if so (c) Would these effects clarify the Subject/Predicate relationship described above?

Method
Procedure. The classification phase of this study was identical to that of Kroll, et al. (1978). Pairs of sentences were rear-projected onto a small screen in front of the participant. The first sentence, the context sentence, was presented for three seconds, and the participant was instructed to read this sentence aloud. Following a one second blank-screen interval, the 'simile', was projected. The participant was instructed to decide as rapidly as possible if this second sentence represented "a reasonably clear figurative communication" and to press one of two keys to convey the decision. Latency from the onset of the simile to the key press was recorded for each trial. A three second interval separated trials.

As with the previous study, the participant was instructed that the first sentence in many cases would be unrelated to the meaning of the simile and, the experimenter discussed the participant's misclassifications after each occurrence. This procedure resulted in conservative classifications; i.e., a stronger tendency to classify Good Similes as Bad than vice versa.

As with the earlier study, the following examples were given in the instructions:
First sentence: "The totem pole was made out of wood."

141

Second sentence: "The arrow was like a totem pole."
Answer: Bad Simile.
Even though both are made of wood and both are possible Indian arti-facts, this would be a literal communication and there is no readily discernible metaphoric communication in the second sentence.
First sentence: "His personality was very pleasant."
Second sentence: "His personality was like an anchor."
Answer: Good Simile.
This sentence is a meaningful metaphor, indicating that his personal-ity was a liability to him. Note that in this case, the first sentence was somewhat misleading in that a pleasant personality would not be 'an anchor'. However, your decision is to be made on the second sentence *by itself.*

The first 24 trials were not included in the analysis. They were considered as practice trials, although the participants were not in-formed of this distinction. The remaining 60 'Good' and 60 'Bad' sim-iles were included in the analysis.

After completing all 144 trials of the classification task, the participant was given a booklet containing the 72 items of the recog-nition test. The participant was instructed that one member of each pair had been presented as a context sentence during the first phase and that the sentence recognized should be circled. A number from one (guessing) to four (absolutely certain) indicated the confidence of the choice. The recognition task was not paced, but was completed by most participants within 10-15 minutes.

Materials. The similes used in the present experiment were essen-tially the same as used previously, with the exception of eight simi-les that were modified or replaced because they either had a high misclassification rate in the earlier study or they were judged as too similar to other similes in the pool.

Context sentences referred to either the Subject or the Predicate of the simile, and were Relevant (literalization of the simile's ground), Irrelevant (no shared tenor/vehicle properties), or Mis-leading (shared tenor/vehicle property, but irrelevant to the simile's ground). See the introduction for an example of context types. Since the Bad Similes obviously could not be preceded by a Relevant context sentence, they had either Irrelevant (no shared property) or Mis-leading (shared property) context sentences.

Two presentations sets were constructed. They differed only in the type of context sentence that was paired with each Good Simile. Thus, when a Good Simile was preceded by a Relevant context sen-tence in the first set, it was preceded by either an Irrelevant of a

Misleading context in the second set. Half of the participants were shown Set 1; the other half, Set 2.

For each of the two simile sets, three recognition test sets were constructed, each of these containing one pair of possible context sentences for each of the Good Similes in the classification task. These six tests each had two forms that differed in their ordering of the alternative choices. The sequence of test trials was the same for all twelve test forms. The first twelve items on all tests corresponded to the 'practice' similes and contained the actual context sentence and a distractor using the same element (Subject or Predicate). For the next 60 items, two-thirds contained the presented context sentence paired with an alternative context sentence as a distractor. The remaining twenty items consisted of the two alternative contexts that had not been presented in the classification task. These items were included in order to measure any tendencies regarding the mediational aspects of the ground of the simile.

Participants. Thirty students from introductory psychology courses participated in the study. Six of these failed to meet a criterion of at least three correct responses in each of the six context conditions and were therefore excluded from the analyses. All students received course credit for their one-hour participation.

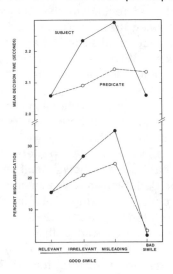

Figure 1. TOP: Mean decision time, in seconds, of correctly classified similes as a function of the context sentence. BOTTOM: Mean percentage of misclassifications as a function of the context sentence.

143

Results

The decision times for the correctly classified similes were averaged for each participant as a function of the type of preceding context sentence. These mean decision times were averaged over participants and these averages are presented at the top of Figure 1. As in our earlier experiment (Kroll, et al., 1978), the classification time of a Good Simile tends to be longer when the preceding context sentence deals with the Subject of the simile than when it deals with the Predicate, 2.20 *vs.* 2.10 seconds, t (23) = 2.370, p < .05, but just the opposite is the case for Bad Similes, 2.06 *vs.* 2.14 seconds, t (23) = 3.116, p < .01. within the Good Similes, comparisons of individual pairs of types of contexts found the simile comprehension time to be slower following Subject contexts than following Predicate contexts for both Irrelevant and Misleading conditions, t (23) = 2.120 and 2.370, p < .05. In addition, within the Subject contexts, the Relevant condition was faster than either the Irrelevant or Misleading conditions, t (23) = 2.908 and 3.526, p < .01. However, within the predicate contexts, the various conditions did not differ significantly. This is essentially the same pattern of results found with the decision times in our earlier experiment: With Good Similes, comprehension times are more sensitive to the relevancy manipulation when the contexts are related to the Subject of the simile and, therefore, similes following Irrelevant and Misleading Subject contexts are more slowly comprehended than are their counterparts with Predicate contexts. With the Bad Similes, however, the Subject-related contexts result in faster comprehension than do the Predicate-related contexts.

The percentage of simile misclassification for each of the various context types are presented at the bottom of Figure 1. While the results here are more definitive than they were in our earlier experiment, they present a very similar pattern. The classification conservatism of the participants shows itself in the virtual absence of misclassification of Bad Similes. Within the Good Similes, there are more misclassification following Subject-related contexts than following Predicate-related contexts, 26.7% *vs.* 20.3%, t (23) = 2.451, p < .05, and this is true with both the Irrelevant and Misleading conditions, t(23) = 1.934 and 2.511, p < .07 and .02. Within the Subject-related contexts, fewer errors follow Relevant than Irrelevant contexts, t (23) = 2.094, p < .05, and fewer follow Irrelevant than Misleading, t (23) = 2.402, p < .05. Within the Predicate-related contexts, only the difference between Relevant and Misleading contexts is significant, t (23) = 3.114, p < .01. Thus, as with the decision time measure, the error measure suggests that the Subject-related contexts have a greater effect on the classification of Good Similes than do the Predicate-related contexts.

In measuring the ability of participants to recognize context sentences, both percentage correct and confidence ratings (scoring the ratings of errors as negative numbers) showed the same pattern, but only the more sensitive confidence ratings will be reported here. Tests for the recognition of context sentences that had preceded a misclassified simile were not included. To increase the number of trials per participant per condition, Subject and Predicate sentences were combined when measuring the recognition of Relevant, Irrelevant, and Misleading sentences as a function of the distractor, and tests with different distractors were combined when measuring the recognition of Subject and Predicate sentences as a function of whether they were Relevant, Irrelevant, or Misleading. (Other, more complicated, methods of combining the data had suggested that there was no interaction of these three variables.)

The average confidence ratings for the recognition of Relevant, Irrelevant, and Misleading sentences, averaged over Subject and Predicate related sentences, are presented in Table 1 as a function of the type of distractor used on the recognition test trial. For the Relevant sentences, the Misleading sentences appear to be more effective distractors than the Irrelevant sentences, although this difference is not significant, $t(23) = 1.953$, $p < .07$. For the Irrelevant sentences, the Relevant sentences appear to be more effective distractors than the Misleading sentences, however the variability between participants is quite large in the Relevant distractor condition and consequently this difference is also not significant, $t(23) = 1.560$, $p < .10$. However, these data suggest that the Relevant sentences provide a more effective distractor for the Irrelevant than for the Misleading sentences, $t(23) = 1.796$, $p < .10$, that the Irrelevant sentences are more efficient distractors for Misleading than for Relevant sentences, $t(23) = 3.269$, $p < .01$, and that the Misleading sentences are more efficient distractors for Irrelevant than for Relevant sentences, $t(23) = 2.134$, $p < .05$.

Of more interest is how participants responded when they had to select between two alternatives that had not been presented in the classification task. In these cases the alternatives were the remaining two types, such that if an Irrelevant context sentence had been presented, the participant's choice was between Relevant and Misleading sentences. For those items in which the participants had seen the Relevant sentence, but had to choose between the other two alternatives, selection was evenly divided between the alternatives, and participants assigned these items the lowest rating of confidence.

Several of the participants indicated that they felt neither alternative had been presented; these finding strongly suggest that Relevant contexts are firmly embedded in memory. For those items in which participants had not seen the Relevant sentence, a different pattern emerges. Participants are attracted more by the Relevant distractors with Subject sentences (average rating = 1.09) than with Predicate sentences (0.46), t (23) = 2.906, $p < .01$. (For these items, ratings for the Relevant distractor were arbitrarily scored as positive and those for the other alternative as negative.) In addition, sign tests showed that more participants chose the Relevant distractor than the other, 22 of 24 for Subject sentences, $p < .001$, and 19 or 24 for Predicate sentences, $p < .006$. When averaging over Subject and Predicate sentences, tests where the correct choice would have been the Irrelevant sentence appear more likely to lead to the participant preferring the Relevant distractor (1.04) than those tests where the correct choice would have been the Misleading sentence (0.58). Unfortunately this comparison resulted in a much greater variability, which meant that this difference was not significant, t (23) = 1.513, $p < .10$. However, this data combination still found that participants chose the Relevant distractor significantly more often than the other, 19 of 24 participants in both cases, $p < .006$.

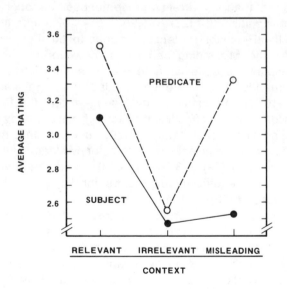

Figure 2. Average confidence rating of the recognition of Subject and Predicate related context sentences as a function of their relevancy to their similes.

146

The average confidence ratings for the recognition of Subject and Predicate sentences, averaged over distractor conditions, are presented in Figure 2 as a function of their relevancy to their similes. Predicate sentences are recognized more confidently than are Subject sentences under both Relevant and Misleading conditions, t (23)= 2.795 and 3.315, $p < .02$ and .01. Among the Subject sentences, the Relevant sentences are rated higher than either the Irrelevant, t (23) = 2.356, $p < .05$, or the Misleading, t (23) = 2.245, $p < .05$. Among the Predicate sentences, the Irrelevant sentences are rated lower than either the Relevant, t (23) = 3.709, $p < .01$, or the Misleading t (23) = 2.246, $p < .05$.

Discussion

The patterns of results for both comprehension time and misclassifications of similes replicated those of the previous experiments. These results suggest that: (a) when the preceding context sentences contains, as its Subject, the Predicate of the simile, that the context sentence is relatively easy to ignore while evaluating the simile, but (b) when the context sentence has the identical Subject as the simile, the simile evaluation becomes much more complicated. With Relevant-Subject contexts, simile processing can still proceed smoothly, since no conflict in meaning is produced by the two sentences. With Irrelevant- and Misleading-Subject contexts, however, participants must deal with different ascriptions about the same Subject term and, ultimately, must actively reject the meaning of the Subject gleaned from the preceding context. This procedure requires more processing time to comprehend the simile and leads to a greater possibility for error since, instead of confirming an already formed construct, as in the Relevant-Subject condition, or presenting all new information, as in the Predicate conditions, these conditions present a conflict between the old and new information which requires the former to be suppressed while the simile is being evaluated. With an Irrelevant context, the need for this suppression is easier to see — and perhaps easier to accomplish — since it is applicable only to the Subject term. The Misleading-Subject context is more difficult since the information gained from the context is about a legitimate relationship between the Subject and Predicate of the simile, but not a relationship expressed by the simile.

We have assumed that since the participant's primary task is the evaluation of the simile, the participant's memory of a given trial should be dominated by the concept gained from making this evaluation. Earlier, based on our previous experiment's cued recall data, we characterized that representation as being composed of the Sub-

147

ject of the simile, elaborated by the appropriately constrained meaning domain of the Predicate of the simile. In the present experiment, the context recognition task was included to test the above characterization of the memory representation and to give us a more detailed picture of the processing involved in the evaluation. For example, we expected that representation to bias the participant's recollection of what had been previously seen, but minimally processed. The results from the 'false recognition' tests, where neither of the choices had been previously seen, support the above characterization. Under those conditions, in which one of the new sentences stated the ground of a seen simile, a significant majority of the participants 'recognized' that sentence as having previously occurred.

The conclusions suggested by the confidence-rating/recognition data for those trials on which one of the choices had been a previously seen context sentence were as follows:

(a) When the context sentence was Irrelevant, regardless of whether it was about a simile's Subject or Predicate, recognition was relatively poor. This result confirms both our assumption that the memory trace left by each trial of the classification task was of the simile, and that during the classification task, the participant's strategy was to dismiss or ignore contexts that did not contribute to the understanding of the simile. In the case of these Irrelevant contexts, this active dismissal was relatively straightforward; i.e., participants were not compelled to spend much time or effort resolving any conflicts between context and simile meanings since this type of context does not link Subject and Predicate.

(b) With Relevant contexts available as a recognition-item, both memory and confidence ratings were significantly higher. Here, again, our assumption about the memory trace was supported: Relevant contexts, because they state the ground of the previously-seen similes, are most likely to be recognized on the basis of the remembered simile. Interestingly, Relevant-Predicate contexts were more confidently recognized than were Subject-contexts of the same type. We interpret this difference to reflect the idea, stated above (and in Verbrugge & McCarrell, 1977) that it is the Predicate (or vehicle) domain that contributes most to the meaning of figurative expressions. Our participants were extremely confident that they had previously seen statements of the ground of remembered similes, especially when the ground was explicitly stated about the Predicate term, whose meaning domain contributed that ground to the simile.

(c) This potency of the Predicate is suggested by the recognition ratings of the Misleading context sentences as well. Here, the largest differences between Subject and Predicate conditions occurred: The Misleading-Predicate sentences were recognized quite confidently, while the Misleading-Subject sentences were rated as poorly as in the Irrelevant condition. To see why this was so, examine the following typical case. The simile "The refugees were like windblown leaves" was preceded by either "The refugees were numerous" or "The windblown leaves were numerous" in the Misleading-Subject and Misleading-Predicate conditions. When participants had seen the former, they entered the simile evaluations with a 'picture' of many refugees. The meaning implied by the simile, however, was that of people scattered aimlessly. To make this interpretation, the full meaning of the subject, gleaned from the prior context sentence, had to be drastically revised since entirely different characteristics were made salient by the predicate of the simile. The work done to revise this representation is shown in the long reaction times which participants produced in this condition. Later, when the sentence "The refugees were numerous" was given as a recognition item, the dissimilar representation recalled from the simile classification interfered with the participants' memory for that context sentence, and their confidence ratings were accordingly low.

Upon encountering the Misleading-Predicate sentence during the first phase of the experiment, participants formed an idea of numerous windblown leaves. Now, when the same simile is encountered, and the image of scattering windblown leaves is applied to the refugees, the context-gained representation of the leaves need not be utterly discarded so much as made a subsidiary, less salient part of the simile's meaning. In this case, numerosity, as old information, merely fades into the background and does not compete with the ground of the simile. During the recognition task, when these participants see the sentence "The windblown leaves were numerous", they are likely to be reminded of the simile with which this context is not inconsistent: Numerosity is a small, but viable feature of the simile's representation. Hence, this context sentence is confidently recognized, though, it might be added, not as confidently as the Relevant-Predicate statements of the ground itself.

More generally, whenever a property is ascribed to a term, the reader will construct a representation of that property as constrained by the term to which it is applied. Subsequently, when that same term is used again, the previous property is brought along. When that term appears as a Subject likened to a Predicate, the contextually supplied property will play an important role in determining the ease of comprehension of the second sentence. When the original property describes the relation that is being emphasized in the second sentence, comprehension is abetted. But when this redundancy does not occur, a revision in understanding becomes necessary.

The situation will be different when the term elaborated by the property in the first sentence is used in the second as a Predicate. Here, even though that property may still be brought along across sentences, its effect upon comprehension will not be as dramatic. This is so, in the above analysis, because the Subject will constrain the elaboration by the Predicate. The Predicate's domain will be exploited only in ways appropriate to that Subject. In the case of a Misleading context, the property ascribed to the simile's Predicate term is, by our definition of 'Misleading', a property shared by the simile's Subject and Predicate, and therefore cannot in this syntactic situation be in conflict with the idea to be ascribed to the Subject in the simile. This explanation accounts for the relative speed of understanding similes preceded by Misleading-Predicate sentences, and, additionally, why these context sentences are so confidently recognized: The property 'brought along' has elicited no need to eliminate it.

REFERENCES

Anderson, R.C., & Ortony, A. (1975). On putting apples into bottles. Cognitive Psychology, 7, 167-180.

Beardsley, M.C. (1967). Metaphor. In P. Edwards (Ed.), The encyclopedia of philosophy. Vol. 5 (pp. 284-289). New York: Macmillan.

Black, M. (1962). Models and metaphors. Ithaca, NY; Cornell University Press.

Bolinger, D. (1965). The atomization of meaning. Language, 41, 555-573.

Cassirer, E. (1953). The philosophy of symbolic forms. New Haven, CT: Yale University Press.

Chafe, W.L. (1970). Meaning and the structure of language. Chicago: University of Chicago Press.

Chafe, W.L. (1972). Discourse structure and human knowledge. In J.B. Carroll & R.O. Freedle (Eds.), Language comprehension and the acquisition of knowledge (pp. 41-69). New York: Wiley.

Chomsky, N. (1957). Syntactic structures. The Hague: Mouton.

Chomsky, N. (1965). Aspects of the theory of syntax. Cambridge, MA: MIT Press.

Clark, H.H., & Haviland, S.E. (1974). Psychological process as linguistic explanation. In D. Cohen (Ed.), Explaining linguistic phenomena (pp. 91-124). Washington, DC: Hemisphere.

Gildea, P., & Glucksberg, S. (1983). On understanding metaphor: The role of context. Journal of Verbal Learning and Verbal Behavior, 22, 577-590.

Haviland, S.E., & Clark, H.H. (1974). What's new? Acquiring new information as a process in comprehension. Journal of Verbal Learning and Verbal Behavior, 13, 515-521.

Inhoff, A.W., Lima, S.D., & Carroll, P.J. (1984). Contextual effects on metaphor comprehension in reading. Memory and Cognition, 12, 558-567.

Katz, J.J., & Fodor, J.A. (1963). The structure of a semantic theory. Language, 39, 170-210.

Kroll, N.E.A., Berrian, R.W., & Kreisler, A.F. (1978). The comprehension and memory of similes as a function of context. In M.M. Gruneberg, P.E. Morris, & R.N. Sykes (Eds.), Proceedings of the International Conference on Practical Aspects of Memory (pp. 663-670). London & New York: Academic Press.

Marks, L.E., & Miller, G.A. (1964). The role of semantic and syntactic constraints in the memorization of English sentences. Journal of Verbal Learning and Verbal Behavior, 3, 1-5.

McCabe, A. (1983). Conceptual similarity and the quality of metaphor in isolated sentences vs. extended context. Journal of Psycholinguistic Research, 12, 41-68.

Ortony, A. (1979). Beyond literal similarity. Psychological Review, 86, 161-180.

Ortony, A., Schallert, D.L., Reynolds, R.E., & Antos, S.J. (1978). Interpreting metaphors and idioms: Some effects of context on comprehension. Journal of Verbal Learning and Verbal Behavior, 17, 465-477.

Pollio, H.R. (1977, August). Metaphoric style: Personal cognition and figurative language. Paper presented at the convention of the American Psychological Association, San Francisco, CA.

Pollio, H.R., Barlow, J.M., Fine, H.J., & Pollio, M.R. (1977). Psychology and the poetics of growth. Hillsdale, NJ: Laurence Erlbaum Associates.

Tourangeau, R., & Sternberg, R.J. (1981). Aptness in metaphor. Cognitive Psychology, 13, 27-55.

Verbrugge, R.R., & McCarrell, N.S. (1977). Metaphoric comprehension: Studies in reminding and remembering. Cognitive Psychology, 9, 494-533.

7

VISUAL LATERALITY AND CEREBRAL HEMISPHERE SPECIALIZATION: METHODOLOGICAL AND THEORETICAL CONSIDERATIONS

Joseph B. Hellige

There is currently considerable interest among psychologists, linguists, and neurologists in information processing differences between the right and left cerebral hemispheres. Investigation of hemispheric specialization in normal individuals often involves presenting stimuli so that they project directly to only one cerebral hemisphere and examining performance as a function of which hemisphere receives the stimulus information directly. Such laterality effects have been studied using visual, auditory, and tactile presentation of stimuli and involve examination of accuracy and latency of overt responses as well as measurement of psychophysiological responses. The present chapter discusses several of the factors that influence visual laterality patterns and considers the resulting methodological and theoretical implications.

In the human visual system, all information from each half of the visual field projects directly to the contralateral cerebral hemisphere and travels only indirectly to the ipsilateral hemisphere via interhemispheric connections. It has been argued that performance is better for a task when the stimuli are projected directly to the cerebral hemisphere that is more efficient for the task (e.g., Kimura, 1966). The prototypical reports of a right visual field, left hemisphere (RVF-LH) advantage for verbal stimuli and a left visual field, right hemisphere (LVF-RH) advantage for complex, non-verbal stimuli are, therefore, consistent with the clinical observation that difficulty with verbal processing occurs more frequently after left-sided brain damage than after right-sided brain damage, while difficulty with complex, visuospatial tasks occurs more frequently after right-sided than after left-sided damage (e.g., Bradshaw & Nettleton, 1983). Both types of results suggest differential hemispheric involvement in verbal versus nonverbal processing of visual stimuli.

In the visual laterality work with normal individuals there are several deviations from the prototypical pattern of results just noted. To understand these deviation it is necessary to know the factors that influence visual laterality and the manner in which they interact. In the present chapter, I discuss several such factors and consider what the effects of each factor imply about information processing differences between the cerebral hemispheres and about the use of visual laterality to investigate hemisphere differences. This discussion will begin with a brief consideration of the ways in which asymmetries in the peripheral visual pathways might influence visual laterality. Following this will be a consideration of stimulus presentation parameters and perceptual quality. Effects of stimulus presentation parameters are often overlooked in laterality research. However, it is important to consider such effects because presentation parameters vary widely among visual laterality experiments. The other factors to be considered might be best characterized as task demand factors and include post-exposure scanning, processing strategy, relative involvement of perception and memory, and selective hemispheric activation and interference.

Peripheral Pathway Factors

There are several asymmetries in the peripheral visual pathways that could contribute to visual laterality effects. For example, there is anatomical and physiological evidence that the crossed visual pathways dominate the uncrossed visual pathways (see White, 1969, for a discussion of such dominance). Consequently, under conditions of monocular stimulus presentation we would expect recognition to be better from the visual field traversing the crossed pathway than from the visual field traversing the uncrossed pathway. The use of binocular stimulus presentation controls for cross-uncrossed pathway differences insofar as each visual field reaches the contralateral cerebral hemisphere via the crossed pathway from one eye and via the uncrossed pathway from the other eye. However, crossed pathway dominance combined with the dominance of one eye over the other could lead to peripheral pathway effects even under binocular viewing conditions (see Wyke & Ettlinger, 1961; Hayashi & Bryden, 1967).

While peripheral asymmetries such as those just considered could contribute to main effects of visual field, it is unlikely that they could account for the various changes in visual field advantages that occur as a function of such things as stimulus and response characteristics and task demands. Therefore, when using visual laterality patterns to draw conclusions about cerebral hemisphere specialization it is probably more fruitful to emphasize Visual Field by Experimental Condition interactions rather than absolute differences between the visual fields (see Hellige, 1983b). As the remainder of this paper focuses primarily on such interactions, there will be little additional consideration of peripheral pathway asymmetries. However, continued investigation of these pathway effects would be valuable both to increase understanding of the peripheral visual system and to more effectively separate pathway effects from effects of later, more central stages of information processing.

Stimulus Presentation Parameter and Perceptual Quality

Every visual laterality experiment begins with the specification of a variety of stimulus presentation parameters: duration, size, luminance, presence or absence of a mask, and so forth. During the last several years it has become increasingly apparent that the values of such parameters can influence the pattern of visual laterality, especially insofar as the parameters influence perceptual quality of the visual stimulus. For example, a number of experiments have indicated that as visual stimuli become perceptually degraded the laterality pattern shifts toward a right hemisphere advantage. This seems to be especially true for tasks that minimize the complexity of cognitive processing requirements. As an illustration, consider the following experiment involving same/different judgments about complex polygons.

On each trial of the experiment two stimuli from a pool of 10 complex polygons were presented simultaneously to the LVF-RH (Left Visual Field-Right Hemisphere) or RVF-LH (Right Visual Field-Left Hemisphere) for 100 msec, one above the other, and the observer indicated whether or not the two polygons were the same shape as each other by pressing one of two keys as quickly as possible. On half of the trials a grid of masking lines was placed over the viewing screen while on the remainder of the trials there was no grid. Several previous experiments using stimuli from this pool and no masking grid have found either no significant field difference (e.g., Hellige, 1975, Experiment 2; Hellige, 1976, Experiment 1) or a very small LVF-RH RT (Reaction Time) advantage averaging 17 msec (Hellige, Cox, & Litvac, 1979, Experiment 2).

An additional variable manipulated in the present experiment can be referred to as stimulus frequency. Hardyck and his colleagues (Hardyck, Tzeng, & Wang, 1978) have suggested that visual laterality effects are enhanced when a small number of stimuli are used very frequently during an experiment compared with the use of different stimuli on each trial. They further suggest that this occurs because a small, well-learned stimulus set allows a comparison-to-memory and that the hemispheres differ more in terms of memory storage (and comparison) than in terms of immediate perceptual pro-

155

cessing. In the present experiment one polygon from the pool of 10 was chosen as the "frequent" polygon and appeared as both members of half of the Same (i.e., physically identical) pairs and as one member of half of the Different pairs. According to Hardyck's hypothesis we would expect a larger visual field difference for the stimulus pairs containing the frequent polygon than for the other stimulus pairs. Furthermore, if the grid manipulation influences relatively early stages of perceptual processing and the frequency manipulation influences later stages related to the relative involvement of memory, then we would expect the two variables to have additive effects on visual field differences.

Figures 1 and 2 show the number of errors and RT in msec, respectively, as a function of visual field. In each figure the results of Same and Different trials are shown in the left and right panels, respectively, and the results for frequent pairs and infrequent pairs are shown in the upper and lower panels, respectively. The parameter in each panel is no-grid condition (intact stimuli) versus grid condition (degraded stimuli).

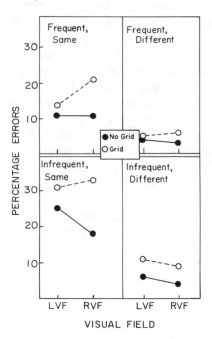

Figure 1.   Percentage of errors as a function of visual field for the no-grid and grid conditions.   Results for Same and Different trials are shown in the left and right panels, respectively, and results for frequent and infrequent pairs are shown in the upper and lower panels, respectively.

156

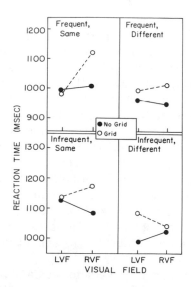

Figure 2. Reaction time in msec as a function of visual field for the no-grid and grid conditions. Results for Same and Different trials are shown in the left and right panels, respectively, and results for frequent and infrequent pairs are shown in the upper and lower panels, respectively.

A comparison of Figures 1 and 2 indicates that the results for errors and RT were very similar. There were no visual field effects on Different trials, a finding that has been reported in several previous experiments and is discussed by Hellige (1976, 1980) and Hellige et al. (1979), but which will not be discussed in detail in the present chapter. Consequently, the remainder of this discussion will focus on the results for same stimulus pairs. Both the stimulus quality manipulation (i.e., grid versus no-grid) and the frequency manipulation interacted with visual field. When the masking grid was superimposed on the screen there was a shift toward an LVF-RH advantage, for both frequent and infrequent pairs. Based on a considerable amount of experimental and clinical evidence, it has been suggested that the right hemisphere is more efficient than the left at extracting complex visuospatial information (for reviews see Bradshaw & Nettleton, 1983; Bryden, 1982; Hellige, 1983a). It is likely that the grid used in the present experiment makes the extraction of visuospatial features and relationships more difficult and it would seem reasonable for the grid to have less disruptive effects on the cerebral hemisphere more efficient at processing those relationships

157

Averaged across grid and no-grid conditions, there was a larger LVF-RH advantage for frequent pairs than for infrequent pairs. This result is similar to the frequency results reported by Hardyck et al. (1978) and will be considered further in a later section of the present chapter. Interestingly, stimulus quality and frequency had additive effects on the laterality pattern. That is, there were no Stimulus Quality by Frequency by Visual Field interactions. This additivity is consistent with the hypothesis that stimulus quality and frequency influenced different stages in the information processing sequence.

Even when visual stimuli can be processed along verbal-analytic dimensions, the initial stages of information processing must involve such things as the extraction of visual features and spatial relationships among those features. Therefore, we might expect to find similar effects of stimulus degradation for tasks that allow or even demand verbal processing. There is, in fact, experimental support for this notion.

Hellige (1976) required observers to indicate whether two simultaneously presented letters of different cases had the same name, a task which requires verbal processing. In one experiment observers performed this task either with or without a masking grid similar to the one described earlier. The right panel of Figure 3 shows the percentage of errors on the Same-name trials of this experiment as a function of visual field. The error percentage results of the Same-shape trials from the polygon experiment described earlier (averaged over the frequency variable) are presented in the left panel for comparison. The parameter in each panel is no-grid versus grid.

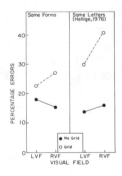

Figure 3. Percentage of errors on Same trials for the no-grid and grid conditions. Results for the polygon form experiment and the letter-pair experiment (Hellige, 1976) are shown in the left and right panels, respectively. (Adapted from Hellige, 1976. Reprinted by permission of The Psychonomic Society.)

158

As Figure 3 shows, the results for the letter-name experiment were very similar to those of the polygon experiment. The imposition of the masking grid interfered more with RVF-LH performance than with LVF-RH performance, thereby introducing an LVF-RH recognition advantage. This shift is especially interesting for a task which requires verbal processing and suggests that the right cerebral hemisphere is more efficient than the left for the extraction of visuospatial features and relationships, even though the stimuli may eventually undergo verbal analysis.

Additional experiments involving recognition of single letters also provide some support for the preceding hypothesis. On each trial of an experiment reported by Hellige and Webster (1979) observers were required to identify which one of ten uppercase letters had been presented to the LVF or RVF. Viewing conditions were chosen so that letter identification was perfect from both the LVF-RH and RVF-RH. To make the extraction of visual features more difficult, a visual pattern mask was presented to both visual fields at various times before and after the target letter. Figure 4 shows the percentage of correct letter recognitions as a function of stimulus onset asynchrony (SOA). Negative and positive SOAs refer to trials on which the mask preceded the target (forward masking) and the target preceded the mask (backward masking), respectively. The parameter is visual field of target presentation.

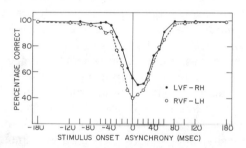

Figure 4. Percentage of correct letter recognitions as a function of stimulus onset asynchrony (SOA). The parameter is left visual field (LVF-RH) versus right visual field (RVF-LH). (after Hellige & Webster, 1979)

When the target and mask were presented simultaneously (SOA = 0 msec), so the target features had to be extracted from a rather complex montage, 15 of 16 observers showed better letter recognition from the LVF-RH than from the RVF-LH. There is considerable evidence in the masking literature that, when the target and mask have equal energy (which they did in this experiment), the central visual

159

system continues to treat the target and mask as a single, composite preperceptual image at short SOAs (up to about 30 msec) in both forward and backward masking (e.g., Hellige, Walsh, Lawrence & Prasse, 1979; Massaro, 1975; Turvey, 1973). In the present experiment the LVF-RH recognition advantage persisted across these short SOAs, up to 30 msec in forward masking and 20 msec in backward masking. Therefore, the present results suggest that the right hemisphere is superior to the left at extracting critical visual features from a complex montage (see also Hellige, 1983c).

The effects of perceptual quality are not limited to presence versus absence of a masking stimulus. During the last decade it has been reported that reductions in stimulus duration, reductions in stimulus luminance, moving stimuli further from the fixation point and blurring a stimulus (Chikashi & Hellige, 1987) can all produce interactions with visual field similar to those just described for the imposition of a masking stimulus (for review see Jonsson & Hellige, 1986; Sergent, 1983; Sergent & Hellige, 1986). In most cases, manipulations that reduce the perceptibility of the stimuli shift the visual laterality pattern toward an LVF-RH advantage.

In an interesting series of articles, Sergent (1982, 1983) has suggested that such effects occur because, at some level of processing beyond the sensory analysis, the two cerebral hemispheres are biased toward or are more efficient for processing different ranges of visual spatial frequency. Specifically, she argues that the left hemisphere requires relatively high visual spatial frequencies for optimal performance whereas the right hemisphere uses information carried by relatively low frequency channels. In order to explain effects such as those described, Sergent considers evidence that many manipulations used to reduce perceptibility have the effect of selectively removing relatively high visual spatial frequencies from the stimulus prior to cognitive processing. This can occur in the physical stimulus itself (as when a stimulus is blurred) or can occur because high frequency visual channels require greater stimulus energy than do low frequency channels to respond (influenced by variables such as duration and luminance).

Evaluation of the visual spatial frequency theory is beyond the scope of the present chapter and, in any case, requires further research. However, there would seem to be an advantage in describing the effects of input parameters in terms of the units of analysis used at an early level in the visual information processing system. At the present time, units tuned to small ranges of visual spatial frequency seem to provide at least a reasonable approximation of these units (e.g. De Valois & De Valois, 1980; Gervais, Harvey & Roberts,

1984). In addition, the visual spatial frequency model appears to be formulated more precisely than some of the other dichotomies used to describe hemispheric asymmetry and is, therefore, more amenable to scientific investigation.

Although reductions of stimulus perceptibility have shifted the laterality pattern toward a LVF-RH advantage in many studies, such effects are not always found. For example, Hellige, Corwin and Jonsson (1984) examined the effects of imposing a grid of small dots on tasks that required observers to make a discrimination among a set of similar male faces or that required a male/female discrimination. In the male/male task, observers indicated on each trial whether a single male face was contained in a "positive" set of five faces chosen randomly from a pool of 10 male faces. Embedding the probe face in a grid of dots increased the error rate more when the probe was presented to the LVF-RH than when the probe was presented to the RVF-LH. In the male/female task observers indicated whether a single probe face was male or female. In this task the grid of dots impaired performance more on RVF-LH trials than on LVF-RH trials, opposite the effect for the more difficult male/male task. Note that the results for the male/female task are similar to the effects shown in Figures 1-4, while the results for the male/male task are not.

In discussing these results, Hellige et al. (1984) suggest that the level of analysis required for optimal performance of an experimental task is as important as the level of information physically present in the stimuli for determining the effects of stimulus perceptibility on visual field differences. If various attributes of a task make the processing of very specific features a necessity (which they suggest is true for their male/male task), then a manipulation that makes those features more difficult to process (e.g., a grid of small dots) should have the most disruptive effect on the hemisphere that is not as efficient for processing those specific features. In an extensive review of laterality effects in face processing studies, Sergent and Bindra (1981) argue that the left hemisphere is superior to the right for the processing of highly specific, local features. The Grid/No-Grid by Visual Field interaction for the male/male task follows from these assumptions.

In contrast, it has been argued that a male/female discrimination can be performed adequately by an analysis of more global characteristics such as the outline of the face and hair (e.g., Sergent & Bindra, 1981). In this case, a grid that makes local features more difficult to process would not be very disruptive to a processing system (the right hemisphere) that used primarily global information anyway. Such a grid would be more disruptive to a processing sys-

161

tem that is biased toward analysis of local detail (the left hemisphere as suggested by Sergent & Bindra, 1981). The Grid/No-Grid by Visual Field interaction for the male/female task is consistent with these assumptions. Whether or not the explanations suggested by Hellige et al. (1984) are judged correct after further research, their results provide additional illustration of the importance of perceptual quality and indicate that such effects may be more complex than originally thought.

In this section we have seen that several stimulus presentation parameters can have important effects of visual laterality patterns. Even if some of the theoretical explanations that have been advanced eventually require modification, stimulus quality effects have important implications for the design and interpretation of laterality experiments even when the primary interest is not in the effects of stimulus quality. Because stimulus quality variables influence visual field differences, it is very difficult to compare experiments that use different parameters of stimulus presentation. At the least, it is necessary to note potential effects of stimulus quality in evaluating existing experiments and to hold stimulus quality constant across other experimental conditions in further visual laterality research.

Additional Effects of Task Demand

There are several ways in which changes in the information processing demands of a visual task can be shown to change the laterality pattern. In fact, the stimulus quality manipulations described in the preceding section may be thought of as changing the demand for complex, visuospatial processing. While stimulus quality certainty varies among laterality experiments, it has often been ignored and not intentionally manipulated. In contrast, the variables to be considered in this section are often the primary variables of interest in visual laterality experiments and are attempts to influence such things as an observer's information processing strategy. A complete review of these task demand factors is beyond the scope of the present chapter. Instead, we will focus on only a few to illustrate some of the methodological and interpretational problems of studying task demand factors. We will begin with a consideration of the effects of post-exposure scanning on visual laterality.

Post-Exposure Scanning. In a review of visual laterality effects, White (1969) noted that many early visual field differences could be accounted for by assuming that English-speaking observers are biased to scan the postexposure visual trace of verbal material from left to

162

right. This trace-scanning hypothesis was proposed to account for (1) an RVF word recognition advantage with unilateral presentation, (2) an LVF word recognition advantage with bilateral presentation (i.e., two different words presented simultaneously, one to each visual field), and (3) an LVF advantage for unilateral presentation of Hebrew words (which are scanned from right to left) to Hebrew speakers. Left hemisphere specialization for verbal processing would predict an RVF advantage for each of these three conditions.

Experiments conducted subsequent to White's (1969) review have found RVF advantages in all three conditions listed above when the stimulus duration is sufficiently short (below 150 msec or so) and when there is more adequate control for eye fixation (see McKeever, 1974 and White, 1972). In addition, horizontal scanning factors would have difficulty accounting for visual field differences for nonverbal tasks and with stimuli oriented vertically rather than horizontally. Further, recent experiments suggest that when the stimuli are briefly presented words rather than random letter strings the RVF advantage is no larger with horizontal than with vertical presentation of the letters (e.g., Turner & Miller, 1975) and that horizontal position effects in word matching cannot be accounted for by a serial trace-scanning hypothesis (Bradshaw, Bradley, Gates, & Patterson, 1977). That is, letters in words seem to be processed in parallel and, therefore, word recognition is less influenced by trace-scanning biases than is the recognition of random letter strings.

While a trace-scanning hypothesis is not sufficient to explain all visual laterality effects, there are conditions where scanning effects do influence the results. Therefore, when the goal is to use visual laterality to study hemispheric specialization it is necessary to use experimental conditions that minimize scanning effects. Based on the available research, cerebral laterality factors seem to become predominant over scanning factors with short exposure durations (less than 150 msec), adequate fixation control, vertically oriented stimuli, and with integrated stimuli such as words and single letters in contrast to random letter strings. Fortunately, the majority of recent visual laterality experiments use conditions that minimize scanning effects and also produce interactions that would be very difficult to explain without reference to cerebral hemisphere specialization.

Information Processing Strategy. It is now generally agreed that the type of processing carried out on a visual stimulus is more important for determining visual field differences than is the nature of the stimuli per se. The earliest distinctions were made between verbal and nonverbal processes, but several experimental and clinical results have suggested that any underlying hemispheric specialization is not based on verbal versus nonverbal distinctions per se. Instead, other processing style dichotomies have been hypothesized, including analytic versus holistic or Gestalt-like processing and sequential or serial versus parallel processing. Whether the information processing differences between the cerebral hemispheres can be adequately captured by any single dichotomy of this sort remains to be determined. Unfortunately, the dichotomies that have been proposed are often not well-defined and may be based more on experimenters' intuitions than on carefully examined converging indications of different information processing strategies. Furthermore, it is often difficult to distinguish among the various dichotomies because they are not defined so as to be mutually exclusive.

There has been a considerable amount of disagreement in the information processing literature on how best to distinguish between such things as serial and parallel processing or between analytic and holistic processing. Visual laterality investigations have not always taken these general information processing issues into account when interpreting visual field effects. It is also unclear whether we should expect the two hemispheres to consistently use different strategies from one another or whether we should expect an observer to use the same strategy regardless of hemisphere-of-presentation, with the advantage going to that hemisphere more efficient at the processing strategy being used. These issues are important to resolve is we are to understand the functional basis of hemispheric specialization and their solution requires carefully designed experiments with converging indications of the processing strategy being employed.

It is instructive to review two experiments conducted by Patterson and Bradshaw (1975) which provide some evidence that the right and left hemispheres are more efficient at holistic and analytic processing, respectively, and which also contain some converging evidence for the hypothesized processing strategies. Paterson and Bradshaw required observers to indicate whether a schematic face presented to the LVF or RVF was identical to a schematic face being held in memory. In one experiment the discrimination was easy. That is, the two faces were either identical or differed on each of three features (eyes, nose, mouth). Patterson and Bradshaw hypothesize that observers in this condition compare the faces in an holistic or Gestalt-like fashion, and the relatively fast responses and the finding that Same responses were faster than Different responses is taken as an indication of holistic processing. In this experiment, an LVF-RH advantage was found.

In a subsequent experiment, the face discrimination was made more difficult by having the Different faces differ from each other on only a single feature. Responses were much slower in this condition and, more importantly, Different responses were much faster than Same responses. This pattern of results would be expected if observers now compare the two faces in a feature-by-feature fashion and terminate the comparison process when either a mismatch if found or all features are found to be identical. In this experiment an RVF-LH advantage was found.

Although there may be alternative interpretations of the Patterson and Bradshaw results, much is gained by the use of an explicit model of analytic versus holistic processing and the presentation of converging evidence that processing strategy changes with discrimination difficulty. Without such explicit models and converging evidence it is too easy to introduce entirely post hoc explanations of almost any laterality pattern and, in a sense, use the very laterality pattern changes that we are trying to explain as evidence for changes in processing strategy. Accordingly, laterality researchers must be very careful in future investigations of processing strategy effects to explicitly define the alternative strategies and include conditions which provide converging evidence that it is, in fact, the processing strategy that has been manipulated.

Perception versus Memory. A number of experiments suggest that visual laterality effects are larger when a comparison-to-memory is required than when little or no memory is required (e.g., Dee & Fontenot, 1973; Hannay & Malone, 1976; Hardyck et al., 1978; Moscovitch, 1979). In fact, some of these investigators argue that there are few, if any, hemispheric differences for recognition processes and that hemisphere differences emerge only at the level of memory storage or perhaps memory comparison. Much of the laterality work to date has been motivated more by the need to determine whether hemispheric differences exist that by a desire to provide a precise examination of the information processing locus of any differences. Consequently, many laterality experiments contain both perception and memory requirements. The distinction between perception and memory effects will continue to become more important as researchers become increasingly more interested in localizing hemisphere differences within the sequence of information processing stages.

The separation of perception and memory effects is not a simple matter, as the history of human memory research indicates. This separation is compounded by the realization that "perception" consists of several subprocesses and storage structures (e.g., iconic storage) and "memory" might mean storage into memory, rate of forgetting (by means of decay or interference), or retrieval from any one of several types of memory. Consequently, from the available research it is impossible to determine whether the "memory" effects represent differences between the cerebral hemispheres in the processes involved in storing various types of information into memory, the quality or strength of the stored representation, the rate at which information is lost from each hemisphere, the process of memory retrieval and comparison, etc.

The interpretation of effects as perception or memory effects also depends on the specific assumptions that are made about the acquisition and forgetting processes. Many of the attempts to separate hemispheric differences in perception from hemispheric differences in memory involve varying the ISI (Initial Stimulus Interval) between an initial target stimulus and a subsequent probe stimulus. The rather straightforward prediction is that if the hemispheres differ in perception processes the visual field difference should remain the same across all ISI values. If the hemispheres differ in memory processes then the visual field difference should increase with increasing ISI. One implicit assumption of this logic is that the rate of forgetting is independent of the initial strength of the stored representation, which may or may not be the case (see Anderson, 1963; and Massaro, 1977, for discussion of various ways of defining rate in psychological models and some resulting implications). The primary point is that effects can be localized at the level of perception or memory only within the context of specific models of the perception and memory processes. It is, therefore, important for future laterality experiments to consider explicitly the underlying models assumed to describe processing as well as to justify the use of one set of assumptions over another.

As noted earlier, Hardyck et al. (1978) have attributed effects of ratio of experimental stimuli to trials (what we have called frequency effects) to a lack of cerebral hemisphere specialization for active ongoing cognitive processing and the presence of cerebral hemisphere specialization for some aspect of memory processing. The polygon matching results in Figure 1 and 2 show similar frequency effects. The frequency effects were also found to be independent of stimulus degradation, a variable that is know to influence stimulus recognition or encoding (cf., Sternberg, 1975). This independence is consistent with the hypothesis that frequency effects occur at some other stage of processing, but the results do not offer any strong evidence for what stages are involved.

166

Although frequently occurring stimulus pairs are more likely to be compared to templates in memory, it is unclear whether the hemispheres differ in the strength with which the templates are stored in memory, the ability to retrieve templates from memory, the ability to compare the incoming information with the stored representation, etc. At this point the stimulus frequency effects are quite interesting and may provide an important converging operation for interpreting visual laterality effects. However, further research is clearly required to both establish the generality of the effects and determine exactly what information processing mechanisms are responsible for them.

Selective Activation and Interference. In a very influential series of papers, Kinsbourne (1970, 1973, 1975) hypothesized that the visual field difference at a given time depends not on the directness of the pathway nor on which hemisphere receives the stimulus but on the balance of hemispheric activation at that time. According to Kinsbourne, an RVF-LH advantage occurs for verbal or analytic tasks because the ongoing verbal/analytic processing activates the left more than the right cerebral hemisphere, thereby biasing attention toward the right side of space. Likewise, an LVF-RH advantage is found for complex visuospatial tasks because the ongoing visuospatial processing activates the right more than the left cerebral hemisphere, thereby biasing attention toward the left side of space. In one test of the attention gradient model, Bruce and Kinsbourne (1974) had observers attempt to recognize complex polygons presented briefly to the LVF or RVF on each trial. When observers were doing only this task a small LVF-RH advantage was found. However, when observers were given a list of words to hold in memory during each recognition trial, an RVF-LH advantage was found (see also Kinsbourne, 1970, 1973, 1975). The attention gradient model hypothesizes that holding words in memory activates the left more than the right hemisphere, biasing attention toward the RVF.

Hellige and Cox (1976) reasoned that if the left hemisphere were required to do too much processing the verbal memory load should have a very different effect. To examine this, they required observers to identify either complex polygon forms (Experiment 1) or four-letter words (Experiment 2) presented to the LVF or RVF. Different groups of observers were required to hold 0, 2, 4, or 6 words in memory during each recognition trial. The results from these experiments are summarized in Figure 5, which shows percentage of correct recognitions as a function of memory set size. The polygon form recognition and four-letter word recognition results are shown in the upper and lower panels, respectively. The parameter in each panel is visual field of presentation.

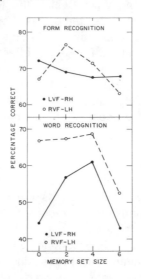

Figure 5. Percentage of correct responses as a function of memory set size. Polygon recognition and word recognition are shown in the upper and lower panels, respectively. The parameter in each panel is left visual field (LVF-RH) versus right visual field (RVF-LH). (Adapted from Hellige & Cox, 1976. Reprinted by permission of the American Psychological Association.)

As the upper panel of Figure 5 shows, an LVF-RH form recognition advantage when there was no concurrent memory load shifted to an RVF-LH advantage with a relatively easy load of 2 or 4 words. This result is very similar to the left hemisphere priming effect reported by Bruce and Kinsbourne (1974). However, when the left hemisphere load was increased, (memory load of 6 words), RVF-LH performance decreased so the an LVF-RH advantage was again found. Furthermore, when the laterality task itself required left hemisphere involvement (i.e., recognition of four-letter words) a concurrent memory load of 2, 4, or 6 words greatly reduced the RVF-LH advantage (Figure 5, lower panel). These results indicate that while a relatively light verbal load may prime the left hemisphere and, thereby, improve its performance relative to the right hemisphere, when the left hemisphere is required to do too much processing its performance is reduce relative to right hemisphere performance.

While the priming effect predicted by Kinsbourne has been difficult to obtain, selective hemispheric interference has been demonstrated in several ways. There are even cases where the introduction of a verbal concurrent task not only reduces an RVF-LH advantage but reverses the visual field advantage. For example, Hellige et al. (1979, Experiments 4 and 5) had subjects indicate whether two letters of different case had the same name and obtained an RVF-LH advantage when the task was performed alone with no memory load. However, when 2, 4, or 6 words were concurrently maintained in short-term memory an LVF-RH advantage was found for the letter comparison task. In another recent experiment, Friedman, Polson, Dafoe and Gaskill (1982) used the recognition of CVC (Consonant Vowel Consonant) nonsense syllables as the lateralized visual identification task and the maintenance in short-term memory of 2, 3 or 4 CVCVC nonsense syllables as the concurrent task. Their subjects were preselected to show an RVF-LH advantage for CVC recognition in the no-memory-load control condition and maintained this advantage in the no-load condition throughout the experiment. Imposing the verbal memory load as a concurrent task again interfered more with the recognition of CVCs from the RVF than from the LVF, with the difference in interference between the two visual fields being greater as the size of the memory load increased from 2 to 4 items. The asymmetry of interference was so great that in some memory load conditions there was an LVF-RH advantage for recognizing the CVCs. That is, the "control" or no-load laterality effect was reverse.

The results just reviewed are difficult to account for in terms of a single pool of completely undifferentiated attentional resources for which all resource-demanding processes must compete. Thus, my colleagues and I (e.g., Hellige & Cox, 1976; Hellige, Cox & Litvac, 1979) have suggested that the two cerebral hemispheres operate as some what separate subprocessors, each with its own limited processing capacity that is at least somewhat independent of the capacity of the other hemisphere. Two tasks that compete for resources from the same cerebral hemisphere will interfere with each other more than two tasks that demand less from the same resource pool (see also Moscovitch & Klein, 1980).

This point of view has been carried to its logical extreme by Friedman and Polson (1981; Friedman et al., 1982) who interpret these effects as evidence for a multiple-resource model of attention such as described by Navon and Gopher (1979). They assert that each hemisphere has processing resources that are completely independent of each other; that is there is no sharing of processing resources across the two hemispheres. Furthermore, they suggest that within a hemisphere the processing resources are completely undifferentiated.

An alternative model has been proposed by Kinsbourne and his colleagues (e.g., Kinsbourne & Hiscock, 1983). They do not discuss attention phenomena in the context of different numbers of resource pools. Instead, they have proposed the principle of "functional cerebral distance" to account for the types of results reviewed in this section. According to this principle, two tasks will interfere with each other to the extent that they require incompatible neural processes. Such tasks are considered to be functionally close to each other in terms of the neural areas involved in performance of the tasks. With a few exceptions functional cerebral distance is proposed to be shorter within a hemisphere than across hemispheres and, thus, hemisphere-specific interference is predicted.

It is beyond the scope of the present chapter to debate the finer points of how models of attention should be changed by the phenomenon of hemisphere-specific interference. Clearly, more research is needed to sharpen the various models so that their differences can lead to critical experiments. Even without this, however, it should be clear that such results do provide information about aspects of human attention that must be incorporated into any complete theory of attention. It is also clear that attentional aspects of task demand must be considered in evaluation of visual laterality results.

Concluding Statement

There is overwhelming clinical and experimental evidence that the left and right cerebral hemispheres process information somewhat differently from each other. Accordingly, it has become difficult for psychologists to ignore the potential implications of these differences. Several paradigms have been very useful for learning more about these processing differences and about their implications for more general issues in human performance. Our conclusions about hemispheric processing can only be as good as our understanding of the factors that are important within the paradigm we use. With this in mind, the present chapter has pointed to the methodological and theoretical consequences of the effects on visual laterality of several types of variables. Although the picture of hemispheric asymmetry that emerges is complex, from the present review it appears that lateralized visual presentation will continue to be a useful technique for learning more about hemisphere asymmetry.

The kind of stimulus quality and task demand factors reviewed in the present chapter provide a flexibility to models of cerebral laterality that is probably necessary if those models are to capture the dynamic nature of central nervous system processing. Of course, much more careful work will be needed to fully understand the mechanisms responsible for many of the effects reviewed here and to determine how these various stimulus quality and task demand factors interact with each other. Given the complexity of visual laterality effects, we are not likely to learn much about the more important questions that have been raised from one-shot experiments that happen to find some interesting difference between the left and right visual fields. Rather, the need is for carefully integrated series of experiments that contain the kinds of control conditions and converging operations that are demanded by the complexity of the problem being studied.

References

Anderson, N.H. (1963), Comparison of different populations: Resistance to extinction and transfer. Psychological Review, 70, 162-179.

Bradshaw, J.L., Bradley, D., Gates, A., & Patterson, K. (1977). Serial, parallel, or holistic identification of single words in the two visual fields? Perception & Psychophysics, 21, 431-438.

Bradshaw, J.L. & Nettleton, N.C. (1983). Human cerebral asymmetry. Englewood Cliffs, NJ: Prentice-Hall.

Bruce, R., & Kinsbourne, M. (1974, November). Orientational model of perceptual asymmetry. Paper presented at the 15th annual convention of the Psychonomic Society, Boston.

Bryden, M.P. (1982). Laterality: Functional asymmetry in the intact brain. New York: Academic Press.

Chikashi, M. & Hellige, J.B. (1987). Effects of blurring and stimulus size on the lateralized processing of nonverbal stimuli. Neuropsychologia, 25, 397-407.

Dee, H.L., & Fontenot, D.J. (1973). Cerebral dominance and lateral difference in perception and memory. Neuropsychologia, 11, 167-173.

De Valois, R.L. & De Valois, K.K. (1980). Spatial vision. Annual Review of Psychology, 31, 117-153.

Friedman, A. & Polson, M.C. (1981). The hemispheres as independent resource systems: Limited capacity processing and cerebral specialization. Journal of Experimental Psychology: Human Perception and Performance, 8, 1031-1058.

Friedman, A., Polson, M.C., Dafoe, C.G., & Gaskill, S.J. (1982). Dividing attention within and between hemispheres: Testing a multiple resources approach to limited capacity information processing. Journal of Experimental Psychology: Human Perception and Performance, 8, 625-650.

Gervais, M.J., Harvey, L.O., & Roberts, J.O. (1984). Identification confusion among letters of the alphabet. Journal of Experimental Psychology: Human Perception and Performance, 10, 655-666.

Hannay, H.J., & Malone, D.R. (1976). Visual field effects and short-term memory for verbal material. Neuropsychologia, 14, 203-209.

Hardyck, C., Tzeng, O.J.L., & Wang, W. (1978). Cerebral lateralization of function and bilingual decision processes: Is thinking lateralized? Brain and Language, 5, 56-71.

Hayashi, T., & Bryden, M.P. (1967). Ocular dominance and perceptual asymmetry. Perceptual and Motor Skills, 25, 605-612.

Hellige, J.B. (1975). Hemispheric processing differences revealed by differential conditioning and reaction time performance. Journal of Experimental Psychology: General, 104, 309-326.

Hellige, J.B. (1976). Changes in same-different laterality patterns as a function of practice and stimulus quality. Perception & Psychophysics, 20, 267-273.

Hellige, J.B. (1980). Effects of perceptual quality and visual field of probe stimulus presentation on memory search for letters. Journal of Experimental Psychology: Human Perception and Performance, 6, 639-651.

Hellige, J.B. (Ed.), (1983a). Cerebral hemisphere asymmetry: Method, theory and application. New York: Praeger.

Hellige, J.B. (1983b). Hemisphere by task interaction and the study of laterality. In J.B. Hellige (Ed.), Cerebral hemisphere asymmetry: Method, theory and application (pp. 411-443). New York: Praeger.

Hellige, J.B. (1983c). Feature similarity and laterality effects in visual masking. Neuropsychologia, 21, 633-639.

Hellige, J.B., Corwin, W.H., & Jonsson, J.E. (1984). Effects of perceptual quality on the processing of human faces presented to the left and right cerebral hemispheres. Journal of Experimental Psychology: Human Perception and Performance, 10, 90-107.

Hellige, J.B., & Cox, P.J. (1976). Effects of concurrent verbal memory on recognition of stimuli from the left and right visual fields. Journal of Experimental Psychology: Human Perception and Performance, 2, 210-221.

Hellige, J.B., Cox, P.J., Litvac, L. (1979). Information processing in the cerebral hemispheres: Selective hemispheric activation and capacity limitations. Journal of Experimental Psychology: General, 108, 251-279.

Hellige, J.B., Walsh, D.A., Lawrence, V.W., & Prasse, M. (1979). Figural relationship effects and mechanisms of visual masking. Journal of Experimental Psychology: Human Perception and Performance, 5, 88-100.

Hellige, J.B., & Webster, R. (1979). Right hemisphere superiority for initial stages of letter processing. Neuropsychologia, 17, 653-660.

Jonsson, J.E. & Hellige, J.B. (1986). Lateralized effects of blurring: A test of the visual spatial frequency model of cerebral hemisphere asymmetry. Neuropsychologia, 24, 351-362.

Kimura, D. (1966). Dual functional asymmetry of the brain in visual perception. Neuropsychologia, 4, 275-285.

Kinsbourne, M. (1970). The cerebral basis of lateral asymmetries in attention. Acta Psychologica, 33, 193-201.

Kinsbourne, M. (1973). The control of attention by interaction between the hemispheres. In S. Kornblum (Ed.), Attention and Performance IV (pp. 239-256). New York: Academic Press.

Kinsbourne, M. (1975). The mechanism of hemispheric control of the lateral gradient of attention. In P.M.A. Rabbitt & S. Dornic (Eds.), Attention and Performance V (pp. 81-97). New York: Academic Press.

Kinsbourne, M. & Hiscock, M. (1983). Asymmetries of dual-task performance. In J.B. Hellige (Ed.), Cerebral hemisphere asymmetry: Method, theory, and application (pp. 255-334). New York: Praeger.

Massaro, D.W. (1975). Experimental psychology and information processing. Chicago: Rand McNally.

Massaro, D.W. (1977). Rate of perceptual processing. Psychological Research, 39, 277-283.

McKeever, W.F. (1974). Does post-exposure directional scanning offer a sufficient explanation for lateral differences in tachistoscopic recognition? Perceptual and Motor Skills, 38, 43-50.

Moscovitch, M. (1979). Information processing and the cerebral hemispheres. In M.S. Gazzaniga (Ed.), The handbook of behavioral neurobiology. Volume on neuropsychology, New York: Plenum Press.

Moscovitch, M. & Klein, D. (1980). Material specific perceptual interference for visual words and faces: Implications for models of capacity limitations, attention, and laterality. Journal of Experimental Psychology: Human Perception and Performance, 6, 590-604.

Navon, D. & Gopher, D. (1979). On the economy of the human processing sytem. Psychological Review, 86, 214-255.

Patterson, K. & Bradshaw, J.L. (1975). Differential hemispheric mediation of non-verbal visual stimuli. Journal of Experimental Psychology: Human Perception and Performance, 1, 246-252.

Sergent, J. (1982). Theoretical and methodological consequences of variations in exposure duration in visual laterality studies. Perception & Psychophysics, 31, 451-461.

Sergent, J. (1983). The role of input in visual hemispheric asymmetries. Psychological Bulletin, 93, 481-512.

Sergent, J. & Bindra, D. (1981). Differential hemispheric processing of faces: Methodological considerations and reinterpretations. Psychological Bulletin, 89, 541-554.

Sergent, J. & Hellige, J.G. (1986). Role of input factors in visual field asymmetries. Brain and Cognition, 5, 174-190.

Sternberg, S. (1975). Memory scanning: New findings and current controversies. Quarterly Journal of Experimental Psychology, 27, 1-32.

Turner, S., & Miller, L.K. (1975). Some boundary conditions for laterality effects in children. Developmental Psychology, 11, 342-352.

Turvey, M. (1973). On peripheral and central processes in vision: Inferences from an information-processing analysis of masking with patterned stimuli. Psychological Review, 80, 1-52.

White, M.J. (1969). Laterality differences in perception: A review. Psychological Bulletin, 72, 387-405.

White, M.J. (1972). Hemispheric asymmetries in tachistoscopic information processing. British Journal of Psychology, 63, 497-508.

Wyke, M., & Ettlinger, G. (1961). Efficiency of recognition in left and right visual fields. Archieves of Neurology, 5, 659-665.

METHODOLOGY

The theme of Chapter 8 by Zalinski and Anderson is that measurement of "importance" is central to many kinds of studies in many areas of psychology, and that all previous methods of measuring importance are arbitrary and ad hoc, and often seriously incorrect. The authors pursue the belief that integration theory provides the first theoretically justified and practicable way to measure importance. And, functional measurement constitutes the theoretical foundation for multiattribute formulations.

Lichtenfels, Schipper, and Oakley describe a method for collecting personal data, especially sensitive information, which is reported to be superior to the direct questionnaire procedure. This randomized response technique (RRT) is a novel version of the simple RRT proposed by Warner in 1965, and subsequently (through 1988) used, revised, and described by others, particularly statisticians. Lichtenfels, et al., describe a randomizing device and two experiments which provide procedures unreported elsewhere.

The contribution of Joan S. Lockard addresses the importance of experimental psychology to the area of human ethology. The author discusses the application of statistical models, experimental designs and techniques to studies on the adaptive significance of hominid behavior.

Arthur Riopelle reports on studies of early deprivation with rats, primates, and humans. He supplies a sample of some of the methods used to study the problem, and a description of the effects resulting from laboratory manipulations and naturally occurring events.

8

MEASUREMENT OF IMPORTANCE IN MULTIATTRIBUTE MODELS

James Zalinski and Norman H. Anderson

A concept of *weight* is basic to most approaches to judgment-decision research. In the standard multiattribute conceptualization, for example, a choice alternative is represented in terms of its *value*, or location, along certain attribute dimensions. Each attribute dimension also has a *weight*, which indexes its importance relative to the other attributes. The overall evaluation is then taken as a weighted integral, typically a sum or average, of its values on the several attribute dimensions.

It follows that psychological measurement is central to judgment-decision research, both cognitive and normative. Values and weights are subjective quantities, not generally amenable to quantification in terms of objective, physical measures. Subjective measurement is clearly essential for cognitive multiattribute theory, but normative theory, it might be thought, could rely on objective measures. Of course, normative theory cannot generally prescribe values, for values naturally differ across persons. Hence normative theory must also face the problem of psychological measurement.

The problem of psychological measurement has long been a focus of controversy. Without a solution to the measurement problem, it was necessary to rely on ad hoc methods. Ad hoc methods are sometimes appropriate, sometimes not—as in measurement of weight. Nearly all indexes of weight in common use are, if not invalid, at best uncertain in psychological significance.

A working solution to the problem of psychological measurement has been provided by functional measurement methodology. This has a solid empirical foundation in studies of cognitive algebra (Anderson, 1974a,b, 1976a,b, 1978a,b, 1981a,b), including various multiattribute models. Functional measurement provided a solution to the problem of measuring weight, although in a manner unforeseen. Measuring weight depends on unique properties of the averaging model of cognitive algebra.

The first section of this chapter summarizes briefly the main problems that arise in attempting to measure importance. An experimental study of job satisfaction is then reported that demonstrates strong differential weighting both between and within attribute dimensions, a result previously conjectured but not well established. These empirical results are related to practical problems of changing job attitudes.

The last section discusses multiattribute analysis, showing how the measurement problem is important for both cognitive and normative theory. Various popular approaches are shown to suffer internal inconsistencies, even for normative application. A unified cognitive-normative approach is proposed, in which the cognitive-prescriptive adding rule (CPAR) combines normative integration with cognitive values obtained from functional measurement.

Measurement of Importance

In many multiattribute formulations, weights may be interpreted as tradeoff factors. In a linear model, a unit change on a given attribute dimension produces an effect proportional to the weight for that dimension. Hence the ratio of two weights measures how much one attribute must be changed to compensate for a unit change in the other. The relative sizes of two weights might thus seem to measure the relative importance of the corresponding attributes.

Indeed, many formulations place substantive interpretations on the weights, as though they really did measure "importance." These weights are then used to make substantive interpretations about importance of various attribute dimensions or of various experimental manipulations.

Rarely are these interpretations justified. Nearly all current multiattribute formulations rely on arbitrary measures of weight that lack any foundation in psychological theory. The difficulties are most easily illustrated with the ordinary linear model, but the same difficulties hold generally for multiattribute formulations. The following discussion illustrates some basic difficulties and shows how integration theory can help resolve some of them.

The Problem of Comparability

A basic problem in measuring weights is to obtain comparability across attribute dimensions. Comparability generally requires that weights for different dimensions be measured on a common linear or ratio scales so that each weight is expressed in the same units.

Comparability is essential for substantive interpretation. Some formulations, it should be recognized, treat weights as arbitrary scaling parameters, without substantive significance (e.g., Keeney & Raiffa, 1976, Section 5.9). This is appropriate for certain purposes, but the present discussion is concerned with substantive comparability.

Unit Confounding. A common method of measuring importance is with weights from a regression analysis. Such weights, unfortunately, are not generally valid as descriptive psychological parameters. Discussion of this point will help explain why comparing importance is so elusive.

The main problem is that regression weights are confounded with their corresponding scale units. To illustrate, consider a regression model for comfort as a function of temperature and humidity. The Fahrenheit and Celsius scales are equally appropriate, but the choice of one over the other will cause the regression weight to change by a factor of 5 to 9. Two different investigators using the very same data could thus reach opposite conclusions about relative importance of temperature and humidity, depending on their arbitrary choice of temperature scale. Because the unit of temperature is arbitrary, so is the value of the regression weight. Hence valid comparison of importance is not generally possible with ordinary regression weights.

Standardized Weights. The unit confounding cannot be avoided by standardization (Anderson, 1974c, 1976a). Suppose that the regression weight is standardized by dividing it, say, by the range or by the standard deviation of the temperature values used in the regression. The standardization factor has the same unit as the value scale, which seems to leave the standardized weight unit-free. In the foregoing example, standardization yields the same answer regardless of choice of Celsius, Fahrenheit, or any other scale. This property presumably accounts for the popularity of standardization procedures.

Unfortunately, standardization introduces another unit confounding: the standardization factor on each dimension depends on the range or distribution of attribute values on that dimension. This could be large or small, depending on arbitrary choice of attribute values. Two different investigators could reach opposite conclusions about relative importance of temperature and humidity, therefore, depending on their arbitrary choice of temperature values. Standardization merely replaces one unit confounding with another.

Attribute Scaling. Interpretation of regression weights as descriptive psychological parameters suffers a further difficulty, one that relates to the validity of the attribute scales. The foregoing example used the physical scale of temperature for simplicity of

179

illustration. But if the weights are to be proper psychological parameters, then the attributes must be measured of linear (equal interval) psychological scales. If the actual scale is psychologically nonlinear, then the weight will be biased. Two different investigators could thus reach opposite conclusions depending on their choice of value scales (see, e.g., Anderson, 1982, pp. 263-264).

Psychophysical studies have shown that physical scales are not generally linear scales of sensation. Hence using physical scales of value will bias the weight estimates. The same must be expected for the arbitrary scales that are typically used in multiattribute analysis. Without a theory of psychological measurement, therefore, weight parameters may not have much meaning.

Model Validity. In regression analysis, weights are estimated by imposing some model on the data. The meaningfulness of these weight estimates depends on the validity of the model. Unless the model has substantive validity, it seems unlikely to yield meaningful estimates.

Unfortunately, few multiattribute formulations have provided adequate tests of the models. This has been obscured with *weak inference methodology*, which seems to test the model but does not really do so. In their discussion of this problem, Anderson and Shanteau (1977) point out three areas of judgment-decision research in which weak inference method made strong but false initial promises that led to much wasted work.

Self-Estimated Parameters. An alternative approach is to ask subjects to tell what weights they used. This approach is attractive, partly from its simplicity, partly because it need not presuppose the validity of some integration model. But self-estimates cannot be taken at face value. Some validational criterion is required. This issue is taken up in the discussion.

Other Concepts of Importance. The present discussion is limited to a weight concept of importance, as in the standard, two-parameter, weight-value representation. Importance may be conceptualized in other ways, among which are a relative magnitude index and a choice importance index (see Anderson, 1982, Sections 6.1 & 7.11). Magnitude indexes refer to the range of effect of an attribute, and are sometimes of practical interest.

Magnitude indexes have limited psychological significance, however, because the same attribute can have small or large effect merely from selection of a small or large range. Most discussions of "importance" refer, explicitly or implicitly, to a weight concept.

Cognitive Algebra

The problem of weights, as the foregoing discussion shows, is at bottom a problem of psychological measurement. Analysis of weights depends, in general, on possession of a theory of psychological measurement that can yield true linear or ratio scales. This longstanding problem can be solved under certain conditions with the theory of functional measurement.

Functional measurement reverses the traditional perspective, which appears in approaches as diverse as Thurstone's paired comparisons and Stevens's magnitude estimation, as well as more recent axiomatic approaches, which make measurement preliminary to substantive inquiry. In the functional perspective, measurement is an organic component of substantive inquiry. Measurement scales are thus derivative from substantive laws.

This functional perspective has been vindicated by the empirical studies, which have demonstrated the operation of a fairly general cognitive algebra. The idea that human judgment may obey algebraic rules has long been popular, but could not be tested without a theory of measurement. Indeed, the studies of cognitive algebra have shown very little correlation between a priori expectation and the rules that have been found empirically. This point may be illustrated with the averaging model, which has been shown to hold for a substantial class of multiattribute tasks.

Averaging Theory. The averaging model of information integration theory provides a basis for measuring both weight and value (Anderson, 1974a, p. 227, 1982, Section 2.3). It thus becomes possible to make valid comparisons between qualitatively different variables, such as salary and status symbols.

The general averaging model represents the response R as a weighted average of information:

$$R = (w_O s_O + \Sigma w_i s_i) / (w_O + \Sigma w_i), \qquad (1)$$

where w_i and s_i are the weight and value of the ith attribute or piece of information. In experimental studies, w_O and s_O represent prior opinion, before integration of the given information.

The potential for separation of weight and value may be seen in Eq. (1). Weights are confounded with scale value in the numerator, for that is just a weighted sum. In the denominator, however, the weights appear alone and so are in principle separable and identifiable.

To illustrate, suppose that prior opinion has zero weight, $w_O = 0$, and consider three attributes, with values, s_i and weights w_i. These attributes are to be judged singly and in pairs, within the same experimental task and session. From Eq. (1), the theoretical values for these judgements are:

$$R_1 = w_i s_i / w_i = s_i ; \qquad (2a)$$

$$R_2 = w_2 s_2 / w_2 = s_2 ; \qquad (2b)$$

$$R_3 = w_3 s_3 / w_3 = s_3 ; \qquad (2c)$$

$$R_{12} = (w_1 s_1 + w_2 s_2) / (w_1 + w_2) ; \qquad (3a)$$

$$R_{13} = (w_1 s_1 + w_3 s_3) / (w_1 + w_3) ; \qquad (3b)$$

$$R_{23} = (w_2 s_2 + w_3 s_3) / (w_2 + w_3) . \qquad (3c)$$

From Eqs. (2), the values of s_i are given directly by the response. These values may be substituted into Eqs. (3) to solve for the weights. Since the unit of the weight scale is arbitrary, it may be fixed by setting $w_1 = 1$. Equations (3ab) may then be solved for the remaining unknowns, w_2 and w_3. These values must also satisfy Eq. (3c)—which thus provides the needed test of goodness of fit to assess whether the model is correct and the weight estimates valid. In practice, regrettably, the estimation is markedly more complex, primarily because the prior weight, w_O, is not in general equal to zero. These technical problems, however, are not of present concern.

Comparability. The averaging model has the remarkable property that it can provide comparable measures of attribute value and of attribute weight (Anderson, 1974a, p. 227, 1976a, p. 687, 1978b). With suitable design, the values for different attribute dimensions will be on linear scales with a common unit and common zero. Hence values may be compared across different attribute dimensions, such as salary and working conditions. The weights will be on linear or ratio scales with common unit and common zero. Hence diverse attributes may be compared in importance.

Unequal Weighting. Averaging theory allows the weight to vary for different levels within a given attribute dimension. Whereas many multiattribute formulations assume that the weight is a characteristic of the attribute dimension, averaging theory considers weight to depend on informational content. Different levels of the same attribute may thus have different weights.

182

Such unequal weighting appears in the present study of job satisfaction. The high and low levels of the attribute of work enjoyment were more highly weighted than the average level. Such extremity weighting would be hard to establish without the averaging model. Extremity weighting makes sense, however, and it may be important in practical studies of job attitudes.

Experimental Method

Subjects judged expected satisfaction of jobs that were described in terms of four attribute dimensions: managerial support, coworker cooperation, pay and opportunity for promotion, and rewards of the work itself. These four dimensions have emerged in numerous factor-analytic studies (see Gillett & Schwab, 1975; Smith, Kendall, & Hulin, 1969) and seem adequate to account for job satisfaction over a broad range of work environments. Subjects were instructed to judge on a criterion of "How satisfied you think you would be with that job and how likely you would be to accept such a job if it were offered to you."

Each job dimension had three levels: very low, average, and very high. These were combined in a complete four-factor design to obtain 81 job descriptions, each with four pieces of information. In addition, all six possible two-factor designs were used, in which only two of the job dimensions were specified. The purpose of these two-factor designs was to vary set size and thereby ensure uniqueness in the estimates of weights and scale values. Also included was one three-factor design that had a filler function and will not be further considered. For these partial job descriptions, subjects were instructed to base their judgments only on the given information.

Each job description was typed on an index card and these were presented at a self-paced rate of approximately six per minute. The subject responded by inserting a pin in a 200-mm graphic rating bar; the experimenter read this to the nearest approximate mm from a scale at the rear of the bar. High and low stimulus end anchors were presented along with the instructions as part of a short practice period. The end anchors were job descriptions in which all four dimensions were either all extremely high or extremely low. Their purpose was to set up the frame of reference and to tie down the ends of the rating scale (Anderson, 1974b, p. 245, 1982, Section 1.1.4).

At the conclusion of the experiment, subjects were asked to make self-estimates of the scale value of the three levels of each job dimension and of the importance or weight of each dimension. Before doing this, the idea of a weighted average model was explained in some detail as a method for conveying the concept of importance. These self-estimates were made using the rating bar in the natural way.

Subjects were 10 male and 10 female undergraduates who served as part of a course requirement in introductory psychology. Each subject judged the total set of 162 job descriptions three times. The descriptions were randomized by shuffling between each replication for each subject. With 5-minute breaks between successive replications, each experimental session lasted approximately 90 minutes.

Results

The general pattern of the data is illustrated in the three graphs of Figure 1. The curves are theoretical predictions; the actual data are given by the points. The three successive panels represent the Pay x Work Enjoyment factorial plots for the low, average, and high levels of the Management factor. All three graphs are for the average level of the Coworker factor.

The expected main effects are clear in the graphs. The upward trend of each curve displays the effect of Work, which is listed on the horizontal axis. The vertical spacing of the three curves in each graph displays the effect of Pay, listed as curve parameter. Finally, the upward trend across the three successive graphs shows the effects of the three corresponding levels of Management.

Main interest is with the shapes of these factorial plots. To a first approximation, each set of three curves is parallel, a pattern that would support a linear model. But closer study of Figure 1 shows systematic deviations from parallelism. Each graph shows a center bulge, being wider in the middle than at either end, with the general shape of a slanted barrel. Graphs similar to Figure 1 were plotted for both of the other two levels of the Coworker factor, and they showed similar barrel patterns. So did the data from the two-way designs (see Figure 2 following). This barrel shape is predicted by the averaging model when the more extreme levels on each dimension have greater importance than the middle level.

Averaging Model versus Linear Model

A critical quantitative test between the averaging and adding hypotheses is shown in Figure 2. The dashed curves are means from the two-factor, Pay x Work design. The solid curves are means from the same two-factor subtable of the full four-factor design, averaged over the other two job dimensions. The critical feature of Figure 2 is that the dashed curves have steeper slope and cross over the solid curves. Such crossovers are predicted by the averaging hypothesis, but cannot be accounted by linear or adding models.

The logic of this averaging-adding test is well known, but it may be useful to indicate how it applies in the present case. This can be seen most simply by comparing the two curves labeled *Med* in Figure 2. The dashed Med curve represents judgments based on just two pieces of information: the medium level of pay and one of three levels of work enjoyment listed on the horizontal axis. The solid Med curve represents judgments based on the same information, plus added information about the other two job dimensions. The test hinges on the effect of this added information.

Under an adding hypothesis, this added information should have the same directional effect at all three curve points. If the added information was positive, it would cause the solid curve to lie above the dashed curve at every point; if the added information was negative, it would cause the solid curve to lie below the dashed curve at every point. Hence the crossover of the two curves cannot be accounted for with an adding hypothesis.

The averaging model, however, provides a straightforward explanation of the crossover. The added information is, in effect, of medium value. If it is averaged, it will pull the points in toward the center of the graph. Thus, it will average up the low level of Work and average down the high level, thereby creating the observed crossover. Similar crossovers were obtained with each of the other five two-factor designs.

This outcome was expected because similar results have been obtained in many other areas (see Anderson, 1974b, 1981a). Such tests had not been made in the area of job satisfaction, however, so it seemed desirable to include them here to support the application of the averaging model for estimating weights.

The mild barrel shape mentioned in the discussion of Figure 1 comes out more clearly in Figure 2. The deviation from parallelism is statistically significant and more substantial than might appear at first glance. For the dashed curves, the vertical spreads between the top and bottom curves are 69, 91, and 76, from left to right. Thus, the center bulge is about 25% greater than the vertical spread at either end. The solid curves show a similar pattern, with theoretically smaller vertical spreads of 55, 68, and 54, respectively.

Within the averaging model, the barrel shape in Figure 2 can be interpreted as an extremity effect: high and low levels of Pay and of Work are more important than the medium level.

Importance Estimates

The primary goal of this study was to use the averaging model to measure the weight parameters. These weights allow valid comparisons of relative importance, both between and within attribute dimensions. For each individual subject, two separate solutions were obtained: an equal-weight solution in which the three levels within each job dimension were required to have equal weight; and a differential-weight solution in which the three levels were allowed different, unequal weights. Technical details are presented in the Appendix.

Equal-Weight Solution. In contrast to previous studies of job satisfaction, the present study found substantial differences in relative importance of the four job attributes. The mean weights from the equal-weight solution are shown in the first data column of Table 1. These weights cover a substantial range, from 1.00 for Managerial support to 2.72 for Work enjoyment. These differences are highly significant, $F(3,57) = 10.28$.

Differential-Weight Solution. The mean weights from the differential-weight solution are shown in the second data column of Table 1. These differential weights show the same hierarchy as the equal weights. The range of importance, however, is about twice as great in the differential-weight solution, with the average weights for the four job dimensions falling roughly in the ratios 5:3:2:1.

The extremity effect foreshadowed in the barrel patterns of Figures 1 and 2 appears in these differential-weight estimates. Thus, the weight of 2.84 for the average level of Work enjoyment is substantially less than the weights of 6.86 and 7.30 for the low and high levels of this job dimension. Similar extremity weighting appears for the Pay-promotion and the Coworker dimensions. This extremity effect was statistically significant on each of these three job dimensions. Only for the low-weight Manager dimension did extremity weighting fail to appear. This unequal weighting *within* the three main job dimensions disagrees with the usual assumption of equal weighting.

Prior Attitude. The analysis also provides estimates of w_0 and s_0, the weight and value of the prior attitude. The values of w_0 in Table 1 are roughly comparable to the average weight for a single piece of information. This agrees with previous results in person cognition (Anderson, 1974b, pp. 254f) and in juror judgment (Ostrom, Werner, & Saks, 1978). The values of s_0 were somewhat below the midpoint of the 200-point scale, which suggests that these subjects feel slightly pessimistic about the likely satisfaction to be obtained from jobs in general.

Self-Estimated Weights. At the end of the experiment, subjects rated the importance of each job dimension. These self-estimates are shown in the first data column of Table 2. Differences in rated importance of the four job dimensions were highly significant, $F(3,57) - 11.62$.

Also included in Table 2 are the weight estimates for the equal-weight solution from Table 1, as well as the mean weight estimates for the differential-weight solution, averaged over the three levels within each job dimension. All three sets of weight estimates show the same rank order of importance. The self-estimates and the equal-weight estimates are roughly comparable, in line with the fact that both apply to the job dimension as a whole. The differential-weight estimates have substantially greater range, however, which suggests that future work should obtain self-estimates for each separate level on each job dimension.

Goodness of Fit. The primary function of the averaging model in this study was to estimate importance weighting; goodness of fit was secondary (see Anderson, 1982, Section 4.4.3). Details are in the Appendix, but a few comments deserve mention here.

The equal-weight solution predicts parallelism and cannot account for the barrel-shaded patterns already noted in Figures 1 and 2. Nevertheless, these weights still reflected the relative importance of the job dimensions. This outcome has practical usefulness because it suggests that the equal-weight solution, which is easier to apply, can provide an approximate guide even with unequal weighting.

The differential-weight solution itself showed some significant discrepancies (see Table 3), but the fit was very close. The mean magnitude discrepancy was only 3.16 points, only 1.6% of the full mean response range, which ran from 2.1 to 196.9 on the 200-point scale. Since the model accounts for the qualitative aspects, discussed in connection with Figures 1 and 2, and does reasonably quantitatively, it would seem to provide an adequate basis for estimating weights.

Related Work

Since this work was completed, Dalal (1978; Dalal & Singh, in press) also found strong support for averaging over adding in job satisfaction. This outcome agrees with Singh in supporting the "traditional theory" of job satisfaction rather than Herzberg's two-factor theory (Herzberg, Mausner, & Snyderman, 1959). This two-factor theory claims that objective "content" factors, such as salary and working conditions, have qualitatively different effects from more subjective "context" factors, such as opportunity for achievement and enjoyment in work itself. The present results support Singh's claim that both kinds of factors have psychologically similar effects.

Singh (1975) and Dalal (1978) used the two-factor theory that they disproved as the basis for their experimental design, taking content and context as the two design factors rather than the job dimensions obtained in the factor analyses referenced earlier. The levels of their factors were accordingly composed of heterogeneous items. Neither study obtained the barrel shape observed here, presumably because their items had only high or low value. The barrel shape in the present data stems from the lower weighting of the average level.

An ingenious analysis for the averaging model was developed by Norman (1976a), who applied it in pioneering work to estimate weights and scale values for three information cues about job applicants (work experience, test score, and interview rating). In Norman (1976c), the data exhibited parallelism, in agreement with the equal-weight case of the averaging model. The results suggested that the same nominal information had different weights for different occupations, as would be expected theoretically (Anderson & Lopes, 1974). The estimated weight of test score, for example, was about .45 for two technical jobs, but only .32 for sales representative. Norman's analyses were done with group data, however, so these and other weighting effects could not be assessed statistically.

Norman (1976b) studied effect of outcome feedback on weights and values. These results also supported the parallelism property, both before and after feedback. However, feedback did appear to affect the parameter values. Before feedback, the differences among the three informational cues were localized in their weight parameters. Feedback had substantial effects on the parameters that depended on specific feedback conditions. In particular, feedback based on the assumptions that just one of the three cues was irrelevant seemed to cause changes in scale values but not in weights. This work, and that of Levin (1973) and Busemeyer (in press), illustrate the potential of information integration theory as an alternative to the lens model formulation (e.g., Hammond, Stewart, Brehmer, & Steinmann, 1975) for analysis of environmental contingencies in modifying behavior.

Job Attitudes and Attitude Change

In the present approach, job satisfaction is viewed from the perspective of general attitude theory (Anderson, 1971, 1981b; Hovland, 1959; Janis & Mann, 1977; McGuire, 1985). In contrast to the tests-and-measurement orientation, with its concern with predictions of job attitudes, the social-psychological orientation is more concerned with changing attitudes. The following comments indicate some ways that the concept of importance weighting relates to problems of changing attitudes.

Unequal Importance

That different job dimensions have unequal importance seems clear to common sense, but evidence has been lacking. Mikes and Hulin (1968, p. 394) noted that nearly all previous studies of job satisfaction had argued that importance measures ought to be taken into account. Their own large field study, however, found that "importance has little value in a prediction situation involving job attitudes and behaviors." Similar conclusions have been reached not only for job attitudes but more generally in attitude and decision theory (e.g., Beckwith & Lehman, 1973; Dawes & Corrigan, 1974; Ewen, 1967; Schmidt, 1971; but see B. F. Anderson, Deane, Hammond, McClelland, & Shanteau, 1981, p. 124). Equally good or even better predictions can often be obtained by assuming that all predictive attributes are equally important.

Present results, in contrast, show large differences in the importance of the four job attributes. Most important was enjoyment in the work itself. Following in rank order were pay-promotion, coworker cooperation, and managerial support. In the unequal-weight solution of Table 2, the relative importance of these four job dimensions is approximately 5:3:2:1. These results provide perhaps the first unambiguous evidence for unequal weighting between attribute dimensions in applied psychology.

Furthermore, unequal weighting within attribute dimensions was also found. Three of the four job attributes showed extremity weighting: the low and high levels had substantially greater weight than the average level. Thus, a low level of work enjoyment is not merely more negative in value than an average level, but also has greater impact on job satisfaction. The same held for the high level of work enjoyment. This extremity effect was substantial, by a factor of about two on each of the three most important job dimensions.

Many multiattribute models disallow unequal weighting within attribute dimensions. That may ignore important aspects of job behavior. A low level of any attribute seems likely to be a continual source of irritation or resentment. A low level of coworker cooperation, for example, could correspond to an atmosphere of friction and jealousy among the workers. Such an atmosphere would be more salient in each worker's life than an average atmosphere, and thereby receive greater weight. A low level of work enjoyment, similarly, would be a continuing source of unhappiness, and a high level would be a continuing source of satisfaction. These plausibility considerations agree with the present results.

Averaging Paradox

Addition of positive attributes can have negative consequences, according to averaging theory. To illustrate, suppose that the scale value is positive but lower on the management dimension than on other dimensions, and that an informational program is instituted to improve management's image. If this program increases the scale value on the management dimension, that will of course increase job satisfaction. But the informational program may only increase management's salience or weight without increasing value. Then the averaging process will decrease overall satisfaction, pulling it down towards the lower scale value on the management dimension. Averaging theory thus shows how seemingly desirable actions can have undesirable consequences.

Attitude Change

Unequal weighting may be important for designing and evaluating programs to change attitudes. Such programs will typically present certain information intended to change values on one or more relevant attributes. The weight parameter indexes how much change would be produced by a unit change in attribute value. Thus, the present weight estimates imply that a unit change in value can have five times greater effect on the work enjoyment dimension than on the management dimension. Similar considerations hold for unequal weighting within attribute dimensions.

Other factors would also operate, of course, having to do with resistance to change and persuasiveness of information. It is clear, however, that information about weights may help evaluate cost-effectiveness of alternative informational programs. Such unequal weighting might be ignored in an attitude prediction study, but it plays a quite different role in attitude change.

190

The importance weights obtained here reflect the job aspirations of a youth population with little work experience. The high weight placed on work enjoyment may reflect the inexperienced idealism of the population. Since many jobs are humdrum, many students may be expected to go through a period of dissatisfaction upon their entry into the labor force. Attitude change programs that focused on orientation adjustment could thus have substantial benefits, for management and labor alike. In model terms, such programs aim to change the parameter values. Scale value of work enjoyment, for example, could be increased by delineating the role of each job in the overall operation. Similarly, company picnics and newsletters build morale and thereby raise both scale value and weight on the coworker and management dimensions. The model thus agrees with common sense and also relates to general attitude theory.

Multiattribute Attitude Models

Multiattribute models have been employed by numerous investigators in attitude studies. General discussions of these models are given elsewhere (see Anderson, 1981a, b; Anderson & Graesser, 1976; Jaccard & Becker, 1985) but two issues, natural settings and self-estimation, deserve present consideration.

The issue of natural settings arises in generalizing results from laboratory studies like the present experiment to everyday life. It seems reasonable to expect the averaging rule and the extremity weighting to hold for job attitudes of more experienced workers in business and industry. It would be desirable to test this, however, and even more desirable to extend the experimental work to this and other natural settings.

Integration theory approaches natural settings with *personal design*. The idea of personal design is to embed a stimulus design, not necessarily of factorial-type, in the relevant natural setting of the individual person. This is done by selecting stimulus materials that are meaningful in the personal context. Functional measurement methodology makes possible complete analysis at the individual level.

A key element of personal design is that it incorporates some measure of experimental control. This is important for cognitive analysis.

Many multiattribute attitude models suffer from reliance on weak inference methods. A prime example is the formulation of Fishbein and Ajzen (1975), which rests on a summation rule that has repeatedly been found invalid. This invalid foundation has been concealed by reliance on weak inference methods of correlation even with experimental data. Ironically, Fishbein's method would, if done properly, cause Fishbein's model to fail even if it were correct (Anderson & Graesser, 1976, Note 1; Holbrook, 1977; see also below). The reliance on weak inference has concealed not only the invalid theoretical foundation, but also the invalid methodology.

Personal design is related to the issue of *self-estimation,* in which subjects rate their own personal values and weights. Self-estimation can markedly simplify design and analysis. This is valuable for studies in natural settings, which often place strong constraints on design. Some methodological considerations are given later. The rest of this section cites some applications of personal design and self-estimation in attitude studies.

One notable instance of self-estimation is the study of dating judgments by Shanteau and Nagy (1976, 1979). Excellent predictions of attitudinal judgments and also of dating choices were obtained from self-estimates of physical attractiveness and probability of acceptance, combined by a multiplying rule.

A study of attitudes generated in group discussion by Anderson and Graesser (1976) is shown in Figure 4. The solid curve shows predictions from the averaging model, based on self-estimates by each individual of value and weight of their own given information and of the discussion input of the other group members. This averaging model fits the data points quite well. The dashed curve shows predictions from a summation model, which did poorly.

A primary advantage of the self-estimates in the foregoing experiment is that they allowed rigorous test of the two models with only four experimental conditions in nonfactorial design. Deviations from the averaging model were statistically nonsignificant. The summation model, despite the very high correlation of .999, showed highly significant deviations from the data, thereby illustrating the difference between weak inference and strong inference.

Personal design with individualized selection of stimulus materials in factorial design has been used in studies of marital satisfaction by Anderson (1981a, Section 4.5.2) and of spouse influence on moral-social attitudes by Armstrong (1984) and Armstrong and Anderson (1985). The latter work illustrated a new approach to socialization processes in marriage.

The most striking case of personal design is the study of contraceptive usage by Jaccard and Becker (1985). Subjects were young, sexually active individuals, each of whom selected the three contraceptive attributes considered personally most important. These three attributes were combined as generalized, hypothetical stimuli in a personalized factorial design. Analyses based on these generalized stimuli yielded excellent predictions of actual contraceptive usage. This study is notable for its thoughtful experimental procedure, as well as for demonstrating the predictive power of personalized hypothetical judgments to behavior in a natural setting.

Multiattribute Theory

This final section takes up four issues in multiattribute theory: multiattribute models as cognitive algebra and the cognitive-normative antinomy; further discussion of weight indexes in current use; a conjoint cognitive-prescriptive adding rule for optimal decision; and problems in the further development of self-estimation methodology.

Multiattribute Models as Cognitive Algebra

Multiattribute models may be treated as part of cognitive algebra. They are thus hypotheses about how people evaluate and integrate information that deserve empirical study. The usefulness of this view is illustrated by the foregoing evidence for the averaging theory of job attitudes.

This cognitive view differs from the predominant approach in judgment-decision. The predominant use of multiattribute models is practical or prescriptive, in which they often seem very useful. This practical success, however, has obscured many cognitive issues.

Two such cognitive issues are considered here. One concerns cognitive algebra; the other concerns the definition and measurement of weight. It is well known that standard multiattribute analysis suffers from weak inference methodology (Anderson & Shanteau, 1977; Fischer, 1977), which seems to test the models but does not really do so. Partly for this reason, standard multiattribute analysis is confused and inconsistent about the psychological concept of weight.

For both issues, the difficulty lies in the fundamental antinomy (Anderson, 1986) between cognitive and prescriptive approaches to judgment-decision. Both approaches are useful in their own way, and each has a good deal to offer the other. Finding a working accommodation is not easy, however, as the following discussion will illustrate.

Sensitivity and Insensitivity. The cognitive-prescriptive antinomy is well illustrated by the issue of sensitivity. Practical studies often find that predictions from multiattribute models are not much affected by changes in the weights. Such insensitivity is often desirable in practical affairs—but not in cognitive analysis.

193

Consider a college graduate choosing among several jobs. The present results indicate that the overall value of each job is a weighted average of its values on the various attribute dimensions, and it would seem sensible to calculate these values and choose the job with the highest overall value. But such calculations may be misleading, for they rest on uncertain expectations about the future. Coworker cooperation, for example, might turn out rather more important than the student had anticipated. It would be reassuring, therefore, if the same job remained in first place even under moderate changes in the importance weights.

To assess this, *sensitivity analysis* may be applied. As Edwards and Newman (1982, p. 93) say, "If the conclusion seems relatively stable under changes of weights . . . you are usually justified in treating it as valid." In practical affairs, in other words, a valid choice is one that is insensitive to changes in weights.

Similar reasoning has been applied to linear regression models. Thus, Dawes (1979, p. 571) discusses the "robust beauty of improper linear models," referring to the fact that using incorrect, suboptimal weights often loses little in predictive power, at least as measured by the correlation coefficient. Robustness, of course, is another name for insensitivity.

But for cognitive analysis, insensitivity is generally undesirable, not to say abhorrent. Weights are indicators of cognitive process. Methodology that is insensitive to weight changes is insensitive to cognitive process. Cognitive theory and practical applications thus require almost opposing outlooks. This exemplifies the fundamental antinomy.

Unequal Weighting. The insensitivity of standard multiattribute methodology appears in the general difficulty, already mentioned, of finding evidence for unequal weighting of different dimensions of job satisfaction. These differences are not small; the present cognitive methodology showed 5 to 1 differences in attribute weights.

The present results go farther, to establish an extremity weighting effect: *within* three of the four job dimensions, high and low levels were weighted more than twice as heavily as the average level. This result is intuitively reasonable and, as already noted, of some practical importance. Previous failures to detect such large weight differences, both between and within dimensions, reflects insensitive methodology.

Model Testing. The insensitivity of standard multiattribute analysis also appears in model testing. Although such analyses typically rest

194

of some algebraic model, the psychological validity of the models is generally left untested and uncertain, owing to the reliance on weak inference.

The weak inference problem may be illustrated with the present data. As Figure 2 has shown, job satisfaction is not an additive or linear function of the attributes. The barrel patterns and the crossovers point instead to an averaging process. But suppose this fact is ignored, and a linear model is applied. This requires fitting a set of six parallel curves to the data. The linear model cannot fit very well, of course, because the six data curves are not parallel. What is surprising is how well the linear model seems to do. Its predictions are shown in Figure 3, plotted as a function of the 18 data points in Figure 2. All the points would lie on the diagonal line—if the linear model was correct and if there was no response variability. The points do lie very close to this diagonal, and the correlation is extremely high, .990. These correlation-scatterplot statistics make it seem that the linear model does very well, which is not true. Correlation and scatterplot conceal what the factorial plot reveals.

Such insensitive methods are inadequate for analysis of cognitive process. The *integration process* involves averaging, but this process analysis requires a more sensitive, cognitive methodology. Again, the *valuation process* involves unequal weighting, but this process analysis also requires more sensitive methodology.

Unified Theory. Anderson (1978b, 1986) has emphasized the desirability of a modus vivendi, in which cognitive and applied approaches can cooperate. This requires understanding of the strengths and weakness of each approach and of their proper areas of application.

An obstacle to such cooperation lies in the general tendency to interpret results from practical analyses as though they had cognitive significance. This is generally unwarranted, because of the insensitivity problem already discussed, and often invalid, as already illustrated with the linear model and with weight estimation. Unfortunately, the usefulness of linear models has blinded many investigator to their limitations, not to mention the relevance of cognitive algebra.

How cognitive theory may be utilized in practical analysis is an important problem. Transplantation of cognitive methodology would not be appropriate, for it requires sensitivity and precision that are not generally necessary or even desirable in practical analysis. Instead, cognitive theory should be used to improve practical analysis.

One locus for improvement lies in self-estimation methodology. People are often asked to judge value and importance of attributes,

195

with these self-estimates being used in the multiattribute models. The most popular methods of obtaining self-estimates, however, have serious shortcomings. Worthwhile improvements may be available with cognitive theory, as discussed in the following sections.

Weight Indexes

Most multiattribute formulations, because they have not been based on viable psychological theory, have been forced to adopt ad hoc or arbitrary indexes of weight. Some formulations recognize this arbitrariness and even capitalize on it. The effectiveness of ordinary regression analysis, for example, depends squarely on the unit confounding discussed earlier. Regression analysis works precisely because the weights need not be comparable across predictor dimensions.

Many investigators, however, do wish to compare importance of different attributes. Such comparisons require explicit justification, which is rarely given. Methods and criteria for assessing proposed weight indexes are illustrated in the following examples.

Averaging Theory. Averaging theory provides a validity criterion for weight indexes that can be used in general multiattribute analysis. The averaging model has been empirically established in a variety of multiattribute tasks, and, as the present experiment illustrates, it can provide proper weight estimates. Other formulations can thus be tested by applying them to tasks already known to satisfy the averaging rule. They must then yield the same weight estimates as the averaging model.

Relative Shift Index. A theoretical method for analyzing one class of weight indexes may be illustrated with the relative shift index used by Frijda (1969) to compare importance of facial and contextual cues in judgment of emotion. Let R_A and R_B be the responses to two separate cues, A and B, and R_{AB} the response to the two-cue combination. Then relative importance is defined as

$$|R_{AB} - R_A| / |R_{AB} - R_B|.$$

This index has face validity. If the two cues are equally important, then R_{AB} seemingly should lie halfway between R_A and R_B, and the ratio should be unity. If A increases in importance, the numerator decreases and the ratio approaches zero. Hence the index might seem to provide a model-free index of relative importance.

In fact, however, the meaning of this index depends on the operative model (Anderson, 1976b, Section 7.3.8). In an adding model, the index equals the ratio of the weight-value products for the two cues.

196

In an averaging model with $w_O = 0$, the index equals the ratio of the weights themselves; in this special case, it is a proper index of relative weight. The index thus has a simple meaning under each model, although these two meaning are rather different.

Empirically, of course, the most frequent case is the averaging model with $w_O \neq 0$. In this case, the ratio is not even a monotone index of relative importance. This flaw reflects the failure of the intuitive presumption that R_{AB} should lie halfway between R_A and R_B when the two cues are equally important. Certain other proposed indexes may be analyzed similarly, in terms of their algebraic form, to see how they agree with the models in question.

Lens Model. The lens model proposed by Brunswik and studied by Hammond (e.g., Hammond, McClelland, & Mumpower, 1978, 1980; Hammond *et al.*, 1975) is an ordinary regression equation. The claim is made, however, that this regression equation forms the basis for a cognitive theory, and such terms as *judgment policy* and *cognitive system* are applied as though the regression equation had psychological significance.

The concept of weight, which is considered basic in the lens model, is used in two ways that purport to be the same, but are actually contradictory. Conceptually, weight is defined as the "relative importance judges place on cues in making judgments of preference or inference (Hammond *et al.*, 1980, p. 217)." Indeed, with objective predictor variables, "all psychological significance resides in the weights. (B. F. Anderson *et al.*, 1981, pp. 254-255)."

But the regression weights in the lens model are psychologically indeterminate, unrelated to the conceptual definition of weight. The roots of the problem lie in the unit confounding, discussed earlier, and in the effects of intercorrelated predictors. This problem has been recognized, and Hammond *et al.* (1975, p. 282) have proposed two methods to resolve the indeterminacy. Both methods are invalid (Anderson, 1982, Note 4.3.1c). The conceptual meaning attributed to the weights and used in theoretical discussions has thus no basis in the lens model itself.

Such double meaning is a general problem with the lens model formulation. The regression model is said to "capture the judgment policy" of the judge, as though this had some psychological significance. Judgment policies can hardly be capture, however, with arbitrary or indeterminate weights.

The basic problem facing the lens model is that of measurement. A quantitative theory of cognition must be able to measure cognitive quantities.

197

Separate Parameter Estimates. A number of multiattribute formulations rely on separate estimates of the weight and value parameters. This has an attractive simplicity that conceals certain difficulties and pitfalls. The following discussion is concerned with practical applications and aims to show how cognitive theory can contribute to practical analysis.

One problem is disordinality. Using separate estimates in a multiattribute integration rule can easily yield results that are disordinally related to the true preferences, as well as to the normative preferences. Such disordinality is undesirable, for it means that choices prescribed by the multiattribute analysis may be systematically suboptimal.

Only the procedure developed by Edwards's group (Edwards, 1977, 1980; Edwards & Guttentag, 1975; Edward & Newman, 1982) will be explicitly considered, in part because it seems generally superior to other procedures, in part because it has been developed through numerous varied applications. It has, moreover, certain similarities with procedures of integration theory, including the use of simple rating-type methods, an emphasis on self-estimated parameters, and the use of an averaging rule for integration. The following considerations, however, are relevant to most multiattribute procedures that use separate parameter estimates.

A first goal in Edwards's procedure is to obtain a common scale of value (measure of location) for each attribute dimension. Accordingly, judges are required to use a 0-100 value scale for each attribute, with the extremes representing the minimum and maximum plausible levels of the attribute. Imposing this common numerical range is, apparently, thought to ensure a common scale of value and thereby provide comparability across attribute dimensions. Self-estimated weights are also obtained, and these weights and values are combined as a weighted average to represent the overall, integrated value of each alternative.

Three basic difficulties appear in this procedure when compared with the present theory. The first difficulty concerns the assumed comparability of the 0-100 value scales for different attributes. Comparability does not lie in the range, but in the unit. Imposing the same numerical range almost guarantees unequal units, for the actual range of each attribute is arbitrary, depending on what particular alternatives happen to be plausible or practical be within a given setting. If some external circumstance caused the upper half-range of one attribute dimension to become unavailable, for example, that would have no necessary effect on the operative values of the re-

198

maining levels of that attribute. Their nominal values, however, would be changed by the rescaling to cover the 0-100 range.

The procedure attempts to allow for such range effects by requiring that any change in range be accompanied by a proportionate change in weight (Edwards & Newman, 1982, pp. 71, 74). A halving of the effective range, for example, would need to be compensated by halving the weight; this would keep the effective unit constant for the attribute itself. Lacking a means for measuring subjective value, however, the procedure has no way of knowing how some change in the objective range changes the effective range—and hence no way of knowing how the weight ought to change. Such compensation, moreover, would only be appropriate if the effective ranges were initially equivalent, which is similarly not determinate and surely not likely.

The second difficulty is that the weights are measured in a way that seems incompatible with the calculation. The calculation requires, as already noted, that weights change in proportion to changes in the value range. The weights are actually measured, however, as self-estimates, under instructions to judge relative importance of each attribute dimension in the overall evaluation. It seems doubtful that halving the range, say, will halve the self-estimated weight as the calculation requires. One reason is that weights may be ranked and estimated for an attribute dimension per se, without information being present about its range. Such judgments can hardly accord with the range if subjects are unaware of what the range is going to be. Intuitively, moreover, the importance of, say, work enjoyment in job satisfaction should be largely unaffected by the available job opportunities and remain roughly constant if the range changed owing to appearance of new jobs or filling of old jobs.

One test of these two arguments can be obtained by considering an attribute with a single level that is common to all alternatives, thus having zero range. The calculational procedure requires that its weight be zero. It may be doubted, however, that work enjoyment would be judged as having zero importance merely because it had the same value for all prospective jobs.

Furthermore, there is empirical evidence that the value range will not affect the weights in the postulated manner. The quantitative tests of the averaging model, in particular, support the hypothesis that weight is a characteristic of the particular entity being judged, regardless of the value range. Collateral support is obtained from the work on self-estimates of weight cited later. Direct experimental evidence could be obtained by manipulating the range to see whether self-estimated weights do change with range in the postulated way. (Anderson, 1982, Note 6.7, 5a).

The two foregoing difficulties can cause disordinality. It can be shown that predictions from multiattribute models with self-estimate parameters can be disordinally related to the true values unless three stringent measurement assumptions are met (see Anderson, 1982, Section 4.3.6a; Anderson & Graesser, 1976, Note 1). First, the weight estimates must be on true ratio scales with common unit. Second, the values must be on true linear scales with a common unit. Both of these measurement assumptions are likely to be false for the reasons indicated in the foregoing discussion of ranges and units. Third, unless the weights are equal across levels within an attribute dimension, the value scales must be true ratio scales, having a known zero. The present results show that equal weighting within attribute dimensions cannot be taken for granted; and the ratio scale assumption seems markedly inconsistent with the requirement that 0 correspond to the lowest plausible level of each attribute, for its true value may be quite positive or quite negative.

Violation of any one of these three measurement assumptions means that even the rank order of the alternatives calculated from the multiattribute model cannot generally agree with the optimal rank order. This disordinality seems undesirable in decision analysis.

The third difficulty, somewhat different in nature, appears in the use of the averaging rule for attribute integration. This is enforced by setting the sum of the weights equal to unity. This agrees with integration theory, to be sure, but the averaging rule is nonnormative and not always appropriate for prescriptive analysis.

To illustrate this cognitive-prescriptive incongruity, suppose that the averaging model holds for two entities that share a common level of some attribute. It might seem, following Edwards and Newman (1982, p. 20), that this common attribute could be ignored in the overall evaluation on the ground that it contributes equally to the evaluation of each alternative. This is not correct for the averaging rule. With averaging, as may readily be shown with numerical examples, omitting the common attribute can easily reverse the preference between the two entities. Integration theory would therefore adopt an additive rule for prescriptive analysis (see following section).

The main purpose of this discussion is to suggest possible improvements in applied multiattribute analysis. The procedure used by Edwards and his associates has been considered in detail because it has been more extensively developed and applied than other multiattribute procedures. No one would quarrel with the view expressed by Edwards and Guttentag (1975) and by Einhorn and McCoach (1977) that rough approximations are entirely adequate for certain purposes and that some measure of accuracy may well be traded for simplicity. It seems clear, however, that current procedures of multiattribute analysis suffer from lack of grounding in cognitive theory and that useful, if modest, improvements can be expected from cognitive-normative interaction of the kind considered here. As Gilbert, Light, and Mosteller (1975. p. 40) point out, "Because even small gains accumulated over time can sum to a considerable total, they may have valuable consequences for society."

Cognitive-Prescriptive Adding Rule: CPAR

This section presents a *cognitive-prescriptive adding rule* (CPAR) for practical applications. A prescriptive rule for multiattribute utility is given by the standard assumption of additivity. Rather than the cognitive averaging rule of Eq. (1), the prescriptive adding rule is:

$$R - w_0 s_0 + \sum w_i s_i. \tag{4}$$

This natural assumption of rationality has been considered by many writers. The cognitive-prescriptive adding rule is novel in that the weights and values are to be obtained form cognitive theory. A primary working assumption is that the averaging model can provide appropriate weights and values for the CPAR.

The CPAR is more general than the typical adding rule in that it allows unequal weighting within each attribute dimension. Weights are not generally identifiable from the formal structure of a weighted adding model, either within or between dimensions. They can be identified with the averaging rule, however, as the present study illustrates (see also Anderson, 1982, pp. 60, 69-70, 193, 277-290). A potentially more general and flexible method for measuring weight is with self-estimation methodology (see following).

The CPAR is a proposal for unifiod theory, with cooperation of cognitive and normative approaches. This proposal entails a conceptual distinction between cognitive and normative integration rules. The averaging rule is cognitive in that it applies to intuitive, holistic judgments in an exact manner. It is nonnormative, however, in that it can lead to presumptively irrational or suboptimal behavior. In prescribing an optimal course of action, therefore, the cognitive rule would be used as a foundation for measurement, whereas Eq. (4) would be used to integrate these weights and values as a basis for decision.

The CPAR thus illustrates one way in which the cognitive and normative approaches, despite their antinomous relation, can work together. Because of the many divergences between cognitive and normative integration rules (Anderson 1981a, pp. 27-29, 33-34,

45-49, 68-69, 71, 83, 128-130, 282-283, 293, 367), separation between their domains of applicability seems advisable. To use the cognitive averaging rule for prescriptive integration, however, may be as inappropriate as to suppose that a linear model can represent cognitive process. Valuation, on the other hand, is largely outside the normative domain but is a proper concern of cognitive analysis.

Experimental analysis plays an important role in this cognitive-prescriptive approach. It is true, as Edwards and Guttentag (1975) observe, that experimental comparisons among alternative courses of action are impracticable or impossible for many decisions. Even so, experimental analysis can be helpful in two ways. One way is with personal design for value measurement, extending the foregoing results of Shanteau and Nagy (1976, 1979) and Jaccard and Becker (1985) from prediction to prescription of decisions. A second way is through experimental development of methods for self-estimation of weights and values, which is taken up next.

Self-Estimation Methodology
Development of a self-estimation methodology has been a continuing concern of the theory of information integration for two decades. It would be extremely useful if people could estimate their own weights and values. Aside from simplicity, self-estimation could be used in many situations in which factorial-type design is impracticable or impossible, as well as for tasks that do not obey any simple algebraic rule.

The problems of self-estimation are by no means easy. Self-estimated weights, in particular, are in an uncertain state. Still, considerable progress has been made, and this area looks promising. A brief overview is given here.

Validity of Self-Estimates. The basic problem with self-estimates concerns their validity. The fallibility of self-reports has been demonstrated repeatedly in psychology. Any use of self-estimates must address this problem of validity.

Cognitive algebra provides a validity criterion. Valid estimates of weights and values can be obtained with functional measurement methodology. the averaging model, in particular, resolves the problem of identifiability of weight parameters. Any proposed method of self-estimation must agree with the estimates provided by the averaging model, and the same holds more generally for cognitive algebra. This provides a foundation for development of self-estimation methodology.

This approach is feasible because cognitive algebra has been reasonable well established in a number of areas. these cases can be used as the developmental ground for a general methodology of self-estimation that may be expected to apply even when no simple algebraic rule holds.

Generality of Self-Estimates. Human values are not constant, but change with experience and with motivational state. Self-estimated values, accordingly, will necessarily lose some generality when they are used outside the immediate situation in which they are measured. This problem arises in almost any major course of action, such as job choice, in which the person must adjust to a new environment. For optimal decision, however, as well as for prediction, it is desirable to maximize generality of self-estimates.

One approach is with personal design, discussed earlier. Valuation is a constructive process that taps into the cognitive background and knowledge systems of the person (Anderson, 1983). Stimulus materials personalized to the individual's past experience and present situation theoretically should evoke deeper levels of personal relevance and meaning. Personal design can become too specific, of course, but it has important potential for increasing generality of self-estimates.

A second approach, commonly used in multiattribute analysis, is to require detailed, explicit consideration of various contingencies and possible outcomes (see Edwards & Newman, 1982). Some writers have even suggested that such consideration leads to clarification of values that is more important than prescription of optimal action (e.g., Pitz, 1983). Such value clarification is naturally expected to increase generality of self-estimates.

Self-Estimation of Values. The fallibility of self-report is well illustrated by the contrast between the method of rating the the method of magnitude estimation advocated by Stevens (1974). Both methods have good face validity and subjects readily adopt either method. But even with well-defined sensations, such as loudness, the two methods give sharply different results. Which—if either—is valid?

This question was resolved with cognitive algebra, which provided a validity criterion for the self-reports. From psychophysics to attitudes, the evidence has shown that ratings are valid in numerous situations and that magnitude estimation is generally invalid (e.g., Anderson 1974a, b, 1981a, Seciton 5.4, 1982, Section 1.1). This outcome, it may be omphaoized, rested on the development of

203

methodological precautions to eliminate various biases that can affect rating responses.

Most of these studies have actually dealt with judgments of multiattribute entities, that is, with integrated attributes, rather than with judgments of their separate components. The two kinds of judgment are similar, however, and a number of studies have used value judgments of single attributes with reasonable success and promise.

One practical issue deserves mention. For direct substitution into a multiattribute integration rule, value estimates may need to be on a ratio scale, with a known zero point, as already indicated. Accordingly, it would be advisable to establish an explicit zero point on the response scale—and check that subjects use this nominal zero as the true zero (see Anderson, 1981a, Note 2.3.2a).

Previous integration studies have generally required only a linear scale or have used linear regression adjustment of zero and unit (Anderson, 1982, Section 4.3.6). Not much is known about establishing proper zero points in self-estimation, therefore, and this issue needs systematic study.

Two theoretical issues in the interpretation of self-estimates also require mention. In averaging theory, judged value of a single attribute is theoretically not a pure measure of value, for the initial state is typically averaged in. In addition, judgments of in situ components of multiattribute stimuli may be expected to include halo effects. These issues cannot be discussed here (see Anderson, 1981a, 1982), but they need to be kept in mind. Also they reemphasize the importance of having a base in cognitive theory for practical multiattribute analysis.

Self-Estimation of Weights. The rating method may be applied to obtain self-estimates of weights in the same way as for values (Anderson, 1981, pp. 290-292). Ordinarily, or course, one end of the scale would be labeled zero importance, as it is usually desirable to have weights on a ratio scale. This rating method has been standard in the work on self-estimated weights in integration theory.

Other response procedures also need consideration. The procedure of dividing 100 points among the attributes has the advantage of making the importance comparison explicit and salient. It has the disadvantage of losing the absolute level of importance; two equally important attributes would each receive 50 points even if both were quite unimportant. This problem is not present with the rating method. Edwards's procedure employs Stevens's method of magnitude estimation, which seems questionable in view of the general failure of magnitude estimation for estimation of values. Not much is known about self-estimated weights, however, and systematic analysis is much needed.

The critical problem, of course, is to provide a validational base for the self-estimates. Previous workers have been generally negative on self-estimation. Studies reviewed by Slovic and Lichtenstein (1971, p. 684) seemed to indicate that "Judges strongly overestimate the importance they place on minor cues" and that all studies "found serious discrepancies" between objective weights and self-estimates. The latter conclusions was reaffirmed in the later review by Slovic, Fischoff, and Lichtenstein (1977). Similarly, Schmitt and Levine (1977, p. 16) state that "Comparisons of objective and subjective weighting policies have consistently shown that statistical and subjective indices of judgment policy disagree." Zeleny (1976, p. 14) notes that "Recent psychological studies indicate that an explicit importance-weighting process in unstable, suboptimal, and often arbitrary."

To the best of the writers' knowledge, however, not one of the studies in question has provided a valid criterion against which to compare the self-estimates. The most popular criterion has been the regression coefficient, which is invalid for reasons indicated in the introduction. The shortcoming may not lie in the subjects, as previous investigators have alleged, but in the methods used by investigators.

In fact, fair agreement was obtained here between self-estimated weights and the actual weights determined with functional measurement. The numerical agreement could be improved, to be sure, but improvement could be expected as better procedures are developed. Indeed, the study of attitudes by Anderson and Graesser (1976) previously shown in Figure 4 yielded excellent agreement between observed attitudes and those obtained using self-estimated values and weights. Other work on self-estimation is summarized in Anderson (1981a, Section 4.4, 1982, Section 6.2; see also Jacard & Sheng, 1984; Schoemaker & Waid, 1982).

The study of self-estimated weights has been held back by the need for determining the actual weights. In principle, the actual weights can be determined with the averaging model. In practice, there has been a technical difficulty that the estimation is unstable for occasional subjects (see Appendix). This difficulty has recently been overcome and the statistical procedures made practicable (Zalinski, 1986). This opens the way to systematic development of self-estimation methodology.

Note. This work was supported by National Science Foundations Grants BNS75-21235 and BNS82-07541 and by grants from the National Institute of Mental Health to the Center for Human Information Processing, University of California, San Diego. We wish to thank G. W. Fischer, B. Fischhoff, I. Levin, J. J. Louviere, K. L. Norman, J. Shanteau, and M. Zeleny for comments on an earlier draft (Zalinski & Anderson, 1977).

REFERENCES

Anderson, B. F., Deane, D. H., Hammond, K. R., McClelland, G. H., & Shanteau, J. C. (1981). Concepts in judgment and decision research. New York: Praeger.
Anderson, N. H. (1971). Integration theory and attitude change. Psychological Review, 78, 171-206.
Anderson, N. H. (1974a). Algebraic models in perception. In E. C. Carterette & M. P. Friedman (Eds.), Handbook of perception (Vol. 2, pp. 215-298). New York: Academic Press.
Anderson, N. H. (1974b). Information integration theory: A brief survey. In D. H. Krantz, R. C. Atkinson, R. D. Luce, & P. Suppes (Eds.), Contemporary developments in mathematical psychology (Vol. 2, pp. 236-305). San Francisco; W. H. Freeman.
Anderson, N. H. (1974c). Algebraic models for information integration. (Tech. Rep. CHIP 45). San Diego: University of California, Center for Human Information Processing.
Anderson, N. H. (1974d). Methods for studying information integration. (Tech. Rep. CHIP 43). San Diego: University of California, Center for Human Information Processing.
Anderson, N. H. (1976a). How functional measurement can yield validated interval scales of mental quantities. Journal of Applied Psychology, 61, 677-692.
Anderson, N. H. (1976b). Social perception and cognition. (Tech. Rep. CHIP 62). San Diego: University of California, Center for Human Information Processing.
Anderson, H. H. (1978a). Progress in cognitive algebra. In L. Berkowitz (Ed.), Cognitive theories in social psychology (pp. 103-126). New York: Academic Press.
Anderson, N. H. (1978b). Information integration theory and its relations to other approaches to judgment and decision. In K. R. Hammond, G. H. McClelland, & J. Mumpower (Eds.), The Colorado report on the integration of approaches to judgment and decision making (Tech Rep. 213, pp. A1-A21). Boulder: University of Colorado, Institute of Behavioral Science.
Anderson, N. H. (1981a). Foundations of information integration theory. New York: Academic Press.
Anderson, N. H. (1981b). Integration theory applied to cognitive responses and attitudes. In R. E. Petty, T. M. Ostrom, & T. C. Brock (Eds.), Cognitive responses in persuasion (pp. 361-397). Hillsdale, NJ: Erlbaum.
Anderson, N. H. (1982). Methods of information integration theory. New York: Academic Press.
Anderson, N. H. (1983). Schemas in person cognition (Technical Report CHIP 118). La Jolla: University of California, San Diego, Center for Human Information Processing.
Anderson, N. H. (in press). A cognitive theory of judgment and decision. In B. Brehmer, H. Jungermann, P. Lourens, & G. Sevón (Eds.), New directions in research on decision making. Amsterdam: North-Holland.

206

Anderson, N. H., & Graesser, C. C. (1976). An information integration analysis of attitude change in group discussion. Journal of Personality and Social Psychology, 34, 210-222.

Anderson, N. H., & Lopes, L. L. (1974). Some psycholinguistic aspects of person perception. Memory & Cognition, 2, 67-74.

Anderson, N. H., & Shanteau, J. (1977). Weak inference with linear models. Psychological Bulletin, 84, 1155-1170.

Armstrong, M. A. (1984). Attitudes and attitude change in marriage, studied with information integration theory. Unpublished doctoral dissertation, University of California, San Diego.

Armstrong, M. A., & Anderson, N. H. (1985). Attitude influence in marriage. Unpublished paper, University of California, San Diego.

Beckwith, N. E., & Lehmann, D.. R. (1973). The importance of differential weights in multiple attribute models of consumer preference. Journal of Marketing Research, 10, 141-145.

Busemeyer, J. R. (in press). Intuitive statistical estimation. In N. H. Anderson (Ed.), Contribution to information integration theory.

Chandler, J. P. (1969). STEPIT — Finds local minima of a smooth function of several parameters. Behavioral Science, 14, 81-82.

Dalal, A. K. (1978). Expected job attractiveness and satisfaction, as information integration. Unpublished doctoral dissertation, Indian Institute of Technology, Kanpur, India.

Dalal, A. K., & Singh, R. (in press). An integration theoretical analysis of expected job attractiveness and satisfaction International Journal of Psychology.

Dawes, R. M. (1979). The robust beauty of improper linear models in decision making. American Psychologist, 34, 571-582.

Dawes, R. M., & Corrigan, B. (1974). Linear models in decision making. Psychological Bulletin, 81, 95-106.

Edwards, W. (1977). Use of multiattribute utility measurement for social decision making. In D. E. Bell, R. L. Keeney, & H. Raiffa (Eds.), Conflicting objectives in decisions (pp. 247-276). New York: Wiley.

Edwards, W. (1980). Multiattribute utility for evaluation: Structures, uses, and problems. In M. W. Klein & K. S. Teilman (Eds.), Handbook of criminal justice evaluation (pp. 177-215). Beverly Hills, CA: Sage.

Edwards, W., & Newman, J. R. (1982). Multiattribute evaluation. Beverly Hills, CA: Sage.

Edwards, W., & Guttentag, M. (1975). Experiments and evaluations; A reexamination. In C. A. Bennett & A. A. Lumsdaine (Eds.), Evaluation and experiment (pp. 409-463). New York: Academic Press.

Einhorn, H. J., & McCoach, W. (1977). A simple multiattribute utility procedure for evaluation. Behavioral Science, 22, 270-282.

Ewen, R. B. (1967). Weighting componenets of job satisfaction. Journal of Applied Psychology, 51 68-73.

Fischer, G. W. (1977). Convergent validation of decomposed multi-attribute utility assessment procedures for risky and riskless decisions. Organizational Behavior and Human Performance, 18, 395-315.

Fishbein, M., & Ajzen, I. (1975). Belief, attitude, intention and behavior. Reading MA: Addison-Wesley.

Frijda, N. H. (1969). Recognition of emotion. In L. Berkowitz (Ed.), Advances in experimental social psychology (Vol. 4, pp. 167-223). New York: Academic Press.

Gilbert, J. P., Light, R.J., & Mosteller, F. (1975). Assessing social innovations: An empirical base for policy. In C. A. Bennett & A. A. Lumsdaine (Eds.), Evaluation and experiment (pp. 39-193). New York: Academic Press.

Gillett, B., & Schwab, D. P. (1975). Convergent and discriminant validities of corresponding job descriptive index and Minnesota satisfaction questionnaire scales. Journal of Applied Psychology, 60, 313-317.

Hammond, K. R., McClelland, G. H., & Mumpower, J. (1978). The Colorado report on the integration of approaches to judgment and decision making (Tech. Rep. 213). Boulder: University of Colorado, Institute of Behavioral Science.

Hammond, K. R., McClelland, G. H., & Mumpower, J. (1980). Human judgment decision making. New York: Praeger.

Hammond, K. R., Stewart, T. R., Brehmer, B., & Steinmann, D. O. (1975). Social judgment theory. In M. F. Kaplan & S. Schwartz (eds.), Human judgment and decision processes, (pp. 271-312), New York: Academic Press.

Herzberg, F., Mausner, B., & Snyderman, B. B. (1959). The motivation to work. New York: Wiley.

Holbrook, M. B. (1977). Comparing multiattribute attitude models by optimal scaling. Journal of Consumer Research, 4, 165-171.

Hovland, C. I. (1959). Reconciling conflicting results derived from experimental and survey studies of attitude change. American Psychologist, 14, 8-17.

Jaccard, J., & Becker, M. A. (1985). Attitudes and behavior: An information integration perspective. Journal of Experimental Social Psychology, 21, 440-465.

Jaccard, J., & Sheng, D. (1984). A comparison of six methods for assessing the importance of perceived consequences in behavioral decisions: Applications from attitude research. Journal of Experimental Social Psychology, 20, 1-28.

Janis, I. L., & Mann, L. (1977). Decision making. New York: Macmillan, 1977.

Kenney, R. L., & Raiffa, H. (1976). Decisions with multiple objectives. New York: Wiley.

Leon, M., & Anderson, N. H. (1974). A ration rule from integration theory tpplied to inference judgments. Journal of Experimental Psychology, 102, 27-36.

Leon, M., Oden, G. C., & Anderson, N. H. (1973). Functional measurement of social values. Journal of Personality and Social Psychology, 27, 301-310.

Levin, I. P. (1973). Learning effects in information integration: Manipulation of cue validity in an impression formation task. Memory & Cognition, 11, 236-240.

McGuire, W. J. (1985). Attitudes and attitude change. In G. Lindzey & E. Aronson (Eds.), Handbook of Social Psychology, (Vol. 2, 3rd ed., pp. 233-346). New York: Random House.

Mikes, P.S., & Hulin, C. L. (1968). Use of importance as a weighting component of job satisfaction. Journal of applied Psychology, 52, 394-398.

Norman, K. L. (1976a). A solution for eights and scale values in functional measurement. Psychological Review, 83, 80-84.

Norman, K. L. (1976b). Effects of feedback on the weights and subjective values in an information integration model. Organizational Behavior and Human Performance, 17, 367-387.

Norman, K. L. (1976c). Weight and value in an information integration task: Subjective weighting of job appliants. Organizational Behavior and Human Performance, 16, 193-204.

Ostrom, T. M., Werner, C., & Saks, M. J. (1978). An integration theory analysis of jurors' presumptions of guilt or innocence. Journal of Personality and Social Psychology, 36, 436-450.

Pitz, G. F. (1983). Human engineering of decision aids. In P. Humpheys, O. Svenson, & A. Vàri (Eds.), Analysizing and aiding decision processes. Amsterdam: North-Holland.

Schmidt, F. L. (1971). The relative efficiency of regression and simple unit predictor weights in applied differential psychology. Educational and Psychological Measurement, 31, 699-714.

Schmitt, N., & Levine, R. L. (1977). Statistical and subjective weights: Some problems and proposals. Organizational Behavior and Human Performance. 20, 15-30.

Schoemaker, P. J. H., & Waid, C. C. (1982). An experimental comparison of different approaches to determining weights in addictive utility models. Management Science, 28, 182-196.

Shanteau, J., & Nagy, G. (1976). Decisions made about other people: A human judgment analysis of dating choice. In J. S. Carroll & J. W. Payne (Eds.), Cognition and social behavior (pp. 221-242). Potomac, MD: Erlbaum.

Shanteau, J., & Nagy, G. F. (1979). Probability of acceptance in dating choice. Journal of Personality and Social Psychology, 37, 522-533.

Singh, R. (1975). Integration theory applied to expected job attractiveness and job satisfaction. Journal of Applied Psychology, 60, 621-623.

Slovic, P., Fischhoff, B., & Lichtenstein, S. (1977). Behavioral decision theory. Annual Review of Psychology, 28, 1-39.

Slovic, P., & Lichtenstein, S. (1971). Comparison of Bayesian and regression approaches to the study of information processing in judgment. Organizational Behavior and Human Performance, 6, 649-744.

Smith, P. C., Kendall, L.M., & Hulin, C. (1969). The measurement of satisfaction in work and retirement. Chicago: Rand-McNally.

Stevens, S.S. (1974). Perceptual magnitude and its measurement. In E. E. Carterett & M. P. Friedman (Eds.), Handbook of perception (Vol. 2, pp. 361-389). New York: Academic Press.

Zalinski, J. (1986). Parameter estimation for the averaging model of information integration theory. Unpublished doctoral dissertation, University of California, San Diego.

Zalinski, J., & Anderson, N. H. (1977). Measurement of importance in multiattribute utility models. Manuscript submitted for publication.

Zeleny, M. (1976). The attribute-dynamic attitude model (ADAM). Management Science, 23, 12-26.

APPENDIX

This appendix gives technical details on model analysis and parameter estimation. Also included is a discussion of imputations about missing information.

Parameter Estimation

Parameter estimates were obtained by fitting the averaging model to the complete set of data, including the 81 data points from the four-way design and the 54 data points from the six two-way designs. The model equation for each data point includes weight and scale value for each of the four or two given items of information and also for the prior attitude. Because of the nonlinearity of the model, Chandler's (1969) iterative numerical routine, STEPIT, was used.

Two different solutions were obtained, corresponding to the two different assumptions about weighting within job dimensions. In the equal-weight solution, a single weight is estimated for each job dimension and a scale value for each level of each job dimension. In the differential-weight solution, both weight and scale value are es-

209

timated for each level of each job dimension. Both solutions also require estimation of the weight and value of the prior attitude.

The weight estimates have already been discussed. Estimates of scale values have no particular interest because the levels within each job dimension were nominal. The estimated values were as expected, namely, near 0, 100 and 200 on the response scale, although the equal-weight solution tended to give scale values more extreme than the ends of the actual response scale. This presumably results from attempting to fit the barrel pattern of Figures 1 and 2 with parallel lines, as is required with equal weighting within job dimension.

Estimation problems require a few comments. A separate fit was made for each subject for both the equal-weight and differential-weight solutions. Estimates based on pooled group data would be biased, and, more seriously, would lose the individual differences that are necessary for a test of goodness of fit.

Estimation of the weights was possible because of the constraints provided by the joint, simultaneous use of two-way and four-way designs. Taken together, the six two-way designs would allow the weights to be estimated on a linear scale with common zero and common unit. Joint use of two-way and four-way designs places the weights on a common ration scale, with known zero and common unit, and also allows estimation of the prior weight (Anderson, 1982, Section 2.3).

Finally, the estimation procedure appeared to be unstable for a few subjects, a difficulty previously reported by Leon, Oden, Anderson (1973). Successive iterations caused the scale values to diverge to impossibly extreme values in return for miniscule improvements in goodness of fit. Fortunately, this had little effect on the weight estimates. For the present study, therefore, the problem was resolved by constraining the scale values to lie within the region from -50 to +250, 50 points more extreme than the endpoints of the response scale.

Substantial improvements in estimation procedure have since been obtained. The main device is to place moderately tight bounds, say, $\pm$ 10% of the scale range, around the starting estimate of each scale value. This bounding procedure has the three-fold benefit of eliminating the divergence, reducing bias, and substantially reducing variability in the weight estimates. Such bounding would usually be justified by prior knowledge about the stimulus values, which are typically selected to cover the range at roughly equal spacing. Fortunately, moderate misbounding of the scale values seems to have relatively little effect on weight estimation (Zalinski, 1986).

Goodness of Fit

Goodness of fit was assessed by a new method that applies generally to nonlinear models (Anderson, 1974c; Leon & Anderson, 1974). For each subject, the estimated parameters were used to generate predicted values for the 81 cells of the four-factor design. These predicted values were subtracted from the observed values to yield 81 deviation scores for each subject. If the model is correct, then these deviations are all zero except for response variability. Accordingly, the model may be tested by applying ordinary, repeated measurements analysis of variance to the four-factor matrix of deviation scores. The model-implied null hypothesis is that every source in the analysis of variance is zero in principle, and so nonsignificant in practice. The estimation forces the grand mean to be zero, but every other source provides a proper test of model-data fit.

This test procedure provides a powerful and statistically valid test of the model. Although the test requires estimation of a substantial number of parameters that are intercorrelated owing to the nonlinearity of the model, these factors are automatically allowed for in the test of goodness of fit (see Anderson, 1982, Chapter 4).

The results of these analyses are in Table 3. The equal-weight solution shows eight significant discrepancies form model prediction. That is no surprise, for the equal-weight solution is effectively a linear model for fixed set size and so cannot account for the significant barrel shapes in Figures 1 and 2.

The differential-weight solution does substantially better. Mean magnitude discrepancy was only 3.16 points on the 200-point response scale. The corresponding value from the 54 data points of the six two-way designs was slightly less, 2.98 points. Nevertheless, 4 of the 15 sources in Table 3 are still significant, so the model may still have some shortcoming.

Imputations about Missing Information

One source of discrepancy from the model lies in the assumption that the weight, w_0, of the prior attitude is constant, the same for sets of two and sets of four information items. This assumption has been supported in person cognition (Anderson, 1981a, Section 2.4), but the present task is different in that several different dimensions of information are explicitly specified. Although instructed to judge only on the basis of the information given in each set of two items, the subject might implicitly impute some value to the missing infor-

211

mation and average in this imputed value. That would cause systematic discrepancies between the observed and predicted values.

Two hypotheses of this type were considered. The first is that an average value is imputed to the missing information. That will cause the response to the sets of two items to be less extreme than the predicted values. The second is that the imputed value equals the average of the given information in the particular set being judged. That will cause the observed response to be more extreme than predicted. The two hypotheses make opposite predictions, therefore, and both can be assessed with the same data.

For this purpose, predicted values were generated for the sets of two items using the parameters of Table 1 for the differential-weight solution. In each two-way design, the three cells with lower than average information were selected, as well as the three cells with higher than average information. Mean response to the former was 1.37 points more negative than prediction; mean response to the latter was .46 points more positive than prediction. This pattern of discrepancy supports the second hypothesis, that the value of the imputed information equals the average of the values of the information at hand.

The complementary pattern of discrepancy should be obtained with the four-item sets, because the predictions are based on parameters estimated from both the two-item and four-item sets. This was confirmed. Mean response to the cells with lower than average information was less negative than predicted, whereas mean response to the cells with higher than average was less positive then predicted. These data also agree with the second hypothesis. The effect is small, however, less than 1 point on the 200-point scale.

The model can take account of imputations about missing information by allowing w_0 to depend on the number of items in the given set. A rough calculation shows that the imputed information would have about 1/20 the weight of a given piece of information. This small effect has little practical significance, although it is a tribute to the power of the statistical analysis. Imputations may well have larger effects under other conditions, and more recent work has found this issue to be of considerable interest for cognitive theory (Anderson, 1983, Section D).

Table 1
WEIGHT ESTIMATES

Job Dimension	Level	Equal-weight Solution	Differential-weight Solution
Management	Low	1.00	.91
	Average	"	1.17
	High	"	.93
Coworker	Low	1.53	3.76
	Average	"	1.30
	High	"	2.01
Pay-Promotion	Low	2.11	3.78
	Average	"	2.25
	High	"	4.26
Work Enjoyment	Low	2.72	6.86
	Average	"	2.84
	High	"	7.30
Prior Attitude		2.58	1.49

NOTE: Weight or mean weight for Management dimension arbitrarily set equal to unity to simplify comarisons.

Table 2
WEIGHT ESTIMATES

Job Dimension	Self-Estimates	Equal-weight Solution	Differential-weight Solution
Management	1.00	1.00	1.00
Coworker	1.68	1.53	2.36
Pay-Promotion	1.99	2.11	3.43
Work Enjoyment	2.28	2.72	5.67

NOTE: Weight for Management dimension arbitrarily set equal to unity. Entries are averaged over subjects

213

Table 3
TESTS OF GOODNESS OF FIT

Source	df	Equal-weight Model	Differential-weight Model
Management (M)	2	.20	.59
Coworker (C)	2	2.00	.09
Pay Promotion (P)	2	5.29*	4.11*
Work Enjoyment (W)	2	5.97*	1.93
MxC	4	2.57*	2.49
MxP	4	3.88*	2.10
MxW	4	2.29	4.18*
CxP	4	3.57*	4.73*
CxW	4	3.99*	2.25
PxW	4	3.95*	1.70
MxCxP	8	1.77	1.41
MxCxW	8	1.78	1.65
MxPxW	8	1.64	1.47
CxPxW	8	3.54*	2.78*
MxPxCxW	16	1.14	1.13

NOTE: Error term for each source is its interaction with subjects and has 19 times as many df.

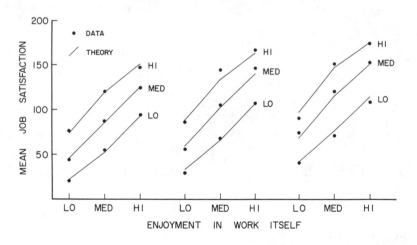

Figure 1. Predicted and observed values of job satisfaction as a function of three job dimensions. (Curve parameter is level of Pay-promotion dimension; successive panels from left to right correspond to low, average, and high levels of Management dimension.)

214

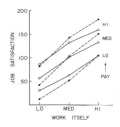

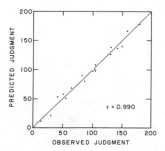

Figure 2. Test of averaging versus adding. Crossover interaction between solid and dashed curves supports averaging, rules out adding hypothesis.

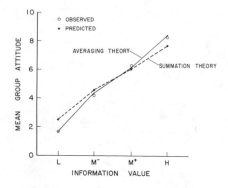

Figure 3. Weak inference test of linear model. Predictions from best linear fit to data of Figure 2 are plotted as a function of the actual data points. Tight scatterplot and high correlation of .990 conceal deviations from parallelism that are clearly visible in Figure 2.

Figure 4. Self-estimated parameters provide good fit of averaging model for attitudes developed in group discussion (Anderson & Graesser, 1976). Data points represent attitudes towards U.S. presidents as a function of given information specified on the horizontal. Solid line gives predictions from averaging theory; dashed line gives predictions from summation theory. (Adapted form Anderson & Graesser, 1976. Reprinted by permission of the American Psychological Association.)

215

9

THE RANDOMIZED RESPONSE TECHNIQUE

Philip Lichtenfels, Lowell Schipper, and Thomas Oakley

The randomized response technique (RRT) for obtaining information appears to be a particularly useful technique for psychologists. Perhaps its greatest virtue is an almost-assured guarantee of anonymity to the respondent — a guarantee almost self-evident on an a priori basis through the operation of the technique itself as carried out by the respondent. Along with this desirable feature of virtual anonymity is a high degree of accuracy in estimating a population proportion possessing traits, characteristics, or attitudes about which the respondent might reasonably be expected to be sensitive.

An initial brief description of one of the simplest uses of the randomized response techniques will provide a "feel" for its application. Consider the question, "Do you sometimes think you're really crazy?" In many contexts this question must have a low probability of being answered truthfully. Now consider the question, "Is the last digit of your social security number zero thru eight?" Put the two questions together on a little two item questionnaire and instruct each respondent to roll a die privately. If it comes up 1, 2, 3, or 4, answer Q_1. If it comes up 5 or 6, answer Q_2. Either question is answered in the same place so that the questioner does not know which question was answered.

Let P	=	probability Q_1 was answered = .67
1 - P	=	probability Q_2 was answered = .33
X	=	(the unknown) proportion of respondents who answer "yes" to Q_1
Y	=	proportion of respondents who have social security numbers ending in 0 through 8 and answer Q_2 (if selected) truthfully. Note that this proportion is unknown for the sample, but is approximately .90 in the population.

Tabulate the responses and record π, the proportion of "yes" responses.

$$\pi = PX + (1-P)Y$$
$$\pi = (.67)(X) + (.33)(.9)$$

And with π already tabulated, it's a simple task to solve for X, the estimated proportion of respondents who have sometimes thought they were really crazy. A mathematically similar type of questionnaire was described by Campbell and Joiner (1973) in summarizing a little classroom demonstration by a colleague. Models of the randomized response technique in this form can be labeled the Unrelated Question Type.

Oddly enough, Grant, Hake, and Hornseth (1951), in describing a study they had carried out in the field of what was then called "verbal conditioning" — a term long since discarded — introduced an equation of the form:

$$P_h = 1 - P_t - P_r + 2P_t P_r$$

where P_h = expected proportion of hits (correct binary predictions)

P_t = proportion of positive trials (light came on)

P_r = proportion of positive responses (light-on predictions)

This expression is nothing more than an expansion of

$$*P_h = P_r P_t + (1 - P_r) (1 - P_t),$$

as shown below

$$= P_r P_t + 1 - P_r - P_t + P_r P_t$$

$$= 1 - P_r - P_t + 2 P_r P_t.$$

Solving for P_r here is the equivalent of solving for X in the former equation. Expression * is the equation used by Warner (1965) in his seminal paper introducing the randomized response to the statistical literature.

This equation was later used by Schipper (1956) in determining whether stimulus sequences were random or non-random depending on whether or not the actual proportion of hits was close to or different from Expected P_h.

The original work by Warner (i.e. Warner, 1965) has been amplified and elaborated frequently in the statistical literature, but, strangely enough, it has received limited attention in psychology (cf. Begin & Boivin, 1980; Bourke, 1984; Fidler & Kleinknecht, 1977; Himmelforls & Lichteig, 1982; Kraemer, 1980; Levy, 1976, 1977; Shotland & Yankowski, 1982; Soeken & Macready, 1982), where it would seem to be most useful because of the multitude of embarrassing questions that could be asked directly with the concomitant high probability of evasive or untruthful answers.

The general progression of statistical papers dealing with RRT has been in the direction of modifications of the basic technique described by Warner: different numbers of alternative questions, different probabilities for responding to alternative questions, calculations of various probabilities for selecting alternative questions to minimize error in estimating true proportions of embarrassing characteristics, various techniques for selecting sensitive vs. non-sensitive questions, and elaboration of the technique to obtain more quantitative information (e.g. Abul-Ela, Greenberg, & Horvitz, 1967; Carr, Marascuilo, & Busk, 1982; Folsom, Greenberg, Horvitz, & Abernathy, 1973; Greenberg, Abul-Ela, Simmons, & Horvitz, 1969; Greenberg, Kuebler, Abernathy, & Horvitz, 1971; Liu & Chow, 1976; Moors, 1971; Poole, 1974; Warner, 1972). What we shall offer here is a summary of these modifications with recommendations for their use and some data obtained using our own innovations which seem to have worked out pretty well.

Actually, the simplest form of the technique is that proposed by Warner (1965). His procedure is reproduced below:

> Suppose that every person in a population belongs to either Group A or Group B, and it is required to estimate by survey the proportion belonging to Group A. A simple random sample of n people is drawn with replacement from the population and provisions made for each person to be interviewed. Before the interviews, each interviewer is furnished with an identical spinner with a face marked so that the spinner points to the letter A with probability p and to the letter B with probability $(1-p)$. Then, in each interview, the interviewee is asked to spin the spinner unobserved by the interviewer and report only whether or not the spinner points to the letter representing the group to which the interviewee belongs. That is, the interviewee is required only to say yes or no according to whether or not the spinner points to the correct group he does not report the group to which the spinner points.

The arithmetic that follows is simple and straightforward. Warner also presents handy tables to show the effects of various proportions of truthful and untruthful responses.

Papers appearing after Warner have tended (1) to improve estimates of anticipated proportions of yes and no responses for unrelated question, (2) to recommend those proportions that will introduce the least amount of error in estimating the "true" proportion of people in the population with the stigmatizing characteristic, and (3) to provide information which will enable the researcher to estimate sample size for specification on the bounds of accuracy. Most of these papers appear in the Journal of the American Statistical Association and are not difficult to read.

219

Perhaps the best summary of developments in the field is the chapter in <u>A Survey of Statistical Design and Linear Models</u> by Horvitz, Greenberg, and Abernathy (1975), although the chapter is short and its latest reference is from 1972. Their section labeled "Some Conclusions" is brief and worth reprinting in its entirety here.

> It seems clear that a very large number and variety of randomized response designs, all of which fit within the framework of Warner's linear randomized response model, are possible. There is still considerable room for further creative thinking and ingenuity in the construction of randomized response designs. The relative efficiencies of competing designs need to be studied somewhat more intensively than has been the case thus far. There is also a need to evaluate respondent reactions to various randomization devices and to alternative designs if more optimum designs are to emerge.
>
> There is little doubt that most of the existing traditional experimental designs can be adapted for use with randomized response. What is not at all clear is whether the randomized response idea has any possible application in areas other than with sensitive data. It appears that those statisticians who are not very concerned with sample surveys might examine developments with respect to randomized response designs and Warner's linear randomized response model to determine possible applications to other problems.

What we propose to show now, hopefully, is a bit of creative thinking and ingenuity with work employing the randomized response technique.

In the studies to be described here the randomization technique is one that can be used by many people, all responding at the same time. Additionally, many questions are asked in a single questionnaire rather than one question per respondent. Procedures like these have not been reported elsewhere. The closest procedure so far is one in which many questions may be asked but only one respondent at a time is involved and each question uses a separate randomization (see, for example, Fidler and Kleinknecht, 1977).

Experiment 1

In this study, estimates of proportions obtained from a group-administered, nine-item direct questionnaire were compared with estimates of proportions obtained for the same set of items using a group-administered, randomized response questionnaire. Questionnaires were administered in two introductory psychology classes in which 99% of the students were freshmen or sophomores. One-hundred and two students completed the direct questionnaire, 97 the randomized response questionnaire.

Items on the questionnaires were somewhat arbitrarily selected to be: (1) relevant to a group of college students, (2) representative of a range of issues from highly personal and sensitive to relatively innocuous, and (3) answerable yes or no.

The nine selected were subsequently scaled by 75 non-sample introductory psychology students using a pair comparisons technique. Every item was paired once with every other item on the questionnaire for the 36 item pairs with the within-pairs order counterbalanced across raters. Raters were instructed simply to select the more sensitive item in each pair. In calculating the scale values, Thurstone's Case V was assumed (i.e., no correlation between discriminal processes and equal discriminal dispersions). The resultant scale values are listed in Table I nest to each of the items with constants added to each scale value so that the least sensitive item has a scale value of 0.000.

Of special interest is the method for randomization used to collect sensitive information as compared with some earlier techniques which permitted the acquisition of only one respondent's data at a time. The randomization device for this study consisted of a sheet of wax paper with nine sticker "units" attached. These stickers were constructed by typing either a "T", "Y", of "N" on a "base" sticker. These letters were then covered with a smaller sticker. The base sticker plus the smaller sticker comprised one sticker unit. In every set of nine sticker units, there were five T's, two Y's, and two N's. The arrangements of these sticker units on each sheet of stickers were randomized across respondents.

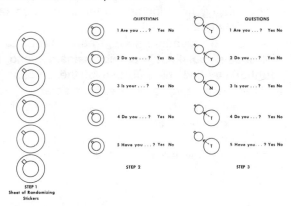

Figure 1. The randomizing device.

Respondents were instructed to remove sticker units from the sheet in any order and place them, in any order in circles next to the questions on the questionnaire. After having done this, respondents were instructed to pull the top stickers off the base stickers revealing the T's, Y's, and N's. A "T" next to an item meant that the respondent was to answer that item truthfully. A "Y" next to an item directed the respondent to answer "Yes" to the item, and an "N" directed a "No" response.

Instructions for using the randomizing device, which included an explanation of the protection it provided for a respondent, had been pretested on a small group of students in other classes in introductory psychology who had expressed their understanding of the purpose of the randomizing device and had provided suggestions for improvement of the instructions.

Procedure

Before the questionnaire was distributed, students were informed that they would be asked to answer a number of questions, some of which were highly personal in nature. They were encouraged to participate, but it was made clear to them that participation was strictly voluntary, and particularly offensive items could be left blank.

The randomized response and direct questionnaires were distributed in alternating fashion such that students sitting next to each other had different forms of the questionnaire. Students were asked to read the instructions carefully before answering any questions. In addition to being asked to answer the questionnaire items, students were requested to indicate their class (e.g., freshman) and sex at the top of the IBM answer sheet that was attached to the questionnaire. To protect confidentiality, no additional information was obtained that could be used to identify individuals.

After completing the questionnaires, respondents turned in the completed IBM sheets, but kept the questionnaires and a debriefing sheet which further clarified the purpose of the study. The classes were also debriefed as a group by the experimenter.

The results of the first study are summarized in Table 1. The entries in Table 1 are estimates of the proportions of "yes" answers of the (very crudely, non-randomly sampled) population of freshmen and sophomores enrolled at Bowling Green State University.

Table 1
Proportion Estimates for Experiment 1

	Scale Values	Direct				Randomized Response			
		Males (n = 31) (N = 2979)	NR*	Females (n = 71) (N = 4256)	NR	Males (n = 33) (N = 2979)	NR	Females (n = 64) (N = 4256)	NR
1. Have you ever masturbated?	1.194	.710 ± .191	(0)	.288 ± .111	(5)	1.006 ± .263	(1)	.440 ± .232	(4)
2. Have you ever shop-lifted?	.958	.484 ± .182	(0)	.257 ± .104	(1)	.725 ± .308	(1)	.350 ± .229	(4)
3. Have you ever considered committing suicide?	.927	.387 ± .177	(0)	.352 ± .113	(0)	.219 ± .302	(1)	.440 ± .232	(4)
4. If available, would you try LSD?	.670	.097 ± .108	(0)	.099 ± .071	(0)	.556 ± .317	(1)	.110 ± .209	(4)
5. If available would you try amphetamines (speed)?	.668	.226 ± .152	(0)	.282 ± .107	(0)	.106 ± .286	(1)	.320 ± .228	(4)
6. Is your parents' income greater than $12,000 a year?	.582	.935 ± .090	(0)	.930 ± .060	(0)	1.175 ± .210	(1)	.830 ± .216	(4)
7. Do you smoke marijuana more than once a week?	.461	.355 ± .174	(0)	.197 ± .094	(0)	.331 ± .312	(1)	.170 ± .216	(4)
8. Are you a democrat?	.143	.267 ± .163	(1)	.373 ± .118	(4)	.106 ± .286	(1)	.290 ± .226	(4)
9. Do you enjoy college?	.000	.968 ± .064	(0)	.901 ± .071	(0)	.950 ± .276	(1)	.860 ± .213	(4)

*NR = no response

Population proportion estimates for the direct questionnaire were calculated using equation 1 (from Mendenhall, Ott, & Schaeffer, 1971):

$$\hat{p} = \frac{y}{n} \qquad (1)$$

where

$\hat{p}$ = proportion estimate of yes responses
y = sample number of yes responses
n = sample size

The bound on the error of the proportion estimate was approximated using equation 2 (also from Mendenhall et al, 1971).

$$b = 2\sqrt{\frac{\hat{p}\hat{q}}{n-1} \frac{N-n}{N}} \qquad (2)$$

$$= 2\sqrt{\hat{V}(\hat{p})}$$

where b is the bound on the error of estimate.

q = $1 - p$

N = population size (i.e., number of male freshmen and sophomores, N_m = 2979, and number of female freshmen and sophomores, N_f = 4256).

$\hat{V}(\hat{p})$ = variance estimate for $\hat{p}$.

The estimated proportions of yes responses for each item on the randomized response questionnaire were obtained using the equation provided by Fidler and Kleinknecht (1977).

$$P_{rr} = \frac{Y_s - Y_f}{p} \qquad (3)$$

where

Y_s = proportion of yesses in the sample
Y_f = expected proportion of forced yes responses
p = expected proportion of truthful responses

A 95% bound on the error of estimation was approximated by doubling the square root of the variance estimate formula derived for use with the randomized response technique by Fidler and Kleinknecht (1977). This bound very probably is an overestimate because of the non-replacement technique used here.

$$b_{rr} = 2\sqrt{\frac{Y_s (1-Y_s)}{nP^2}} \qquad (4)$$

Two of the parameters in equation (3) are the expected number of forced yesses and truthful answers. To the extent that the actual proportions of forced yesses and truthful answers deviate from the expected values, the estimated proportion of yes responses will be unreliable. It is this type of "method" variance which makes it possible to obtain proportion estimates from formula (3) greater than 1.00 or less than 0.000. This method variance casts some doubt upon the validity of proportion estimates obtained (1) from unreplicated administrations of randomized response questionnaires, or (2) with small samples.

Experiment 2

In this study, proportion estimates obtained from a mailed-out, 10-item direct questionnaire were compared to the proportion estimates obtained for the same set of items using a mailed-out randomized response questionnaire.

Subjects. Subjects in this study were on-campus students selected at random from a campus telephone directory. Four hundred ninety-nine direct questionnaires and 474 randomized response questionnaires were sent out through campus mail. Two-hundred and six completed randomized response questionnaire answer sheets were returned for a response rate of 43%, while 192 completed direct questionnaire answer sheets were returned for a response rate of 38%.

Item Selection and Scaling. Four items were retained from experiment 1 and six new items were added. Again, the items were selected to (1) be relevant to a college sample, (2) range in sensitivity from innocuous to highly personal, and (3) be answerable with a yes or no.

These items were also scaled for sensitivity by the same subjects that did the scaling in experiment one (plus two additional subjects). Again, the method of pair comparisons was used, although this time there were 45 pairs of items to be compared. The resultant scale values are listed in Table II next to each of the items. A constant has been added to each of these values so that the least sensitive item has a scale value of 0.000.

Randomization Device.   The randomization device was identical to that used in the first study, except that this time there were 10 sticker units (6 "T's," 2 "Y's", and 2 "N's").   Their order was randomized across subjects.

Procedure.   Subjects received an envelope that contained either a direct or randomized questionnaire.   A cover letter explained the purpose of the study and emphasized that participation was encouraged but strictly voluntary and that partially filled out questionnaires would be useful.   Subject confidentiality was guaranteed.   Subjects placed the completed IBM answer sheets in campus envelopes addressed to the authors.

Results of Experiment 2

Responses to the questionnaire were analyzed in a manner identical to that described for Experiment 1.   Table 2 shows the analysis for only those freshmen and sophomores on campus in the mail survey while Table 3 presents the results for the complete more heterogeneous group of freshmen through seniors.   Table 4 provides a handy comparison for those questions that were the same in both studies.

A multitude of comparisons from question to question, survey techniques (RRT vs. direct), and mail vs. in-class could be made with the data reported here.   To us, the actual proportions of affirmative responses are of little interest.   That the RRT technique in its various forms "works" is also of little novelty.   What we should like to emphasize is that adaptation of the basic one-on-one original technique to group or survey procedures.   With judicious choices of proportions of forced yesses, noes and truthful responses and with proper basic sampling procedures a great deal of reliable and inexpensive information can be obtained which hitherto would have been difficult to uncover.

Table 2

Proportion Estimates for Experiment 2 (Freshmen and Sophomores, On-Campus)

		Direct				Randomized Response			
	Scale Values	Males (n = 41) (N = 2172)	NR*	Females (n = 80) (N = 3482)	NR	Males (n = 41) (N = 2172)	NR	Females (n = 97) (N = 3482)	NR
1. Have you ever masturbated?	1.864	.821 ± .123	(2)	.351 ± .111	(6)	.708 ± .240	(1)	.596 ± .168	(2)
2. Have you ever cheated on a college test?	1.689	.512 ± .157	(0)	.338 ± .106	(0)	.480 ± .260	(0)	.500 ± .170	(1)
3. Have you ever shop-lifted?	1.527	.512 ± .157	(0)	.425 ± .110	(0)	.561 ± .258	(0)	.413 ± .168	(1)
4. Would you mind having a roommate of a color other than you own?	1.137	.439 ± .155	(0)	.350 ± .106	(0)	.683 ± .242	(0)	.577 ± .167	(1)
5. Do you smoke marijuana more than once a week?	.999	.439 ± .155	(0)	.138 ± .077	(0)	.236 ± .221	(0)	.148 ± .120	(0)
6. Do you believe in a supreme being?	.957	.875 ± .105	(1)	.913 ± .063	(0)		(0)		(0)
7. Is the SGA a worthwhile organization?	.714	.634 ± .152	(0)	.467 ± .115	(5)	.667 ± .248	(1)	.622 ± .165	(1)
8. Do you enjoy college?	.523	.878 ± .103	(0)	.988 ± .024	(0)	.764 ± .221	(0)	.990 ± .034	(0)
9. Do you hold a part-time job during the school year?	.406	.317 ± .146	(0)	.350 ± .106	(0)	.195 ± .206	(0)	.440 ± .168	(0)
10. Do you enjoy outdoor sports?	.000	.951 ± .068	(0)	.988 ± .024	(0)	.846 ± .188	(0)	.951 ± .073	(1)

*NR = no response

227

Table 3
Proportion Estimates for Experiment 2 (Freshmen and Sophomores, Juniors, Seniors; Combined)

	Scale Values	Direct				Randomized Response			
		Males (n = 52) (N = 2955)	NR*	Females (n = 109) (N = 4592)	NR	Males (n = 51) (N = 2955)	NR	Females (n = 135) (N = 4592)	NR
1. Have you ever masturbated?	1.864	.860 ± .098	(2)	.417 ± .097	(6)	.767 ± .199	(1)	.531 ± .144	(2)
2. Have you ever cheated on a college test?	1.689	.500 ± .139	(0)	.402 ± .096	(7)	.517 ± .233	(0)	.469 ± .143	(0)
3. Have you ever shop-lifted?	1.527	.538 ± .138	(0)	.431 ± .094	(0)	.647 ± .223	(0)	.351 ± .137	(1)
4. Would you mind having a roommate of a color other than you own?	1.137	.404 ± .136	(0)	.358 ± .091	(0)	.582 ± .230	(0)	.580 ± .142	(0)
5. Do you smoke marijuana more than once a week?	.999	.500 ± .139	(0)	.138 ± .066	(0)	.222 ± .194	(0)	.123 ± .094	(0)
6. Do you believe in a supreme being?	.957	.882 ± .090	(1)	.927 ± .046	(0)	.974 ± .074	(0)	.105 ± .000	(0)
7. Is the SGA a worthwhile organization?	.714	.577 ± .137	(0)	.697 ± .087	(0)	.633 ± .227	(1)	.605 ± .140	(0)
8. Do you enjoy college?	.523	.904 ± .082	(0)	.991 ± .018	(0)	.843 ± .170	(0)	.988 ± .031	(0)
9. Do you hold a part-time job during the school year?	.406	.808 ± .109	(0)	.385 ± .093	(0)		(0)	.457 ± .143	(0)
10. Do you enjoy outdoor sports?	.000	.962 ± .053	(0)	.972 ± .031	(0)	.843 ± .170	(0)	.914 ± .080	(0)

*NR = no response

Table 4
Proportion Estimates for Items Repeated in Experiments 1 & 2

| | Experiment 1 | | | | Experiment 2 (Fr. and So., On-Campus) | | | |
| | Direct | | Randomized Response | | Direct | | Randomized Response | |
	(n = 31, N = 2979) NR*		(n = 33, N = 2979) NR		(n = 41, N = 2172) NR		(n = 41, N = 2172) NR	
MALES								
1. Have you ever masturbated?	.710 ± .191	(0)	1.006 ± .263	(1)	.821 ± .123	(2)	.708 ± .240	(1)
2. Have you ever shop-lifted?	.484 ± .182	(0)	.725 ± .308	(1)	.512 ± .157	(0)	.561 ± .258	(0)
3. Do you smoke marijuana more than once a week?	.355 ± .174	(0)	.331 ± .312	(1)	.439 ± .155	(0)	.236 ± .221	(0)
4. Do you enjoy college?	.968 ± .064	(0)	.950 ± .276	(1)	.878 ± .103	(0)	.764 ± .221	(0)
	Direct		Randomized Response		Direct		Randomized Response	
	(n = 71, N = 4256) NR*		(n = 64, N = 4256) NR		(n = 80, N = 3482) NR		(n = 97, N = 3482) NR	
FEMALES								
1. Have you ever masturbated?	.288 ± .111	(5)	.440 ± .232	(4)	.351 ± .111	(6)	.596 ± .168	(2)
2. Have you ever shop-lifted?	.257 ± .104	(1)	.350 ± .229	(4)	.425 ± .110	(0)	.413 ± .168	(1)
3. Do you smoke marijuana more than once a week?	.197 ± .094	(0)	.170 ± .216	(4)	.138 ± .077	(0)	.148 ± .120	(0)
4. Do you enjoy college?	.901 ± .071	(0)	.860 ± .213	(4)	.988 ± .024	(0)	.990 ± .034	(0)

*NR = no response

Note: Lowell Schipper, who recently passed away, was a student of Dave Grant. The first and third authors were students of Lowell Schipper at Bowling Green State University. Order of authorship was determined randomly. The authors express their appreciation to the various people at the Air Force Human Resources Laboratory at Williams Air Force Base, Arizona, for some of the time and assistance involved in the completion of this chapter.

REFERENCES

Abul-Ela, A.A., Greenberg, B.G., & Horvitz, D.G. (1967). A multiproportions randomized response model. Journal of the American Statistical Association, 62 (319), 990-1008.

Begin, G., & Boivin, M. (1980). Comparison of data gathered on sensitive questions via direct questionnaire, randomized response technique, and a projective method. Psychological Reports., 47, 743-750.

Bourke, P.D. (1984). Estimation of proportions using symmetric randomized response designs. Psychological Bulletin, 96 (1), 116-133.

Campbell, C., & Joiner, B.L. (1973). How to get the answer without being sure you've asked the question. The American Statistician, 27 (5), 229-231.

Carr, J.W., Marascuilo, L.A., & Busk, P. (1982). Optimal randomized response models and methods for hypothesis testing. Journal of Educational Statistics, 7, 295-310.

Fidler, D.S., & Kleinknecht, R.E. (1977). Randomized response versus direct questioning: Two data-collection methods for sensitive information. Psychological Bulletin, 84 (5), 1045-1049.

Folsom, R.E., Greenberg, B.G., Horvitz, D.G., & Abernathy, J.R. (1973). The two alternate questions randomized response model for human surveys. Journal of the American Statistical Association, 68, (343), 525-530.

Himmelforls, S., & Lichteig, C. (1982). Social desirability and the randomized response technique. Journal of Personality and Social Psychology, 43 (4), 710-717.

Grant, D.A., Hake, H.W., & Hornseth, J.P. (1951). Acquisition and extinction of a verbal conditioned response with difference percentages of reinforcement. Journal of Experimental Psychology, 42 (1), 1-5.

Greenberg, B.G., Abul-Ela, A.A., Simmons, W.R., & Horvitz, D.G. (1969). The unrelated question randomized response model: Theoretical framework. Journal of the American Statistical Association, 64 (326), 520-539.

Greenberg, B.G., Kuebler, R.R., Jr., Abernathy, J.R., & Horvitz, D.G. (1971). Application of the randomized response technique in obtaining quantitative data. Journal of the American Statistical Association, 66 (334), 243-250.

Horvitz, D.G., Greenberg, B.G., & Abernathy, J.R. (1975). Recent developments in randomized response designs. In J.N. Strivastava (Ed.), A survey of statistical design and linear models (pp. 271-285). Amsterdam: North-Holland.

Kraemer, H.C. (1980). Estimation and testing of bivariate association using data generated by the randomized response technique. Psychological Bulletin, 87 (2), 166-172.

Levy, K.J. (1976). Reducing the occurrence of omitted or untruthful responses when testing hypotheses concerning proportions. Psychological Bulletin, 83 (5), 757-761.

Levy, K.J. (1977). The randomized response technique and large sample comparisons among the parameters of K independent binomial populations. Psychological Bulletin, 84 (2), 244-246.

Liu, P.T., & Chow, L.P. (1976). A new discrete quantitative randomized response model. Journal of the American Statistical Association, 71 (353), 72-73.

Mendenhall, W., Ott, L., & Schaeffer, R.L. (1971). Elementary survey sampling. Belmont, CA: Duxbury Press.

Moors, J.J.A. (1971). Optimization of the unrelated question randomized response model. Journal of the American Statistical Association, 66 (335), 627-629.

Poole, W.K. (1974). Estimation of the distribution function of a continuous type random variable through randomized response. Journal of the American Statistical Association, 69 (348), 1002-1005.

Schipper, L.M. (1956). Prediction of critical events in contexts of different numbers of alternative events. Journal of Experimental Psychology, 52 (6), 377-380.

Shotland, R.L., & Yankowski, L.D. (1982). The random response method: A valid and ethical indicator of "truth" in reactive situations. Personality and Social Psychology Bulletin, 8 (1), 174-179.

Soeken, K.L., & Macready, G.B. (1982). Respondents perceived protection when using randomized response. Psychological Bulletin, 92 (2), 487-489.

Warner, S.L. (1965). Randomized response: A survey technique for eliminating evasive answer bias. Journal of the American Statistical Association, 60 (309), 63-69.

Warner, S.L. (1972). The linear randomized response model. Journal of the American Statistical Association, 66 (336), 884-888.

FROM EXPERIMENTAL PSYCHOLOGY TO HUMAN BEHAVIOR AS A NATURAL SCIENCE

Joan S. Lockard

In the excitement of a new specialty such as biological mechanisms of behavior, students and colleagues alike often lose sight of the precursors which spawned the immediate scientific productivity. An historical perspective, although not popular, makes explicit the continuity of a discipline, giving credit to those ideas and individuals which provided the impetus, as well as indicating the past mistakes and dead ends to avoid in the future. From Pavlov's time on, experimental psychologists have demonstrated a precision in methodology (Boring, 1959) which far exceeded the scientific value of their data. Clad in white coats and working industriously in laboratories instrumented to reveal "basic principles of learning", they practiced an art of experimental design and mathematical analysis unequaled by most other related disciplines. Yet the animal under study, white rat or human, could not be understood by its lever press or eye blink alone. These were responses which awaited a serious commitment to biology and natural selection before their quantification became meaningful. Since 1970, the methodological promise of experimental psychology is being realized, though the nomenclature may be different. From laws of learning (e.g., Thorndike, 1898) to neuromechanisms of memory (e.g., Ojemann, 1979); from classical conditioning (e.g., Pavlov, 1906) to biofeedback (e.g., Wyler, Lockard, Ward & Finch, 1976); from operant rate (e.g., Ferster & Skinner, 1957) to normative behaviors (e.g., Lockard, 1980a, 1980d); whatever the terms, psychology is fast becoming a life science. Nowhere is this metamorphosis more evident than in the study of human social behavior (Hinde, 1982; Lockard, 1980b).

Human Behavior as a Natural Science

While the evolutionary foundation for the study of the adaptive significance of human social behavior was laid by Darwin (1859, 1871, 1872) and the statistical tools readied by Fisher (1925, 1935, 1949, 1956), only more recently has the theoretical sophistication been sufficient to merit serious focus. Behaviorism essentially devoid of biology spanned the interim (e.g., McDougall, 1908; Thorndike, 1911; Watson, 1913; Skinner, 1938; Hull, 1943; Spence, 1956). The impetus was a little noticed concept (at the time) called **inclusive fitness** (Hamilton, 1964). It embodied the idea that reproductive success could be assessed not only in terms of number of offspring of breeding age, but also the accumulation of genes held in common with all other close relatives. Thus, an individual's inclusive fitness came to be regarded as the sum of its own fitness (i.e., reproductive success: number of offspring) plus all its influence on the fitness of its relatives (Wilson, 1975). In its simplest interpretation, the concept suggested that there were alternative ways to contribute to the gene pool of future generations. In its more global ramifications, it crystallized the adaptive significance of helping others (altruism; Hamilton, 1963) who are able to return the favor (reciprocal altruism; Trivers, 1971), especially kin (kin selection; Kurland, 1980), and revealed the benefit of manipulation of others (deceit; Trivers, 1985), particularly non-kin, to one's genetically selfish ends (Dawkins, 1982).

In essence, the concept of inclusive fitness brought such complex subjects as nepotism, reciprocity and deception under the rubric of biology. In its satirical manifestations it pits population against population (evolutionary stable strategy; Maynard-Smith, 1976); man against man (sexual selection; Trivers, 1972; deception; Wallace, 1973; Lockard, Kirkevold, & Kalk, 1980); brother against brother (sibling rivalry; Alexander, 1974); husband against wife (different mating strategies; Trivers, 1972); parent against child (parent-offspring conflict; Trivers, 1974); mocks mother love (parental manipulation; Alexander, 1974); and leads to the revelation that individuals are gene machines (Dawkins, 1976) who are self-deceived biologically (Lockard, 1980c; Lockard & Paulhus, 1988) and who communicate with other to manipulate their musculature to one's own advantage (Dawkins, 1982). In its practical applications, it provides insights into such mundane phenomena as the adoring qualities of infants, the dotingness of grandparents, and the indulgence of favorite uncles (e.g., Robinson, Lockard, & Adams, 1979). However, in its most dangerous form, it may explain all and provide little in the way of additional scientific knowledge and understanding.

The problem in utilizing evolutionary theory as a basis to study human behavior rests mainly with the lack of specificity of the research hypotheses proposed. Sometimes the predictions have been altered after the fact to be consistent with accumulated data. Even when the hypotheses have been expounded prior to the gathering of data, their generality has frequently rendered them nonrejectable. Therefore, a paucity of relevant data has derived from a failure to sort out single variables for study, to effectively randomize irrelevant variables or to discard unsupported hypotheses. Statistically testable questions of human behavior suffer less from these errors, especially when they are coupled with good experimental design and procedures.

An application of statistical techniques in experimental psychology to research in human ethology is depicted in several studies (e.g., Lockard, McDonald, Clifford, & Martinez, 1976; Lockard, Schiele, Allen, & Wiemer, 1978; Lockard & Adams, 1980; Gunderson & Lockard, 1980) in which animal models of human behavior were proposed. In the past, the application of such models to human social behavior has had limited scientific return (e.g., Morris, 1967; Tiger and Fox, 1966). The research challenge lay with precise questions which could, in fact, be answered.

Peripheral Males. A study by Lockard and Adams (1980) proposed a human analogy of an adolescent primate subgroup. Observations in the literature (Chivers, 1971; Cohen, 1971; Hall & Devore, 1965; Harcourt, Steward, & Fossey, 1976; Hinde, 1983; Hrdy, 1977; Schaller, 1963; Sugiyama & Ohsawa, 1974) suggest that males of several nonhuman primate species exhibit a subadult stage not shared by females. While females appeared to be gradually integrated into the group upon reaching reproductive age, some older juvenile males remain apart (i.e., peripheral), associating largely with same-sex peers. Evidence regarding a comparable stage in the development of human males (18-20 year olds) was sought by an analysis of the relative frequencies of various age/sex groupings in public.

An ethological approach was utilized in the research, where the number and age-sex classification of individuals within groups passing along a definable path were recorded. Data gathering was carried out in public places where a demographic cross-section of a city was likely to be seen and where there were no apparent rigid constraints on group composition. Five trained observers with a statistically significant (p<.01) interobserver reliability coefficient ranging from .75 to .98 (for all possible pairs of observers and for each of the study locations) recorded collectively the age and sex of the members of 11,536 groups of from 1 to 6 members, of which 4,574 were appropriate to this study. Prior to the conduct of the research, the observers were well practiced in age estimation to a mean directional variance (for both female and male subjects) of less than 1 1/2 years for the age range (12-26 year olds) under study. The estimated age and sex of members of all groups exiting along well-defined paths from two large shopping malls were recorded from 7 to 9 p.m. weekdays and 1 to 5 p.m. weekends.

The hypothesis tested was whether there would be revealed a disproportionately higher frequency than expected of subadult (age 18-20 years), all-male groups (with three or more members). It was assumed that for subadult males such an outcome would be indicative of difficulty in sexual competition as compared to older males, a greater likelihood of separation from natal units, and an increased association with more than one same-sex peer. The data were subjected to computer analysis and observed frequencies of specified age-sex groupings were compared by chi square statistics to expected frequencies based on a binomial distribution (Table 1). For example, in considering dyadic groups only (i=j=2), the probability of either a female or a male being observed in public alone was assumed to be 0.50 and, therefore, $R_2 = 1.00$. The expected coefficient for a same-sex dyad was then the product of the probability of a same-sex dyad and the probability of a dyad in general, i.e. $(0.50)^2$ x 1.00 = 0.25. The expected coefficient of a mixed dyad was simply obtained by subtraction from 1.00, the sum of the expected coefficients of same-sex dyads, i.e., 1.00-(0.25 + 0.25) = 0.5. The observed frequency of all dyads of a group age category was then multiplied by these expected coefficients to manifest the expected frequencies of occurrence for the same-sex dyads and mixed-sex dyads, as shown in Figure 1. In a similar fashion, the expected frequencies for triads (i=j=3), quadrads (i=j=4), and triads and quadrads combined (i=3, j=4) were computed.

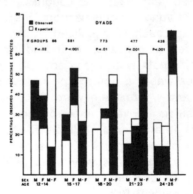

Figure 1: Dyads: For five age categories, the percentage of male, female and mixed-sex pairs observed in public vs. percentage expected based on a binomial distribution. Subadult males (18-20 years old) are the focus in which a no greater than expected frequency of same-sex male dyads are seen, but their frequency does differ from same-sex female and mixed-sex pairs. Statistical significance using a chi-square test is indicated by a probability statement (e.g., p<.01). (Adapted from Lockard & Adams, 1980. Reprinted by permission of The Psychonomic Society.)

236

Table 1
Determination of Expected Frequencies with a Binomial Model

i	=	lower limit of group size
j	=	upper limit of group size
Gij	=	observed frequency of groups of size i to j that meet group age category requirement(s)
Gk	=	observed frequency of groups of size k, k = i, j

$$Gij = \sum_{k=1}^{j} Gk$$

m	=	# males in the entire population that meet age category requriement(s)
f	=	# females in the entire population that meet age category requirement(s)
T	=	m + f
P_M	=	m/T
P_F	=	f/T
Rk	=	Gk/Gij, k = i, j (probability of k group in the Gij groups)

Expected coefficients:

$$E_{ij}^{M} = \sum_{k=1}^{j} (P_M)^k \cdot Rk \qquad \text{(males)}$$

$$E_{ij}^{F} = \sum_{k=1}^{j} (P_F)^k \cdot Rk \qquad \text{(females)}$$

$$E_{ij}^{X} = 1 - \left(E_{ij}^{M} + E_{ij}^{F} \right) \qquad \text{(mixed)}$$

Expected coefficients:

$$N_{ij}^{M} = E_{ij}^{M} \cdot Gij \qquad \text{(males)}$$

$$N_{ij}^{F} = E_{ij}^{F} \cdot Gij \qquad \text{(females)}$$

$$N_{ij}^{X} = E_{ij}^{X} \cdot Gij \qquad \text{(mixed)}$$

With respect to the hypothesis under study, Figure 2 shows the percentage comparisons for groups of triads and quadrads. It is evident from the data that groups of 3 to 4 subadult males (18-20 years old) were out in public in much greater frequency than would be expected and in greater frequency than comparable-age female groups (x^2=105.86, df=8, p<.001). This finding was further emphasized by the fact that, while the differential between the observed and expected frequencies of male triads was increasing from ages 15-20, the differential for female triads was decreasing over the same age range.

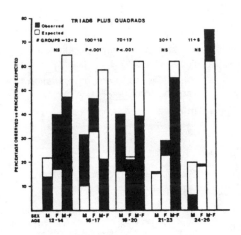

Figure 2: Triads and quadrads: For five age categories, the percentage of male, female and mixed-sex groups of three to four individuals (e.g., 70+17=87 triads and quadrads) observed in public vs percentage expected, based on a binomial distribution. Subadult males (18-20 years old) are the focus in which a greater than expected frequency of same-sex male groups are seen compared to either all-female or mixed-sex groups. Statistical significance using a chi-square test is indicated by a probability statement (e.g., p<.001); NS=not significant. (Adapted from Lockard & Adams, 1980. Reprinted by permission of The Psychonomic Society.)

Since the initial hypothesis was supported by the results, other questions were subsequently entertained as to why subadult males group together. The prevalence of male triads was not simply a function of the sex ratio in this category, as in total numbers (singletons, dyads, triads, etc.) there were more female (N=1,269) than male (N=1,143) 18-20 year olds observed. As has been suggested for other primate species, it is possible that human subadult males are sexually mature, but neither physically nor experientially developed sufficiently to compete with older males for either females or essen-

238

tial resources in their society. However, if males showed a simple developmental lag equivalent to the national age difference at marriage, namely, males 2.4 years older (Presser, 1975), the groupings of males and females of these two age categories should be roughly mirror images of one another, which they were not. The data were not a matter of straight economics either (i.e., females pairing with older males of "means") as an excess of younger males was not evident in a greater than expected number.

Perhaps these male groupings reflect and, therefore, convey a message of "availability." It could be that at 18-20 years of age, pairs of individuals, be they male, female, or mixed-sex dyads, represent an already accomplished transition to adulthood. Supportive of this view, Konner (1976) suggests that only older juvenile males in hunter-gatherer and nonhuman primate societies should form same-age peer groups. He reasoned that late-adolescent males benefit the least from cross-age groups in that, for example, they have little need for practicing alloparental behavior. In modern human societies, subadult males may, in fact, be practicing to become adult males by testing their abilities against males of similar ages while waiting for an opportunity to pair with females. That subadult males are seen with some prevalence in groups of three or four in shopping malls may be indicative of an even greater tendency for them to band together in less adult-oriented areas of a city (i.e., literally peripheral males). The latter hypothesis was tested in a recent study (Lockard, Schemann & Adams, manuscript in preparation).

All-night food stores (18 individual stores of the 7-11 food chain) in Seattle, Washington, were utilized as peripheral sites, i.e., they were regarded as not part of the usual adult shopping routine. The age-sex groupings (N~4000) of the patrons (N~10,000) for all hours of the day and night were recorded by 14 trained observers over a period of six months (January through June, 1980). The data strongly indicated that a disproportionate number of subadult males in groups of 3 or more frequented these stores, particularly after midnight. This finding suggested that not only are older juvenile males peripheral in location, they are also out of phase with "The Establishment."

Sharing Behavior. In psychology, and science more generally, no one study is all encompassing. As was the case above, initial research is usually conducted to establish a phenomenon for subsequent, more selective pursuit. Replication is also an essential ingredient of any precise discipline, as unique events are not amenable to further inquiry. Moreover, systematic manipulation of the variables under scrutiny to produce the predicted outcome helps to establish the extent to which they control the phenomenon and, thus, how well the phenomenon is understood. As a second example in tracing some of the methodological roots from experimental psychology to the study of human social behavior, two projects on resource sharing by Lockard, McDonald, Clifford, & Martinez, (1976) will be considered. A pilot effort (N=79) provided empirical support for the idea that donating money stems from evolved tendencies to food share. A second larger study (N=447) ascertained the likelihood that implied reciprocity may be a crucial factor in giving. Again a primate model was used to select the variables on which to concentrate.

Food sharing among nonhuman primates has been documented only for chimpanzees (Teleki, 1973a; 1973b) and gibbons (Ellefsom, 1967; Schessler & Nash, 1977) while baboons (Strum, 1975) sometimes tolerate the stealing of food. In chimpanzees, food sharing occurs among relatives (van Lawick-Goodall, 1972), such as between a mother and her offspring or between siblings, or among non-relatives such as a "hunting party" of adult males who divide the spoils among themselves (Teleki, 1973b) according to certain "rules-of-the-game." In either case, getting one's share is a function of exhibiting appropriate behaviors.

The evolution of sharing food with relatives could be mediated by kin selection (Hamilton, 1963), with the sharing increasing the fitness of individuals with common genes. Sharing food with non-kin may be mediated by reciprocal altruism (Trivers, 1971) where a "favor" now by one individual is returned at some later time by the recipient. As is well known, the sharing of food and other resources among humans is an established practice (Dumond, 1975). However, the essential behaviors, rules, and contexts have not been well defined (Feinman, 1979).

Panhandling was selected as an appropriate social context since supposedly a needy individual request or begs for money from a potentially more solvent stranger. Observations of several panhandlers had suggested that sex, eye contact, postural stance, dress, weather and the amount of money requested may be important factors in successfully acquiring a donation. In the studies proper, several confederates were used as panhandlers since the research time involved to acquire a sufficient number of sightings of actual panhandlers would have been excessive.

The studies were designed to answer four specific questions: Which individuals share with strangers? What characteristics of the panhandlers facilitate sharing? What aspects of the environment influence the process? And, what percentage of people share when kin selection is not applicable and reciprocity unlikely?

In the pilot study two male "panhandlers" (college students) approached 79 different target groupings — either a single male, a single female, two males, two females, or a male and a female together. The approach was either with a submissive posture (bent head, stooped shoulder, no eye contact, and the right hand extended in a begging gesture) or with a dominant stance (upright posture, erect head, eye contact and no begging gesture). Panhandlers were dressed either nicely or shabbily and each time requested 10 cents without explanation. Target individuals who were either obviously at the moment consuming food or who were not eating and had no food in sight were approached in public places on sunny and overcast days during spring.

The more comprehensive second study compared the success rate of male and female panhandlers and an additional target category was included, namely, a family grouping consisting on one adult female, one adult male, and at least one child. The panhandlers were two female and two male (the same as in the first study) college students who dressed casually (neither nice nor shabby) and again asked for 10 cents without explanation, but this time during the autumn season.

The main effects of both studies are shown in Table 2 and are largely self-explanatory. The clothes the panhandler wore or whether the sun was shining (both not shown in Table 2 were not significant in achieving 10 cents in the first study. However, the season was important since the rate of success for the male panhandlers in spring (53%) was considerably higher than for the same males in autumn (26%).

The interactions of the main study are shown in Figure 3 and indicate that male panhandlers were comparatively successful only when submissively approaching females who were eating, and females were considerably more successful than male panhandlers, particularly when submissively approaching males who were eating, or when approaching in a dominant posture, a single female or a single male who was not eating. Targets of more than one individual, but especially a family or a male and a female together, were resistant to giving in this situation. The most potent variable was whether the target individuals were eating. Moreover, many target individuals who were eating tended to offer some of their food to the panhandler in addition to giving 10 cents.

Table 2

Panhandling 10¢

	Pilot Study (N=79) During Autumn			Main Study (-447) During Spring		
Variables	% Success	X^2	P	% Success	X^2	P
Panhandler's Sex:						
Female	—			41.0		
		34.0 <			11.21	<.001
Male	53.2			26.0		
Food:						
With	69.8			45.8		
		8.95	<.055		26.06	<.001
Without	36.1			22.9		
Approach:						
Dominant	58.6			38.1		
		1.12	<.25		3.14	<.10
Submissive	49.3			30.1		
Target Grouping:						
(a) M+MM	22.2	22.60(a, b)	<.001			
(b) F+FF	88.0	5.08(a, c)	<.05			
(c) FM	51.9	7.96(b, c)	<.01			

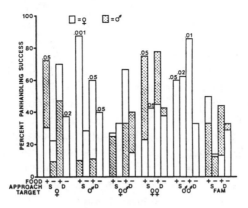

Figure 3: Comparative success of female and male "panhandlers" individually approaching an approximately equal number of target groupings of (a) one or two females or males, (b) a female and male pair, (c) a family with at least one child. Significant differences between male and female panhandlers using a chi-square test are shown in terms of probability statements above the respective bars. Panhandlers approached either submissively (S) or dominantly (D) a target target consuming food (+) or not (-); FAM=family. Panhandling was generally more successful if targets were eating, and families were most resistant to giving. (Adapted from Lockard, McDonald, Clifford, & Martinez, 1976. Reprinted by permission of the American Association for the Advancement of Science.)

The salient points of this research are missed if the reader focuses mainly on situational interpretations (i.e., proximal explanations) of the data (Knowles, 1977; Lockard, 1977). Although the panhandlers were college students, the target groups were not, and the panhandling was done at locations for the general public, not on a college campus. Even more to the point, in spite of the fact that a donated dime is a small cost in our society today and would most probably not be viewed by the donor as either a great expenditure or as a great benefit to the recipient, the various target groups were differentially resistant to giving to a panhandler. The resistance of family groups to being panhandled and the importance of food consumption by the targets for successful panhandling are findings compatible with distal explanations (i.e., ultimate causation based on evolution by natural selection). In other words, the common practice among humans of trading resources may have its origin in primitive food sharing tendencies.

There has been considerable bias against explanations based on evolution since largely proximal questions have been asked. Moreover, distal and proximal explanations of the same behavior may often be superficially inconsonant with one another. For instance, to explain that we eat because we are hungry or we take care of our children

243

because we love them are proximal reasons (based in part on our physiological state and hormonal levels) and may have little intuitive similarity to distal relationships (with which they are undoubtedly intimately correlated) of food availability and survival, or parental investment and reproductive success.

Smiling versus Laughter. In utilizing animal models to facilitate the study of human behavior, the underlying assumption most often made is that the similarity in behavior between the model and the human is analogous (of like function) but not necessarily homologous (of common ancestry). This is the case also for comparative psychology, however, here each animal species being studied may be of interest in itself and not as a model of human behavior. Alternatively, the focus could include human behavior where the animal species under consideration are not regarded as models **per se** but where the behaviors being compared are thought to be homologous. The third example in this discourse on the study of human social behavior is in this latter category and suggests not only a phylogenetic difference in origin of smiling and laughter but a homologous similarity of each behavior respectively, across several species of primates (e.g., guenons, macaques, baboons and chimpanzees) including hominids (Kirkevold, Lockard, & Heestand, 1983).

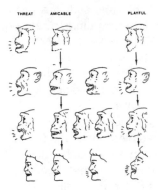

Figure 4: Sketches illustrating the possibly differing origins of human smiling and laughter. The threat (left), silent-bared teeth submissive grimace (amicable), and relaxed-open mouth display of play (right) are shown for the vervet monkey (top), rhesus, macaque, chimpanzee and human (bottom). The last three species have intermediate expressions between amicable and playful. (Adapted from van Hooff, 1972. Reprinted by permission of the Cambridge University Press.)

The consensus in the literature had placed the facial expression of smiling and laughter on either a continuum of graded intensities

244

(Andrew, 1963, 1965) or suggested that initially they were of two different origins (Figure 4) that have converged essentially one display with several degrees of intensity (Hinde, 1972, 1974; Jolly, 1985; van Hooff, 1967, 1971, 1972). Smiling was thought to have its origin in the silent-bared teeth submissive grimace of primates (Figure 4, amicable) and laughter to have come from the relaxed open-mouth display of play (Figure 4, playful). However, in a study by Lockard, Smith, Fahrenbruch, & Morgan (1977), it was proposed that whereas smiling and laughter may be converging, the process is incomplete and that evidence of the distinctiveness in function of the two expressions is still apparent in humans today (Figure 5). In that study it was hypothesized that if the two behaviors were originally of different origin and still served to some extent their initial functions, then they should be either temporally distinct or mutually exclusive in certain types of social situations.

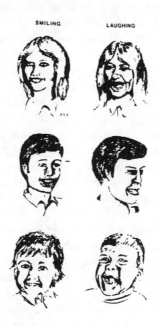

Figure 5: Sketches illustrating the differences between the facial expressions of smiling (left) and laughter (right). Teeth biting edges (particularly lower jaw) and round mouth corners are evident in laughter, whereas front teeth surfaces showing (particularly upper jaw) and sharp mouth corners characterize smiling.

The facial grimaces associated with each behavior were distinguished by the extent of teeth exposure, degree of lip retraction, and

245

the curvature of the corners of the mouth. Smiling was defined as either closed lips, or front-teeth exposed (more intense form) but jaws mainly closed, and with sharp mouth corners (slightly turned up) in both cases. The laughter mouth was defined as open jaws, teeth-biting edges showing (particularly lower jaw) and rounded mouth corners. The vocal aspect of laughter was defined in terms of upper torso movements. A mild chuckle involved some vertical chest movement and sometimes eye closure, i.e., in frank laughter the head moved backward and then forward (with eyes closed) and the chest movements were very exaggerated.

The form, frequency and temporal occurrences of smiling and laughter, respectively, were observed and systematically recorded between pairs of adults (N=141) in situations where either the two individuals: a) did not know one another but were engaged in a business transaction, b) they were acquaintances at work only, c) they were good friends but it was a chance encounter, and d) they were good friends in a planned leisure context. Only the initiating individual of the different dyadic interactions was observed from the beginning to the end of the exchange. Two female and two male observers were utilized and the interobserver reliability in recording periodically the same dyads ranged from a correlation of .75 to .95.

The finding supported the hypotheses that teeth-together smiling and the open-mouth expression associated with laughter still have distinct human functions. Smiling was evident at times of greeting and departure of strangers or good friends but frank laughter was seen almost exclusively between good friends in a recreational context (play). The frank laughter that only rarely occurred in other exchanges did so during the later stages when the situation was more relaxed or less formal.

Another study on smiling and laughter by the present author (Lockard, 1978) addressed whether face-to-face interaction is necessary to discern the differences in function between smiling and laughter. The frequency of each behavior was recorded for individuals engaged in telephone conversations (N=65). The procedure was the same as in the previous study except that after the completion of each observed telephone call, the callee was approached by the observer and asked several questions concerning the nature of the call (e.g., a social or business call) and how well the caller knew the recipient (e.g., an acquaintance only, a good friend or a relative).

The differences in frequency of smiling and laughter during telephone conversations were consistent with the dyadic data in face-to-face exchanges in spite of the fact that smiles cannot be heard over a telephone. Good friends and relatives both smiled and laughed often

246

but smiled considerably more than they laughed, and laughed more after the initial segment of the conversation. Acquaintances smiled at the beginning or at the end of a conversation and rarely laughed, or did not laugh at all if it were a short business call.

Departure behavior. The comparative method in psychology has been utilized not only to compare different animal species but to compare human behavior in different cultures. This is the focus taken in the last example to be discussed. In the studies on smiling and laughing, smiling occurred with a certain degree of regularity at the beginning (as a greeting) and at the end of an interaction (as a signal of leave-taking). Laughter also occurred at the beginning of a chance encounter among good friends or among close relatives who had not seen one another for awhile (e.g., at times of arrival at airports), but most often it occurred some time after the initial segment of a conversation or just prior to departure.

In other studies on departure signals, postural cues of leave-taking were compared among U.S. Whites, African Blacks and U.S. Native Indians. The initial study (Lockard, Schiele, Allen, & Wiemer, 1978) indicated that unequal weight stance and stance weight shifts served as intention movements of imminent departure among Whites (N=142) in Seattle, Washington. Using similar procedures, the second study (N=96) was conducted in Dakar, Senegal (Gunderson and Lockard, 1980). Stance data were gathered on adult dyads of the Wolof tribe. The observations were taken in city streets and open markets. Every 10 seconds from the beginning to the end of a dyadic interaction the following information was recorded on a randomly selected member of a pair: Body weight equally or unequally distributed on both legs; weight shifts and social distance changes of the focal subject; and whether after the exchange the observed member left with or without the other member.

As in the first stance study, the data of the first, middle and last observational intervals of all African subjects were analyzed and indicated that the frequency of unequal-weight stances increased from the beginning to the end of the exchange (x^2=4.84, df=2, p<.05). A trend analysis of the frequency of weight shifts of these individuals (Table III, right column) revealed a linear component (F=19.94, df=1 and 190, p<.001) in contrast to a quadratic component (Table III, left column) for Whites (F=15.17, df=1 and 168, p<.05) from the first to the middle to the last interval. In other studies, length of interaction was not a significant factor and in the Dakar study only, males exhibited more weight shifts in the first interval than females (t=2.02, df=1, p<.05).

247

Table 3
Stance, Weight Shift, and Social Distance Analysis

	Interval Comparison	Study I: U.S. Whites			Study II: African Blacks		
A. Stance (dyads)		X^2		P	X^2		P
McNemar non-parametric analyses	First vs. middle	8.83		<0.01	0.52		NS
	First vs last	26.26		<0.001	4.84		<.05
	Middle vs. last	6.25		<0.02	2.20		NS
B. Weight Shifts							
Trend analysis (dyads)		df	F	P	df	F	P
Source: Sex		1	1.29	NS	1		NS
Ss/gps		84	1.11	NS	95		NS
Intervals		(2)	3.66	<0.05	(2)	8.46	<.001
Linear		1	2.15	NS	1	19.94	<.001
Quadratic		1	15.17	<0.05	1	0.43	NS
Intervals x sex		2	0.14	NS	NA		
Ss x intervals/gps		168			190		
Total		257			288		
Student Tests			t	P		t	P
Source: Singletons	Last vs. middle		1.96	0.05		1.06	NS
Dyads, together	Last vs. middle		1.95	0.05		<1.0	NS
Dyads, separate	Last vs. middle		4.63	<0.001		2.81	<.005
C. Social distance (SD)			X^2	P		X^2	P
McNemar non-parametric analyses	SD↑ Last vs first		5.30	<0.02		13.50	<.001
	SD↓ Last vs. first		0.41	NS		0.30	NS
	Dyad Comparison						
Parametric contingencies	SD↑ M-M, M-F, F-F, F-M		6.95	<0.10			
	SD↓ M(M-M, M-F), vs. F(F-F, F-M)		6.24	<0.02			

Consistent with the U.S. White data, the West African data indicated that members of dyads departing separately weight shifted more in the last than in the middle interval (t=2.81, df=1, p<.005). This was not the case when individuals departed together. Weight shifts away (increases in social distance) from the non-focal member of the dyad increased in the last interval (x^2=13.50, df=1, p<.001), especially for male-male dyads whether the members of the dyads left separately (x^2=6.10, df=1, p<.02) or together (x^2=5.90, df=1, p<.02).

For the most part, the African Wolof and U.S. White data were compatible. The main exception was the linear as opposed to the quadratic component of the weight shifts. The tribal nature of the West African societies may account for this difference. As a consequence of their extended kinship ties, individuals encountering one another may be more comfortable initially than urban Americans and therefore, do not shift their weight as frequently upon meeting one another. This idea of "ease of interaction" is supported by the finding that Dakar females showed fewer postural changes (i.e., were more at ease) in the first interval than Dakar males. Moreover, the outcome of the third study on departure signals of American Indians (Suchoski and Lockard, 1980) is consistent with this interpretation.

The study design was similar to the earlier research. The frequency of weight shifts of stationary Native American adults (20 to 60 years of age) were recorded every 10 seconds from the beginning to the end of a dyadic exchange. Only those individuals who were stationary 50 seconds to 5 minutes before departure were included as subjects and only the weight shifts of one member of each dyad was recorded.

The observer was herself a Native American and gathered the data on three different occasions: An Indian college student pow wow, a tribal pow wow conducted by a Northwest coastal tribe, and a national Indian conference held in the Northwest. Each subject was assigned to one of two groups **prior** to the taking of the data. Group I (traditional, N=100) consisted of those individuals known by the observer to have had a traditional background and/or whose biological parents were both American Indian. Group II (acculturated, N=100) were those individuals with less traditional backgrounds and/or only one biological parent was American Indian.

Similar to the Dakar data, the results of the last study implicated weight shifts as a departure signal for acculturated American Indians but to a much lesser extent than U.S. urban Whites (Figure 6). For the traditional American Indians, weight shifts were infrequent. Intent to depart was indicated by either a very slight head nod and/or turning or walking away. Verbal cues or other preparatory movements of leave-taking were rare.

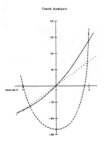

Figure 6: Comparing the curve fits of weight shifts of the African stance data (solid line: N=96 dyads; Gunderson and Lockard, 1980) with the U.S. data for Whites (dark dashed line; N=86 dyads; Lockard et al., 1978) and an idealized linear plot (light dashed line). The acculturated American Indian data (N=100 dyads; not shown) are similar to the African data while the traditional American Indian data (N=100 dyads; Suchoski & Lockard, 1980) showed very few weight shifts at all.
The empirical values are

$$\sum_{j\,=\,1}^{N} X_{ij} - Mdn_{x_i}, \text{ where the } X_{ij}$$

are the observations for the jth individual in the ith interval and the median is taken from the total weight shifts for the three intervals for each population, respectively. (Adapted from Gunderson & Lockard, 1980. Reprinted by permission of Baillière Tindall.)

There are at least two likely and interdependent explanations of the lack of prominence of weight shifts as departure signals for traditional American Indians. Although "...bipedal stationary postures of humans are difficult to maintain for any length of time" (Lockard, Schiele, Allen, & Wiemer, 1978, p. 223), the traditional American Indian value system discourages drawing attention to oneself in any way and encourages the endurance of "self-control" even to such a proximate level as postural behavior. Moreover, most Native Americans have a different concept of time than do industrialized Whites. They readily engage in long visits back and forth between households and reservations with little concern for the exigencies of the nine-to-five world. "Indian time" is measured by days and seasons and not by minutes and hours. American Indian social gatherings, even those held in urban settings, are generally designated as starting at either "White time," e.g., "7:30 p.m. sharp" or at "Indian time," e.g., "7:30 p.m. or a few hours later." Therefore, it is not surprising that individuals so little concerned with the sweeping hand of the clock should appear to make few restless shifts involved in social interactions.

This last study has taken us "full circle" back to "learned behaviors," but not in ignorance. A weight shift is a behavior exhibited by all normal adult individuals in every society. In some cultures, time-conscious individuals weight shift often when preparing to leave a social exchange. For them this behavior reliably serves an an intention to depart. In other cultures, the same behavior in the same situation may be unacceptable, repressed or at least not encouraged. However, the finding that was consistent in the three cultures studied was that weight shifts and "ease of social interaction" seem to be inversely correlated. A likely test of this hypothesis would be to assess weight shifts of Dakar Blacks or acculturated American Indians while interacting with White strangers and compare their frequency, respectively, with those in the second and third stance studies above in which they were interacting with individuals of their own culture.

Overview. The investigatory techniques of a specific research area have been presented to illustrate some of the contributions of previous training in experimental psychology to the study of human behavior as a natural science. While admittedly much of the focus is not the exclusive predilection of psychology, the expounded research design and control have been the academic heritage of behavioral scientists for nearly a hundred years. One might ask then, what has taken us so long to incorporate biology as an essential factor in the study of behavior, especially human behavior. In my opinion, it was not a problem in recognizing the importance of evolution and "natural" observations to the understanding of behavior. Rather, it was the motivation for rigor and the rush of psychologists to be accepted as scientists that resulted in an omission of a descriptive phase in their discipline and that promoted and perpetuated their sometimes sterile laboratory approach. I would also like to believe that experimental psychology was somewhat ahead of its time, with research concepts and statistical methods awaiting the acceptance of behavior into biology.

Moreover, it is very difficult to be objective about one's own species. Many zoologists, psychologists, anthropologists, and sociologists today do not take the theory of natural selection seriously when it comes to human behavior. In fact, it may well be adaptive to be self-deceived as to the actual mechanisms which influence our behavior (Lockard, 1980c; Lockard & Paulhus, 1988). For ex-

251

ample, to explain that we help friends and other non-relatives because we care about them (i.e., it provides us with a feeling of satisfaction — proximal reward) is a seemingly more palatable reason than that we do so because their cooperation now or in the future (reciprocal altruism) may augment our ability to contribute differentially to future gene pools. To know that much of what we hold dear, such as our sociality, artistry, creativity, and cultural achievements are means by which we increase our inclusive fitness is a sobering thought at the very least, if not outright depressing (Barkow, 1980; Dawkins, 1978; Lockard, 1980c). Experimental psychologists have erred no more than other relevant scientists in regarding humans as infinitely malleable, as superficially they appear to be. The problem in the past rested with not recognizing the finite survival and reproductive functions to which their motivations and varied behaviors are being employed.

ACKNOWLEDGEMENT

The author wishes to express her appreciation to The Harry Frank Guggenheim Foundation in providing the research funds for the studies reviewed in this chapter. Indebtedness is also owed her graduate mentor, Dr. David A. Grant, in memory of whose exacting mind this chapter is dedicated.

REFERENCES

Alexander, R.D. (1974). The evolution of social behavior. Annual Review of Ecological Systems, 5, 325-383.

Andrew, R.J. (1963). Evolution of facial expression. Science, 142, 1034-1041.

Andrew, R.J. (1965). The origins of facial expressions. Scientific American, 213, 88-94.

Barkow, J.H. (1980). Biological evolution of culturally patterned behavior. In J.S. Lockard (Ed.), The evolution of human social behavior (pp. 277-296). New York: Elsevier.

Boring, E.G. (1959). A history of experimental psychology. New York: Appleton-Century-Crofts, Inc.

Chivers, D.J. (1971). Spatial relations within the siamang family group. Proceedings of the 3rd International Congress of Primatologists, Zurich, 3.

Cohen, J.E. (1971). Casual groups of monkey and men. Cambridge, MA: Harvard University Press.

Darwin, C. (1859). Origin of species. London: John Murray.

Darwin, C. (1871). Descent of man. London: John Murray.

Darwin, C. (1872). Expression of the emotions in man and animals. London: John Murray.

Dawkins, R. (1976). The selfish gene. London: Oxford University Press.

Dawkins, R. (1978). Replicator selection and extended phenotype. Zeitschrift für Tierpsychologie, 47, 61-76.

Dawkins, R. (1982). The extended phenotype. Oxford, England: W. H. Freeman & Co.

Dumond, D.E. (1975). The limitation of human population: A natural history. Science, 187, 713-721.

Ellefson, J.O. (1967). A natural history of gibbons in the Malay Peninsula (Doctoral dissertation, University of California, Berkeley.)

Feinman, S. (1979). An evolutionary theory of food sharing. Social Science Information, 18, 695-726.

Ferster, C.B., & Skinner, B.F. (1957). Schedules of reinforcement. New York: Appleton-Century-Crofts, Inc.

Fisher, R.A. (1925). Statistical methods for research workers. Edinburgh: Oliver and Boyd.

Fisher, R.A. (1935). The design of experiments. Edinburgh: Oliver and Boyd.

Fisher, R.A. (1949). The theory of inbreeding. Edinburgh: Oliver and Boyd.

Fisher, R.A. (1956). Statistical methods and scientific inference. Edinburgh: Oliver and Boyd.

Gunderson, V.M., & Lockard, J.S. (1980). Human postural signals as intention movements to depart: African data. Animal Behaviour, 28, 966-967.

Hall, K.R.L., & DeVore, I. (1965). Baboon social behavior. In I. DeVore (Ed.), Primate behavior (pp. 53-110). New York: Holt, Rinehart and Winston.

Hamilton, W.D. (1963). The evolution of altruistic behavior. American Naturalist, 97, 354-356.

Hamilton, W.D. (1964). The genetical evolution of social behaviour. I and II. Journal of Theoretical Biology, 7, 1-52.

Harcourt, A.H., Steward, J.J., & Fossey, D. (1976). Male emigration and female transfer in wild mountain gorilla. Nature, 263, 226-227.

Hinde, R.A. (Ed.) (1972). Non-verbal communication. New York: Cambridge.

Hinde, R.A. (1974). Biological bases of human social behaviour. New York: McGraw-Hill.

Hinde, R.A. (1982). Ethology. Oxford, England: Oxford University Press.

Hinde, R.A. (Ed.) (1983). Primate social relationships. Oxford, England: Blackwell Scientific Publications.

Hrdy, S.B. (1977). The langurs of Abu: Female and male strategies of reproduction. Cambridge, MA: Harvard University Press.

Hull, C.L. (1943). Principles of behavior: An introduction to behavior. New York: Appleton-Century-Crofts.

Jolly, A. (1985). The evolution of primate behavior (2nd edition). New York: Macmillan.

Kirkevold, B.C., Lockard, J.S., & Heestand, J.E. (1983). Developmental comparisons of grimace and play mouth in infant pigtail macaques (Macaca nemestrina): Implications for human facial displays. American Journal of Primatology, 3, 277-283.

Konner, M.J. (1976). Relations among infants and juveniles in comparative perspective. Social Science Information, 15, 371-402.

Knowles, P.O. (1977). Panhandling as an example of the sharing of resources. Science, 198, 857-858.

Kurland, J.A. (1980). Kin selection theory: A review and selective biography. Ethology & Sociobiology, 1, 255-274.

Lockard, J.S. (1977). Panhandling as an example of the sharing of resources. (A reply to Knowles, 1977). Science, 198, 858.

Lockard, J.S. (1978). Comparison of smiling and laughing during telephone conversations. Unpublished raw data.

Lockard, J.S. (1980a). The biological synthesis of behavior. In J.S. Lockard (Ed.), The evolution of human social behavior (pp. 297-318), New York: Elsevier.

Lockard, J.S. (Ed.) (1980b). The evolution of human social behavior. New York: Elsevier.

Lockard, J.S. (1980c). Speculations on the adaptive significance of self-deception. In J.S. Lockard (Ed.), The evolution of human social behavior (pp. 257-276). New York: Elsevier.

Lockard, J.S. (1980d). Studies of human social signals: Theory, method and data. In J.S. Lockard (Ed.), The evolution of human social behavior (pp. 1-30). New York: Elsevier.

Lockard, J.S., & Adams, R.M. (1980). Peripheral males: A primate model for a human subgroup. Bulletin of the Psychonomic Society, 15, 295-298.

Lockard, J.S., Kirkevold, B.C., & Kalk, D.F. (1980). Cost/benefit indexes of deception in crime. Bulletin of the Psychonomic Society, 16, 303-306.

Lockard, J.S., McDonald, L.L., Clifford, D.A., & Martinez, R. (1976). Panhandling: Sharing of resources (reciprocal altruism or kinship selection). Science, 191, 406-408.

Lockard, J.S., & Paulhus, D.L. (Eds.). (1988) Self-deception: An adaptive mechanism. New Jersey: Prentice-Hall.

Lockard, J.S., Schemann, J., & Adams, R.M. (manuscript in preparation). Peripheral males: Out of phase with "The Establishment".

Lockard, J.S., Schiele, B.J., Allen, D.L., & Wiemer, M.J. (1978). Human postural signals: Stance, weight shifts, and social distance as intention movements to depart. Animal Behavior, 26, 219-224.

Lockard, J.S., Smith, J.L., Fahrenbruch, C.E., & Morgan, C.J. (1977). Smiling and laughter: Different phyletic origins? Bulletin of the Psychonomic Society, 10, 183-186.

Maynard-Smith, J. (1976). Evolution and the theory of games. American Scientist, 64, 41-45.

McDougall, W. (1908). Introduction to social psychology. Boston: J.W. Luce and Co.

Morris, D. (1967). The naked ape. London: Cape.

Ojemann, G. (1979). Altering memory with human ventrolateral thalamic stimulation. In E. Hitchcock, H. Ballentine, & B. Beyerson (Eds.), Modern concepts in psychiatric surgery (pp. 103-110). New York: Elsevier.

Pavlov, I.P. (1906). The scientific investigation of the psychical faculties or processes in the higher animals. Science, 24, 613-619.

Presser, H.B. (1975). Age differences between spouses: Trends, patterns, and social implications. American Behavioral Scientist, 19, 190-205.

Robinson, C.L., Lockard, J.S., & Adams, R.M. (1979). Who looks at a baby in public. Ethology and Sociobiology, 1, 87-91.

Schaller, G.B. (1963). The mountain gorilla: Ecology and behavior. Chicago: University of Chicago Press.

Schessler, T., & Nash, L.T. (1977). Food sharing among captive gibbons. (Hylobates lar). Primates, 18, 677-689.

Skinner, B.F. (1938). The behavior of organisms: An experimental analysis. New York: Appleton-Century.

Spence, K.W. (1956). Behavior theory and conditioning. New Haven: Yale University Press.

Strum, S.C. (1975). Primate predation: Interim report on the development of a tradition in a troop of olive baboons. Science, 187, 755-757.

Suchoski, J., & Lockard, J.S. (1980). Native American postural signals as intentional movements to depart. Unpublished report.

Sugiyama, Y., & Ohsawa, T. (1974). Population dynamics of Japanese macaques at Ryozenyama, Suzuka Mts., 1. General review. Japanese Journal of Ecology, 24, 50-59 (in Japanese).

Teleki, G. (1973a). The omnivorous chimpanzee. Scientific American, 228, 33-42.

Teleki, F. (1973b). The predatory behavior of wild chimpanzees. Lewisburg, PA: Bucknell University Press.

Thorndike, E.L. (1898). Animal intelligence: An experimental study of the associative processes in animals. Psychological Monographs, 2, No. 8.

Thorndike, E.L. (1911). Animal intelligence. New York: Macmillan.

254

Thorndike, E.L. (1911). _Animal intelligence_. New York: Macmillan.

Tiger, L., & Fox, R. (1966). The zoological perspective in social science. _Man_, 1, 75-81.

Trivers, R. (1971). The evolution of reciprocal altruism. _Quarterly Review of biology_, 46, 35-57.

Trivers, R. (1972). Parental investment and sexual selection. In B. Campbell (Ed.), _Sexual selection and the descent of man 1871-1971_. Chicago: Aldine.

Trivers, R.L. (1974). Parent-offspring conflict. _American Zoologist_, 14, 249-264.

Trivers, R.L. (1985). _Social evolution_. Menlo Park, CA: Benjamin/Cummings.

van Hooff, J.A.R.A.M. (1967). The facial displays of the catarrhine monkeys and ages. In D. Morris (Ed.), _Primate ethology_ (pp. 7-67). London: Widenfeld and Micolson.

van Hooff, J.A.R.A.M. (1971). _Aspects of the social behavior and communication in human and higher non-human primates_. Rotterdam: Bronder Offset.

van Hooff, J.A.R.A.M. (1972). A comparative approach to the phylogeny of laughter and smiling. In R.A. Hinde (Ed.), _Non-verbal communication_ (pp. 209-241). New York: Cambridge University Press.

Van Lawick-Goodall, J. (1972). Expressive movements and communication in the Gombe stream chimps. In P. Dolhinow (Ed.), _Primate patterns_ (pp. 25-84). New York: Holt, Rinehart and Winston.

Wallace, B. (1973). Misinformation, fitness and selection. _American Naturalist_, 107, 1-7.

Watson, J.B. (1913). Psychology as the behaviorist views it. _Psychological Review_, 20, 158-177.

Wilson, E.O. (1975). _Sociobiology, the new synthesis_. Cambridge, MA: Belknap Press of Harvard University.

Wyler, A.R., Lockard, J.S., Ward, A.A., Jr., & Finch, C.A. (1976). Conditioned EEG desynchronization and seizure occurrence in patients. _EEG Clinical Nerophysiology_, 41, 410-512.

EARLY NUTRITIONAL DEPRIVATION AND DEVELOPMENT

Arthur J. Riopelle

More than 30% of the world's children die from malnutrition and disease before the age of 5 (McGovern, 1979). If world circumstances produce such extensive nutritional deprivation and disease in infants and children, we can be sure that adults also are undernourished. "The ominous prospect of some 300 to 500 million malnourished children growing up to become brain-damaged adults, who, in turn, will parent another deprived, mentally subnormal generation is a real one in every respect.... There is no question that severe malnutrition during early life is associated with varying degrees of cerebral degeneration and mental subnormality. To what degree the cerebral inadequacy is causally related to protein or protein-calorie deficiency and its variously associated disturbances remains to be determined. However, a large body of cumulated evidence suggests that the longer and more severe the malnutrition is during the first two years of life the more serious the effects will be on subsequent intellectual development. Thus the potential for reversibility of the defects is drastically decreased if the dietary inadequacy overlaps the most rapid phases of brain growth. The special vulnerability of the central nervous system to insult during early childhood is a well established fact, since the critical period for brain development in humans is in fetal life to approximately the third to fourth year of postnatal life. Thus, most nerve cells are formed in utero, while glial cells form primarily during the first years of life and myelin accumulates most rapidly during the second postnatal year. Although prenatal nutrition of the mother remains the most important consideration with respect to brain development, we should emphasize that, unless nutritional adequacy is also maintained for the infant and young child, both physical and mental development will be impaired" (Morgane et al., 1978, pp. 137-138).

The implication that malnutrition during early life, when the brain is most vulnerable, leads to inadequate cerebral development and impaired mental capacity, which, in turn, leads to economic and social impoverishment that causes more malnutrition when the next generation is developing, makes the nutritional argument profoundly significant and points precisely to the kinds of intervention programs that might interrupt the cycle and, once interrupted, would have long lasting improvement in the culture, way of life, and intellectual capacity, as well as the health of the populations participating in such an intervention program. In addition to being completely plausible, the hypothesis of nutritionally induced brain damage would appear to be testable by examining the intellectual status of children who had experienced severe undernutrition during their gestation or early postnatal period. This is exactly what Stoch and Smythe (1963) did. They followed the development of 20 infants, grossly undernourished during infancy for a period of 11 years after rehabilitation. They examined their growth, including head circumference, height, weight, and their intellectual and psychological competence and concluded that the undernutrition left them with a significant reduction in brain size and an impairment in intellectual capacity.

This important study is provocative but not conclusive because the children who were undernourished most came from homes in which illegitimacy, alcoholism, and parental separation were characteristic. Moreover the degree of intellectual isolation of the infants was undocumentable. Consequently, it is not certain whether the deficits these children showed when tested at later ages were attributable to malnutrition itself, to lack of intellectual stimulation and encouragement, or to other factors such as intervening disease. It would seem then, that conclusions about the relation of brain growth to intellectual achievement are not readily determinable from studies of humans regardless of how many times they are replicated.

In point of fact, the strength of our conviction regarding the role of early nutrition and brain growth and subsequent adaptive capacity is due more to the credibility of the theory and to the acceptance of the validity of the animal models on which data are collected to validate the theory than they are to the actual assessment of the human data.

It is at this point that one is reminded of David A. Grant's cautious empiricism: because a datum fitted with a theory did not guarantee that its interpretation would be correct. We might rephrase this skepticism by acknowledging that theories and models are devices we use which allow us to believe that we know more about something than we actually do. Internal consistency of the data or of the theory is no guarantee of its validity. My point is not to disparage the use of either one, but rather to continue to maintain the kind of caution that Professor Grant instilled in us in the years following World War II during which we were graduate students. Neither should one infer that I am disparaging the study of nutrition and development in rats or in primates for the principal purpose of understanding rat of primate behavior. The issue concerns the selection of one or the other as a model for man and of the applicability of the data collected from either for the solution of human problems.

The problem to which attention is addressed is straight forward: If millions of children are born of mothers who are malnourished during pregnancy and who themselves may be malnourished subsequently, are they as a consequence incapacitated in any way that is reflected in their comportment and in their adaptive capacity. Several alternatives to resolve the question are available to us. We may, first, deny it, stating that children from these populations are as competent intellectually and physically as are children from populations that are healthy and well-fed. We might, secondly, deny the question in part by acknowledging that although such populations have limited competence, the diminished capacity is due to social and educational factors rather than to nutrition. Because of the coincidence of malnutrition and the absence of social and intellectual stimulation during growth, the finding of reduced intellectual capacity among such populations would not be revealing of its origin. The third possibility entails experimental study either in the laboratory in which animals are involved or in experiments of nature which may not be well controlled.

Sufficient evidence exists of studies of prolonged starvation (Keys, Brozek, Henschel, Mickelsen, & Taylor, 1950) to indicate that although starvation during adulthood produces distinct changes in physical competence, in motivation, and in attitude, the changes are reversible upon rehabilitation and no permanent loss in competence is usually discerned. If a vulnerable period is to be found, it probably will be found early in life. Accordingly, emphasis in research has been directed toward the period of early development. Teratological studies point to the vulnerability of the central nervous system during prenatal life or early childhood. From this experience has emerged the notion that critical or vulnerable periods for brain development exist in the period between early fetal life to approximately the third or fourth year of postnatal life. Most nerve cells are formed during gestation but glial cells develop during the first year after birth and myelin develops during the second postnatal year.

Two theoretical approaches have been developed to rationalize the vulnerability of the organism to malnutrition during early development. The studies of Enesco and Leblond (1962) establish that growth on any organ (except for those few like blood, skin, and reproductive cells which regenerate throughout life) is by two definable processes. The first is an increase in cell number (hyperplasia). During this period the daughter cells, products of cell division, are equal is size to the others. The second is by an increase in cell size (hypertrophy).

These two processes overlap in time so that the sequence is: hyperplasia, combined hyperplasia with hypertrophy, and hypertrophy alone. The onset and cessation of hyperplasia and the onset of hypertrophy are relatively fixed in time, probably due to genetic control. Cell size probably reaches a maximum under ideal conditions at a certain time as well, but cell size can be reduced or increased depending on the nutrition; starvation causing a reduction in cell size but not in cell number. If, however, undernutrition curtails the rate of cell division and if the predetermined time for cell proliferation is passed without the genetically possible number of cells having been formed, the animal will be permanently deficient in the number of cells. Rehabilitation after this time may increase the size of the cells but it will not restore the cell number to its maximum.

A closely related theory by Dobbing (1968) emphasizes that the brain grows quite rapidly over a precisely defined period of time. It is referred to as the "growth spurt" of the brain and occurs either in late fetal or early postnatal life, depending on the species. Many of the brain's components undergo rapid changes during this growth spurt. Especially important is the fact that the major nerve cell processes, axons and dendrites, develop during the growth spurt period, and synaptic connections between these processed do, too. Any disruption of the growth spurt will result in fewer or abnormal synaptic connections, the proliferation of glial cells, and myelin formation. It will have less effect on the number of nerve cells. The precise distinction between the two theories is of considerable theoretical import. However, our current state of technical capability does not permit the determination of the processes and events which are controlled by either theoretical mechanism. For example, changes in either brainwaves or cortical thickness due to malnutrition can be caused by numerous factors among which are deficits in the number of glial cells, the elaboration of neural processes and synaptic connections, and in the overlapping total amount of myelin. Furthermore, no mechanism is available for precisely differentiating the number of cells of neuronal as opposed to glial origin that are lost during malnutrition. At any rate, distinction between the theoretical positions will not be resolved by behavioral studies.

Ample studies reveal the vulnerability of the prenatal and infant rat to malnutrition. Wigglesworth (1964) partially ligated the artery to one horn of the rat uterus. The infants that were attached in the neighborhood of the ligation were undersized and underdeveloped when born. Internal organs of these animals were characteristic of small malnourished babies. They had small livers but large well-developed brains. The histological maturity of the organs was in accordance with their gestational age. The most likely explanation of the diminished organ and body size is that the partial ligation reduced the nutrients available to the fetus, although it's possible that the elimination of waste products was similarly compromised by the operation.

Two parallel studies were conducted on rhesus monkeys. In this species the placenta usually has two discs. The infant is directly attached to the larger of the two. Myers, et al., (1971) ligated the fetal vessels attached to the secondary placental disc at the 100th day of gestation, thus isolating the fetus from it. These investigators noted a high rate of pregnancy interruption, but seven of the 13 animals reached 150 to 160 days of gestation, when they were delivered by Cesarean section. The smallest of the experimental animals weighed about 2/3 the average of the control animals. Most affected were the lungs, pancreas, liver and spleen. The brain, adrenals, kidney and pituitary glands were least affected (Myers et al., 1971). Biochemical studies of these animals by Hill, Myers, Hold, Scott, & Cheek (1971) revealed that the cerebellar DNA of the experimental animals was less than normal. In a similar experiment Portman et al. (1977) ligated the vessels bridging the two discs of the placenta at the 90th day of gestation. Portman and his colleagues had somewhat better reproductive fortunes than did Myers et al., benefiting, perhaps, from the earlier reports of difficulties, for all the animals survived to day 155 (of the approximately 165-day gestation length), when they, too, were delivered by Cesarean section. Three of the animals died within 2 weeks. The animals that survived were maintained on a low-protein diet containing only 3% of the energy as protein. When sacrificed 40 days after delivery, significant reductions in brain weights and in the weights of brain stems and cerebellums were found, but the DNA content, the protein content, and the lipid constituents of the cerebellum and cerebrum were not significantly reduced. Glycolipid deficiency was found in the brain stem. How much of this deficiency can be ascribed to the period of pregnancy and how much to the postnatal deprivation period cannot be determined from this study. The results do, however, point to the possible reserve capacity of the monkey placenta and to the resistance of brain DNA against undernutrition created by placental vessel ligation.

Since the placenta is the proximate source of nutrients for the fetus, direct mechanical reduction in the capability of the placenta to provide nutrients to the infant would, if resulting clearly in a smaller brain with fewer constituents, point directly to a mechanism for intrauterine growth retardation and thus would answer an important question concerning the correlation that has been observed between placental size and infant size. It has long been known that large babies usually have large placentas and small babies small placentas, but two questions arise about this fact. The first concerns the magnitude of the correlation between the two sizes. The ratio of the fetal weight to the placental weight varies between 5:1 and 11:1 (Behrman, Seeds, Battaglia, Hellegers, & Bruns, 1964; Garrow and Hawes, 1971). This variation in feto-placental ratio is as large for babies that have been declared to be victims of intrauterine growth retardation as it is for normal, well-developed, full-sized babies at term. The great variation in the ratios strongly suggests either that the coupling between the baby and the fetus is a loose one or that remarkable placental reserve often exists for even the intrauterine retarded babies. The second question based on the correlation between infant and placental weight concerns which of the two is the moving force. Do small placentas produce small babies or do small babies cause the development of small placentas? In light of these questions, it is unfortunate that the placental ligation studies are not entirely clear in their conclusions or their interpretation. The best that can be said is that the effects are greater in rats than they are in rhesus monkeys.

Had the placental ligation studies been conclusive, they would have pointed directly to the mechanism involved in intrauterine growth retardation. Despite our failure to identify the mechanism, the problem of determining whether or not the starvation and the malnutrition experienced by many persons, particularly the pregnant, is itself the causative factor in low birthweight and in behavioral and physiological incompetence still remains. We have already seen that the epidemiologic studies among humans can at best only suggest factors that might be involved in the relation of malnutrition to low birthweight. Ignorance, lack of intellectual and social stimulation, and the social disorganization among individuals who suffer severe malnutrition complicate the interpretation. These studies can only identify the problem, not point to the causative factor. For that reason, animal studies are necessary.

In any extrapolation we make from animals to man, we expose ourselves to a number of risks. One that has been indentified specifically with respect to the role of prenatal vs. early postnatal deprivation in development arises because the act of birth occurs for different species at different stages of fetal development.

A second hazard concerns the choice of the nutrient to be fed in deficient amounts. Malnourished human populations normally are deficient in calories, in protein, and in vitamins and minerals as well. The term protein-calorie malnutrition has achieved widespread adoption because it has within it the ambiguity necessary to cover a broad spectrum of possible deficiencies. Although this ambiguity may be superficially appropriate for the human situation at large, there is reason to believe that the problem actually is less complicated than that because whether the protein alone is deficient or the deficiency is in both protein and calories the basic deficit is thought to be of protein. For one thing, protein deficiency alone is as disastrous in effect as is calorie deficiency. The young of rats fed a protein-deficient diet during pregnancy were small when born and had difficulty in learning (Bandera & Churchill, 1961; Caldwell & Churchill, 1967). Other studies with rats suggest that protein deficiency may actually produce more serious effects on the central nervous system than does food restriction alone. Because of its expense, protein is one of the components of the diet which may be eliminated because of economic factors. Moreover, Miller (1970) noted that baby rats during the suckling period accumulate fat, which implies that they take in an excess of calories. When these animals were placed on a diet that was low in protein the weight gain was severely restricted.

Direct studies of the brains of the offspring of rats maintained on an 8%-protein diet show that the brains contain less DNA (number of cells) and protein than do the progeny of well-fed females. Since the rat brain at birth is mostly neurons (the glial and myelin are yet to be formed), the reduced DNA implies that the dietary restriction results in a brain neuron deficiency (Zamenhof, van Marthens, & Margolis, 1968). Numerous other investigations have shown that the offspring of rats prenatally deprived of protein are undersized at birth. In general, the adverse effects on the offspring of rats occur if the mothers are deprived of calories during pregnancy as well as if they are deprived of protein (Chow & Lee, 1964; Zamenhof, van Marthens, & Grauel, 1971; Smart, Adlard, & Dobbing, 1972). Clark, Zamenhof, van Marthens, Grauel, & Crugar (1973), who studied the effect of prenatal malnutrition on dimensions of the cerebral cortex, found that the cortical thickness was significantly reduced in baby rats born of calorie-deficient mothers. The reduction in cortical thickness was approximately twice that which would be expected by the reduction in cerebral weight. This finding suggested to the authors that the cerebral cortex is more affected by such malnutrition than is the cerebrum as a whole.

The rodent data are not entirely confirmatory, however. Suggesting that the fetus lives as a parasite having a prior claim on the nutrients circulating in the maternal blood stream, Naismith (1969) found that a 54% reduction in dietary protein intake reduced fetal weight by no more than 11%. Morgane et al. (1978) in an extensive

263

study, found no difference in brain weight or body weight at birth in infants of mothers maintained on an 8%-casein diet throughout pregnancy when compared with those whose mothers were fed an isocaloric 25%-casein diet. They concluded that the brain of the offspring as expressed in weight measures was spared despite the maternal protein restriction.

The primate data on prenatal protein deprivation have come from four different laboratories, but remarkable agreement is found among the data. Diets affording 1.2g of protein per kg per day during pregnancy resulted in infants that weighed an average of about 4% less than the control group infants did when delivered by Cesarean section at the 157th day of gestation. No statistically significant changes occurred in protein, in DMA, in RNA, in cholesterol, in phospholipid, in water, or in cloride space in the brain. This diet contained about 5% of the calories as protein (Cheek et al., 1976).

A similar study was conducted by Portman and coworkers (1977). When they were delivered at the 160th day of gestation the control infants weighed 485g and the infants from protein-deficient mothers 408g. Their infants were not sacrificed at Cesarean delivery but, instead, were maintained on a low-protein diet for 5 weeks. Protein supplied 3.6% of the calories in this diet. The protein-deprived infants were smaller in body weight, in brain weight, and in the weights of the cerebrum, cerebellum, and brain stem. Protein and lipid contents of the brain stem were significantly reduced. Because the animals were deprived postnatally, one cannot determine the extent to which the prenatal deprivation was a contributing factor.

The data from our laboratory represent another portion of the published information available comparing the effects of protein deprivation in pregnant animals with those in nonpregnant animals. When isocaloric diets containing 13.4%, 6.7%, 3.35%, or 1.68% protein (as casein) were fed to nonpregnant rhesus monkeys, significant weight losses occurred in those fed the lowest protein concentrations despite continued high caloric intake. These diets, if consumed at the rate of 120 calories per kg of body weight per day, provided 4, 2, 1 or .5 g of protein per kg of body weight. The animals fed the lowest concentration of protein lost 35% of their body weight within 6 weeks, even though at the time they were eating as much food each day as they did at the beginning of the experiment. When returned to the high-protein diet, they rapidly regained the weight lost during the deprivation period despite their still not eating any more than they did during the deprivation period. Serologic studies confirmed the drastic effects of the low protein diet (Riopelle et al., 1974).

The experiment was repeated later in pregnant monkeys, omitting a group fed the lowest (1.68%) protein diet. The animals fed the diet highest in protein ate slightly more than did the animals which were fed the intermediate or the lowest protein diets and, as expected, they gained the most weight during their pregnancy. When we examined food consumption relative to body weight, we noted that the animals fed the highest protein diet consumed slightly less per unit body weight than the other two groups did (Riopelle et al., 1975). The weight gains of the different groups during pregnancy paralleled the differential food intakes, so that food consumption per kg of body weight was not drastically different in any of the three groups. The low-protein animals gained a little weight during pregnancy on the diets that caused nonpregnant animals to lose weight. A further interesting finding was that when the animals were returned to the high-protein diet after delivery, their weights remained the same for several weeks (Riopelle & Shell, 1978). This finding indicated to us that the pregnant animals were not themselves deprived despite eating a low-protein diet during their pregnancy.

The crucial question is, what happened to the infants? In Table 1 is presented a summary of the individual findings over a series of experiments analyzing birth weight, neonatal physical status, food consumption, growth, and behavior (Hale, Hillman, & Hendricks, 1976; Riopelle, Hale, & Watts, 1976; Riopelle & Favret, 1977; Riopelle, Hale, & Hill, 1976; Hillman, Khalid, & Riopelle, 1978). It is evident from the right-most column of the table that the null hypothesis is alive and well in our laboratory. The infants, themselves, were not deprived. Within the range of protein concentrations used, 3.35% to 13.4%, the pregnant mothers can increase their metabolic efficiency enough to enable the fetus to grow normally with no demonstrable cost to the mother. It follows as the night to the day that if the infants were not deprived during gestation, and if they were fed adequately after birth, then no behavioral, physiological, or anatomical test so far constructed or planned for the future would differentiate among the groups. Accordingly, our behavioral data are exactly as we would expect them to be.

There obviously is some limit to the range within which the mother can adapt her metabolic processes to accommodate the low-protein diet and it would appear that Kohrs, Harper, and Kerr (1976) have identified the lower limit. She and her colleagues fed pregnant rhesus monkeys a standard infant formula that was made isocaloric with supplemental lactose to compensate for the 75% reduction in protein. The deprived animals consumed about .5g protein per kg of body weight per day, but during the latter part of pregnancy reduced their food intake about 20%. The birth weights of the infants delivered at the 165th day of pregnancy by Cesarean section were lower by about 15% than those of infants from normally fed animals. Both maternal and fetal mortality were high in the experimental animals. An important fact to be noted is that the low-protein monkeys reduced their food intake about 20% during the latter part of pregnancy.

The infants in which differences in birth weight due to diet occurred were delivered by Cesarean section. This point deserves noting because terminating the pregnancy at a certain specified time robs the mother of one of the important adaptive mechanisms which she possesses to overcome the nutritional inadequacy, namely, to extend the gestation length. We have found (Riopelle & Hale, 1975) that the monkeys fed a high-protein diet had a shorter gestation period than did those fed the low-protein diets. It is conceivable that some of the differences in Cesarean delivery weights would have disappeared had the mothers been allowed to carry their infants to normal spontaneous delivery.

One cannot escape concluding that moderately low-protein and probably low-calorie intakes during pregnancy (Cheek et al., 1976) are tribulations for the rodent but trivialities for the primate. Cheek (1973) was the first to point out the difference between rodent and primate responses to prenatal calorie restriction, thinking that the syndrome described for rats may be peculiar to small animals. He noted that the metabolic stress of pregnancy for primates is considerably less than that for nonprimate animals (Payne & Wheeler, 1968). Whereas the pregnant rat must produce a litter of perhaps a dozen pups which collectively weigh 25% of her body weight and must do it in 21 days, the primate produces a single infant weighing, perhaps, 5 to 10% of the mother's weight and she has 5 1/2 months (in the case of the rhesus monkey) to accomplish the task. The rat's protein and water accretion rate is 25 times higher than that of the monkey and 60 times higher than that of the human.

It would seem that the most significant factors in the adaptability of the monkey to low-protein and low-calorie diets during pregnancy are two: the singleton infant and the long gestation period. Because the rhesus mother produces only a single infant she can monitor the condition of the pregnancy to keep the development of the fetus within some significant limits. Not only the sex of the infant but its weight, too, affects its gestation length. Because the rodent produces a large litter, the mother is unable to adjust the individual food supplies to the requirements of each of the fetuses, which differ among themselves in their size, sex, and development; consequently some pups get shortchanged.

Obviously, quite different evolutionary adaptations have been adopted by the rodent and the primate. The rat, which is highly vulnerable to inadequate nutrient conditions during pregnancy, can avoid the effects by deferring mating until the optimal conditions are present. Since the gestation period is short, delivery most likely occurs in the same season and in the same nutritional environment as conception. Because of the long time, 5 1/2 months, between conception and delivery in the primate, two seasons are certainly encountered, during one of which the food supplied to the mother is probably reduced either in quality or in quantity. Many monkey species living in temperate climates deliver their babies just before or just after the beginning of the rainy season in spring (Lancaster & Lee, 1965). Even the Japanese Macaque which lives in the northernmost parts of Japan conceives in September or October and delivers in spring. Because of the snow cover prevailing during that period, the food intake to the mother is minimal. Such long gestation periods would not have evolved in primates living in temperate climates had not the animals also evolved ample means to accommodate periods of suboptimal nutrition during pregnancy.

Another relevant consideration is the evolutionary adaptive significance of single versus multiple births. Any species that produces only single infants at each gestation and normally has only one reproductive opportunity per year must, if it is to continue, produce infants that are competent to withstand the rigors of the circumstances in which they find themselves after birth. Rodents, producing litters of 10 to 12 infants conceived and delivered in periods of optimal nutrition, depend on the surplus of offspring to be reduced by the environmental rigors, with only a sufficient number living until reproductive age to keep the species going. Each individual rat pup does not have to be as robust as a primate in order for the species to be perpetuated; only the strongest need survive. It does not surprise us then that rodents because of their high vulnerability are the appropriate species for assessment of environmental pollutants, carcinogens, and other toxic agents.

What we can conclude from the above comparison of rats and primates is that diets containing as little as 3 or 4% protein, if the intake of calories and other nutrients is adequate and if the mother is in good health and well nourished at time of conception, are adequate for the production of infants that are fully as competent as are infants born of mothers fed a higher plane of nutrition during pregnancy. It should be noted that diets containing fewer than 5% of the calories as proteins are quite atypical of human diets.

267

If the robustness of primates during pregnancy is as I have claimed, that conclusion ought to apply to humans as well. A number of findings point in this direction. For example, Habicht, Yarborough, & Klein (1974) reported that protein was not the limiting dietary factor for birth weight in women of a Guatemalan village. An interesting illustration of the strategy of timing birth season so that the period of pregnancy, when metabolic efficiency is greatest, is made to coincide with a period of low-nutritional intake is seen in the Kalahari San in Botswana (Wilmsen, 1978). This group in the Kalahari Desert of Africa experiences periodic feast and famine conditions but the people are not malnourished. The modal number of births occurs during the months of March and April; the peak months of meat consumption, however, are in April, May, and June, after the birth peak has passed. Cucumbers and berries, foods which are low in protein, are the most common constituents of the diet during the latter part of pregnancy. The Kalahari San is a large group of people occupying a wide variety of ecological niches; one cannot, therefore, attribute to any particular environment the adaptive propensity to deliver the young after a protein-lean season. These people, like our ancestors of millennia ago, experience seasonal fluctuations in diet. Such fluctuations in nutriture must have been adapted to by our ancestors, or our species would not have survived.

Especially pertinent to the concept of improved metabolic efficiency during pregnancy is the report by Montgomery and Pincus (1955) describing the fate of a young woman made metabolically inefficient by the therapeutic loss through surgery of much of her small intestine. Her regular state of health was precarious at best. Upon becoming pregnant she felt better, gained weight and delivered a normal, healthy infant, after which she returned to her former state of poor health.

Before closing, we should recognize that restrictions must be placed on the exegesis of these results. None of the experimental studies described above was intended to represent the normal human situation. They were, instead, intended to identify mechanisms and periods of vulnerability and its counterpart, adaptability. Although we are confident that primates, including man, are more robust than rodents during pregnancy, we have produced no evidence on the effects of long term malnutrition, which characterizes the situation encountered by many human populations. Moreover, our animals were subjected to single-nutrient deficits and were maintained in conditions of good sanitation and minimal environmental stress. Finally, our infants were removed from the mother the day they were born, so that we have no idea whatsoever of the capability of the deprived animals to provide milk for the young. Thus we can by no means dismiss the human problem as a nonnutritional artifact. It still exists. The point of human experience most like our precisely defined experimental situations is that of war-time in which a siege of a country originates and terminates at a certain time, and even that comparison is of limited generality because foods other than protein are also limited during such periods. Some small validation of the laboratory data with primates for this circumstance is seen, however, in the finding of Stein, Susser, Saenger, and Marolla (1975) on infants whose mothers were pregnant during the siege of the western Netherlands during the winter of 1944-1945 affecting 40,000 children conceived and born during this period. When tested upon entry into the armed forces the soldiers subjected to prenatal nutrition suffered no impairment of mental ability.

A final word can be said about the relation of the present data to the theories that originally provoked the study. Both the Winick and the Dobbing (1968) theories proposed the existence of vulnerable periods during which the infant, if deprived of nutrients, suffers permanent loss. It is clear that the data and arguments presented in this paper do not contradict these theories; instead they limit their scope by excluding their applicability to the prenatal period of primates, probably including man. This fortunate exclusion for representatives of our order comes about because the primate mother can improve her metabolism during her pregnancy, thus sparing the infant of any deprivation of critical nutrients. It is an open question as to what can happen if the infant is itself deprived, as often occurs during early postnatal life. The tragic scenes of gross starvation presented nightly on the television news reminds us again of the potential consequences of early malnutrition.

Footnote

[1]The author's research was supported by a grant HD07479 from the National Institute of Child Health and Human Development, National Institute of Health, U.S. Public Health Service.

REFERENCES

Bandera, E., & Churchill, J. (1961). Prematurity and neurological disorders. Henry Ford Hospital, 9, 414-418.

Behrman, R.E., Seeds, A.E., Jr., Battaglia, F.C., Hellegers, A.E., & Bruns, P.D. (1964). The normal changes in mass and water content in fetal rhesus monkey and placenta throughout gestation. Journal of Pediatrics, 65, 38-44.

Caldwell, D.F., & Churchill, J.A. (1967). Learning ability in the progeny of rats administered a protein deficient diet during the second half of gestation. Neurology, 17, 95-99.

Cheek, D.B. (1973). Brain growth and nucleic acids: The effect of nutritional deprivation. In F. Richardson, (Ed.), Brain and intelligence: The ecology of child development (pp. 237-256). Hyattsville, MD: National Educational Press.

Cheek, D.B., Holt, A.B., London, W.T., Ellenberg, J.A., Hill, D.E., & Sever, J.L. (1976). Nutritional studies in the pregnant rhesus monkey—the effect of protein-calorie or protein-deprivation on growth of the fetal brain. American Journal of Clinical Nutrition, 29, 1149-1157.

Chow, B.F., & Lee, C.J. (1964). Effect of dietary restriction of pregnant rats on body weight gain of the offspring. Journal of Nutrition, 82, 10.

Clark, G.M., Zamenhof, S., van Marthens, E., Grauel, L., & Crugar, L. (1973). The effect of prenatal malnutrition on dimensions of cerebral cortex. Brain Research, 54, 397-402.

Dobbing, J. (1968). Vulnerable period in developing brain. In A.M. Davison & J. Dobbing (Eds.), Applied neurochemistry (pp. 287-316). Oxford, England: Blackwell.

Enesco, M., & Leblond, C.P. (1962). Increase in cell number as a factor in the growth of the organs of the young male rat. Journal of Embryology and Experimental Morphology, 10, 530-561.

Garrow, J.S., & Hawes, S.F. (1971). The relationship of the size and composition of the human placenta to its functional capacity. Journal of Obstetrics & Gyneacology, British Commonwealth, 78, 22-28.

Habicht, J.P., Yarborough, C., & Klein, R.E. (1974). Assessing nutritional status in a field study of malnutrition and mental development: Specifically, sensitivity and congruity of indices of nutritional status. In J. Cravioto, L. Hambraeus, & B. Vahlquist (Eds.), Symposium of the Swedish nutrition foundation, Vol. 12, Early malnutrition and mental development (pp. 35-42). Uppsala: Almqvist and Wiksell.

Hale, P.A., Hillman, N.M., & Hendricks, D. (1976). Protein deprivation in primates. IX. Individual and social behaviors of infants born of deprived mothers. Unpublished manuscript.

Hill, D.E., Myers, R.E., Holt, E.B., Scott, R.E., & Cheek, D.B. (1971). Fetal growth retardation produced by experimental placental insufficiency in the rhesus monkey, II. Chemical composition of the brain, liver, muscle, and carcass. Biological Neonate, 19, 68-82.

Hillman, N.M., Khalid, S.R., & Riopelle, A.J. (1978). Protein deprivation in primates. X. Test performance of juveniles born of deprived mothers. American Journal of Clinical Nutrition, 31, 388-393.

Keys, A., Brozek, J., Henschel, A., Mickelsen, O., Taylor, H.L. (1950). The biology of human starvation, (Vols. 1 and 2). Minneapolis: The University of Minnesota Press.

Kohrs, M.B., Harper, A.E., & Kerr, G.R. (1976). Effects of a low-protein diet during pregnancy of the rhesus monkey: I. Reproductive efficiency. American Journal of Clinical Nutrition, 29, 136-145.

Lancaster, J.B., & Lee, R.B. (1965). The annual reproductive cycle in monkeys and apes. In I. DeVore (Ed.), Primate behavior. Field studies of monkeys and apes (pp. 486-513). New York: Holt, Rinehart & Winston.

McGovern, G. (1979). Human rights and world hunger. National Forum, The Phi Kappa Phi Journal, 49, 7-10.

Miller, S.A. (1970). Nutrition in the neonatal development of protein metabolism. Federation Proceedings, 29, 1497-1502.

Montgomery, T.L., & Pincus, I.J. (1955). A nutritional problem in pregnancy resulting from extensive resection of the small bowel. American Journal of Obstetrics & Gynecology, 69, 865-868.

Morgane, P.J., Miller, M., Kemper, T., Stern, W., Forbes, W., Hall, R., Bronzino, J., Kesane, J., Hawrylewicz, E., & Resnick, O. (1978). The effects of protein malnutrition on the developing nervous system in the rat. Neuroscience & Biobehavioral Reviews, 2, 137-230.

270

Myers, R.E., Hill, D.E., Holt, A.B., Scott, R.E., Mellits, E.D., & Cheek, D.B. (1971). Fetal growth retardation produced by experimental placental insufficiency in the rhesus monkey, I. Body weight organ size. Biological Neonate, 18, 379-394.

Naismith, D.J. (1969). The fetus as a parasite. Proceedings of the Nutrition Society, 28, 25-31.

Payne, P.R., & Wheeler, E.F. (1968). Comparative nutrition in pregnancy and lactation. Proceedings of the Nutrition Society, 27, 129-138.

Portman, O.W., Alexander, M., Neuringer, M., Novy, M., Illingworth, R., & Uno, H. (1977). The effects of perinatal malnutrition on lipid composition of neural tissues from rhesus monkeys. Journal of Nutrition, 107, 2228-2235.

Riopelle, A.J., & Fabret, R. (1977). Protein deprivation in primates: XIII. Growth of infants born of deprived mothers. Human Biology, 43, 221-233.

Riopelle, A.J., & Hale, P.A. (1975). Nutritional and environmental factors affecting gestation length in rhesus monkeys. American Journal of Clinical Nutrition, 28, 1170-1176.

Riopelle, A.J., Hale, P.A., & Hill, C.W. (1976). Protein deprivation in primates. VIII. Early behavior of progeny. Developmental Psychobiology, 9, 465-476.

Riopelle, A.J., Hale, P.A., & Watts, E.S. (1976). Protein deprivation in primates: VII. Determinants of size and skeletal maturity at birth in rhesus monkeys. Human Biology, 48, 203-222.

Riopelle, A.J., Hill, C.W., Li, S-C., Wolf, R.H., Seibold, H.R., & Smith, J.L. (1974). Protein deprivation in primates, I. Nonpregnant adult rhesus monkeys. American Journal of Clinical Nutrition, 27, 13-21.

Riopelle, A.J., Hill, C.W., Li, S-C., Wolf, R.H., Seibold, H.R., & Smith, J.L. (1975). Protein deficiency in primates. IV. Pregnant rhesus monkeys. American Journal of Clinical Nutrition, 28, 20-28.

Riopelle, A.J., & Shell, W.F. (1978). Protein deprivation in primates. XI. Determinants of weight change during and after pregnancy. American Journal of Clinical Nutrition, 31, 394-400.

Smart, J.L., Adlard, P.F., & Dobbing, J. (1972). Effect of maternal undernutrition and other factors in the birth weight in the rat. Biological Neonate, 20, 236-244.

Stein, Z., Susser, M., Saenger, G., & Marolla, F. (1975). Famine & human development. New York: Oxford University Press.

Stoch, M.B., & Smythe, P.M. (1963). Does undernutrition during infancy inhibit brain growth and subsequent intellectual development? Archives of Disturbed Childhood, 38, 546-552.

Wigglesworth, J.S. (1964). Experimental growth retardation in the fetal rat. Journal of Pathological Bacteriology, 88, 1-13.

Wilmsen, E.N. (1978). Seasonal effects of dietary intake on Kalahari San. Federation Proceedings, 37, 65-72.

Zamenhof. S., van Marthens, E., & Margolis, F.L. (1968). DNA, cell number, and protein in neonatal brain: Alteration by maternal dietary restriction. Science, 160, 322-323.

Zamenhof, S., van Marthens, E., & Grauel, L. (1971). DNA (cell number) in neonatal brain: Alteration by maternal dietary caloric restriction. Nutrition Reports International, 4, 269-274.

271

Table 1
Comparison between young of protein-deprived and of adequately fed monkeys

Test	Significance of difference
Neonatal Status	
Birthweight	Not Significant
Radius Length	" "
Weight: Rad. Length	" "
Skeletal Maturity	" "
Daily Food Consumption	" "
Food Intake Per Unit Body Weight	" "
Food Efficiency Index	" "
Early Behavior (Days 1-60)	
Rooting	" "
Visual Orientation	" "
Extending	" "
Body Orientation	" "
Clasping	" "
Righting	" "
Placing	" "
Rod Walking	" "
Rope Crawling	" "
Tunnel	" "
Platform	" "
Startle	" "
Visual Cliff	" "
Perceptual-Learning Tasks (Juveniles)	
Twenty-trial Problems	Not Significant
Multiple Discrimination Learning	" "
Concurrent Discrimination Learning	" "

INDEX